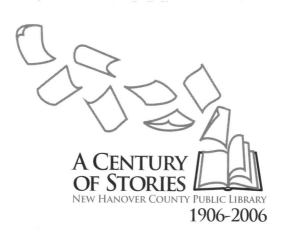

A CENTURY
OF STORIES

NEW HANOVER COUNTY PUBLIC LIBRARY
1906-2006

100 Best Paintings in London

100 Best Paintings in London

Geoffrey Smith

Interlink Books

An imprint of Interlink Publishing Group, Inc.
Northampton, Massachusetts

In memory of my father Kenneth William Smith
and for Victoria, Roland, Lucian and Gabriel with much love

First published in 2006 by

Interlink Books

An imprint of Interlink Publishing Group, Inc.

46 Crosby Street, Northampton, Massachusetts 01060

www.interlinkbooks.com

Library of Congress Cataloging-in-Publication Data

Smith, Geoffrey, 1969-
    100 best paintings in London / by Geoffrey Smith.-- 1st American ed.
      p. cm.
    Includes index.
    ISBN 1-56656-618-5 (pbk.)
    1. Painting, Modern. 2. Masterpiece, Artistic. 3.
Painting--England--London. 4. Museums--England--London. I. Title: One
hundred best paintings in London. II. Title.
    ND160.S59 2005
    750'.74'421--dc22

                                        2005013187

Printed and bound in China

Contents

Introduction 7

List of Paintings by Artist 9

Courtauld Institute Gallery 14

Dulwich Picture Gallery 36

Estorick Collection 42

Kenwood House 46

National Gallery 54

Sir John Soane's Museum 156

Tate Britain 160

Tate Modern 188

Victoria and Albert Museum 218

Wallace Collection 222

Acknowledgements 235

Index 240

Introduction

There are two primary reasons for writing this book.

First, there is no other book which can be used as a guide to the best art in London. It seemed that it was necessary to plug that gap. The busy visitor or tourist will, I hope, welcome a pointer to where the best paintings can be seen. London is such a vast and unfathomable city that it is hard for someone who has limited time to focus on how to spend their time. If one of the reasons you have come to London is to explore the visual arts (and that is increasingly the reason why very many people travel to the great cities of the world) then I believe that this book will be invaluable. If you are a harassed resident then you will already know that the greatest paintings in London do not all reside in the National Gallery and the two Tates. You will know about the riches which can be seen in other galleries but you may have been too busy to have visited the outlying collections such as Kenwood in Hampstead (especially if you live in Tooting or Lewisham) or Dulwich. I hope this book might give you the push that you need to make that journey.

Second, I am a sucker for lists, usually the domain of popular music, film, football, celebrities and TV. I suspect that there might be an anorak in my closet. But coming up with lists, and justifying their contents is an enjoyable way of concentrating the mind and stimulating debate. My list, put before you in the form of a book, will I hope do just that.

Of course the choices I have made will be open to criticism — any subjective choice by one individual is bound to be challenged. That is a large part of the *raison d'être* for this book — to excite discussion and dissension is part of the fun. And that is why you, the reader, are cordially invited to put me straight, to show me the error of my ways, to enlighten me as to which of these paintings do not deserve their top 100 slot and which works should replace those in the book. Who knows, a new edition might take note of your input.

Visit **www.interlinkbooks.com/100bestpaintings/haveyoursay**

If I was pressed to choose my top ten from the 100 paintings in this book then the order would look something like the list below.

1	Rembrandt	*Self Portrait with Two Circles*	Kenwood House
2	J.M.W. Turner	*Norham Castle*	Tate Britain
3		*Wilton Diptych*	National Gallery

4	Jan van Eyck	*The Arnolfini Portrait*	National Gallery
5	Giorgio de Chirico	*The Uncertainty of the Poet*	Tate Modern
6	Mark Rothko	*Seagram Murals*	Tate Modern
7	Claude Lorrain	*The Enchanted Castle*	National Gallery
8	Jan Gossaert	*Adoration of the Kings*	National Gallery
9	J-A. Watteau	*The Music Party*	Wallace Collection
10	Georges Seurat	*Bathers at Asnières*	National Gallery

You can also enter your own top ten in the form provided at our website.

Above all, these are not the choices of an art professional but of a committed gallery visitor, an enthusiastic layman, a person who has queued for entry to exhibitions only to find that so many of us have been admitted that it is impossible to see the paintings, and a person who has on some occasions travelled many miles only to find that the gallery is closed.

The book is arranged by gallery and within each gallery section the paintings are listed chronologically. Most collections are organised in some sort of chronological order (the main exceptions being Tate Modern and to some extent the Wallace Collection) and so it was felt that arranging the book in this fashion would enhance its usefulness. Two pages are devoted to each chosen painting and to the artist concerned. The biographical chronology gives the reader as much information as we have about the artist, or as much as space will allow. The listing of selected paintings by contemporaneous artists will, I hope remind the reader of what was happening elsewhere at about the time that the chosen work was being produced. In each case I have given the current geographical location of the work — when the work is located in London then I have also given the gallery where it can be seen.

I hope you will enjoy looking at these wonderful paintings, but don't forget to let me have your views by visiting our dedicated website at:
www.interlinkbooks.com/100bestpaintings/haveyoursay

List of Paintings by Artist

Antonello da Messina
St Jerome in his Study   National Gallery   **76**
Bacon, Francis
Three Studies for Figures
at the Base of a Crucifixion   Tate Britain   **182**
Balla, Giacomo
The Hand of the Violinist   Estorick Collection   **44**
Beckmann, Max
Carnival   Tate Modern   **202**
Bellini, Giovanni
Agony in the Garden   National Gallery   **74**
Bonnard, Pierre
Coffee   Tate Modern   **198**
Bosch, Hieronymus
Christ Mocked   National Gallery   **86**
Botticelli, Sandro
Venus and Mars   National Gallery   **82**
Braque, Georges
Clarinet and Bottle of Rum on a Mantelpiece Tate Modern   **194**
Bronzino
An Allegory with Venus and Cupid   National Gallery   **108**
Bruegel, Pieter, The Elder
Landscape with the Flight into Egypt   Courtauld Institute   **18**
Burne-Jones, Edward
King Cophetua and the Beggar Maid   Tate Britain   **176**
Canaletto
Old Walton Bridge   Dulwich Picture
                                            Gallery   **40**

Caravaggio
Supper at Emmaus   National Gallery   **114**
Cézanne, Paul
Lac d'Annecy   Courtauld Institute   **30**
Chardin, Jean Siméon
The Young Schoolmistress   National Gallery   **130**
Chirico, Giorgio de
Uncertainty of the Poet   Tate Modern   **196**

Claude Lorrain
  Landscape with Psyche outside the Palace of Cupid
  (The Enchanted Castle)   National Gallery   124
Constable, John
  Sketch for Hadleigh Castle   Tate Britain   162
Correggio
  School of Love
  (Venus with Mercury and Cupid)   National Gallery   102
Cranach, Lucas, the Elder
  Adam and Eve   Courtauld Institute   16
Crivelli, Carlo
  Annunciation with St Emidius   National Gallery   84
Cuyp, Aelbert
  View of Dordrecht   Kenwood House   48
Dadd, Richard
  The Fairy Feller's Master Stroke   Tate Britain   172
Dalí, Salvador
  Metamorphosis of Narcissus   Tate Modern   208
David, Jacques-Louis
  Jacobus Blauw   National Gallery   138
Degas, Hilaire-Germain-Edgar
  Two Dancers on the Stage   Courtauld Institute   20
Delvaux, Paul
  Sleeping Venus   Tate Modern   210
Duccio di Buoninsegna
  Annunciation   National Gallery   56
Dürer, Albrecht
  Saint Jerome   National Gallery   88
Dyck, Anthony van
  Equestrian Portrait of Charles I   National Gallery   118
Ernst, Max
  Celebes   Tate Modern   204
Eyck, Jan van
  Portrait of a Man   National Gallery   62
  The Arnolfini Portrait   National Gallery   64
Fragonard, Jean-Honoré
  The Swing   Wallace Collection   230
Friedrich, Caspar David
  Winter Landscape   National Gallery   140
Gainsborough, Thomas
  Mary, Countess Howe   Kenwood House   52
Gauguin, Paul
  Nevermore   Courtauld Institute   32
Geertgen tot Sint Jans
  Nativity at Night   National Gallery   80
Giorgione
  The Sunset (Il Tramonto)   National Gallery   94

Gogh, Vincent van
Sunflowers   National Gallery   152
Gossaert, Jan (Mabuse)
Adoration of the Kings   National Gallery   98
Goya, Francisco de
Portrait of the Duke of Wellington   National Gallery   142
Greco, El
Christ driving the Traders from the Temple   National Gallery   112
Grosz, George
Suicide   Tate Modern   200
Hals, Frans
The Laughing Cavalier   Wallace Collection 224
Hilliard, Nicholas
Young Man leaning against a Tree among Roses
                                                 V & A   220
Hobbema, Meindert
The Avenue, Middelharnis   National Gallery   128
Hockney, David
A Bigger Splash   Tate Britain   184
Hogarth, William
The Rake's Progress, III, The Rose Tavern   Sir John Soane's
                                                 Museum   158
Holbein, Hans, the Younger
The Ambassadors   National Gallery   104
Christina of Denmark, Duchess of Milan   National Gallery   106
Hooch, Pieter de
Interior with a Woman drinking with Two Men   National Gallery   122
Hunt, William Holman
The Awakening Conscience   Tate Britain   170
Ingres, Jean-Auguste-Dominique
Madame Moitessier   National Gallery   146
Inshaw, David
The Badminton Game   Tate Britain   186
Kiefer, Anselm
Parsifal III   Tate Modern   216
Klein, Yves
IKB 79   Tate Modern   212
Klimt, Gustav
Portrait of Hermine Gallia   Tate Modern   190
Leonardo da Vinci
Virgin of the Rocks   National Gallery   92
Manet, Édouard
Bar at the Folies-Bergère   Courtauld Institute 24
Mantegna, Andrea
Agony in the Garden   National Gallery   72
Martin, John
The Great Day of His Wrath   Tate Britain   168

Masaccio
  Virgin and Child   National Gallery   **60**
Matisse, Henri
  Portrait of André Derain   Tate Modern   **192**
Memling, Hans
  The Donne Triptych   National Gallery   **78**
Millais, John Everett
  Ophelia   Tate Britain   **166**
Monet, Claude
  Antibes   Courtauld Institute   **28**
Picasso, Pablo
  The Three Dancers   Tate Modern   **206**
Piero della Francesca
  Baptism of Christ   National Gallery   **68**
Piero di Cosimo
  A Satyr mourning over a Nymph   National Gallery   **90**
Pisanello
  The Vision of St Eustace   National Gallery   **66**
Pissarro, Camille
  The Quays at Rouen   Courtauld Institute   **26**
Poussin, Nicolas
  A Dance to the Music of Time   Wallace Collection   **226**
Puvis de Chavannes, Pierre-Cécile
  The Beheading of St John the Baptist   National Gallery   **148**
Raphael
  Pope Julius II   National Gallery   **96**
Rembrandt
  Girl at a Window   Dulwich Picture
                                                    Gallery   **38**
  Self Portrait with Two Circles   Kenwood House   **50**
Renoir Pierre-Auguste
  (La Loge) The Theatre Box   Courtauld Institute   **22**
Reynolds, Joshua
  Nelly O'Brien   Wallace Collection   **232**
Rothko, Mark
  Red on Maroon (The Seagram Murals)   Tate Modern   **214**
Rousseau, Henri
  Tiger in a Tropical Storm   National Gallery   **154**
Rubens, Peter Paul
  *Autumn Landscape with a view of Het Steen
  in the Early Morning*   National Gallery   **116**
Sargent, John Singer
  Carnation, Lily, Lily, Rose   Tate Britain   **178**
Seurat, Georges
  Bathers at Asnières   National Gallery   **150**
Spencer, Stanley
  The Resurrection, Cookham   Tate Britain   **180**

Stubbs, George
Whistlejacket   National Gallery   132
Tintoretto, Jacopo
St George and the Dragon   National Gallery   110
Titian
Bacchus and Ariadne   National Gallery   100
Toulouse-Lautrec, Henri de
In the Private Room at the Rat Mort   Courtauld Institute   34
Turner, J. M. W.
The Fighting Temeraire tugged
to her Last Berth to be broken up   National Gallery   144
Norham Castle, Sunrise   Tate Britain   164
Uccello, Paolo
St George and the Dragon   National Gallery   70
Unknown
The Wilton Diptych   National Gallery   58
Velázquez, Diego
Toilet of Venus (The 'Rokeby Venus')   National Gallery   120
Vermeer, Johannes
A Young Woman Standing at a Virginal   National Gallery   126
Vigée le Brun, Elizabeth Louise
Self Portrait in a Straw Hat   National Gallery   136
Watteau, Jean-Antoine
The Music Party   Wallace Collection   228
Whistler, James Abbott McNeill
Nocturne in Blue and Gold:
Old Battersea Bridge   Tate Britain   174
Wright of Derby, Joseph
An Experiment on a Bird in the Air Pump   National Gallery   134

The Courtauld Institute Gallery contains some of the most important works of art in Britain. It is principally made up of three private collections; that of Samuel Courtauld with gifts in 1932 and a bequest in 1947, the bequest of Viscount Lee of Fareham in 1947, and the bequest of the collection of Count Antoine Seilern in 1978.

The Courtauld collection is a superb accumulation of Impressionist and Post-Impressionist paintings and the other two major bequests contain excellent works from many schools of European painting from the mid-fourteenth century through to the twentieth century. Other gifts have added more twentieth-century paintings and sculpture to the mix.

Courtauld Institute Gallery

Somerset House, Strand, London WC2R 0RN
www.courtauld.ac.uk

Opening Hours

Every day 10am – 6pm (Last admissions 5.15pm)
Closed 24 – 26 December

Admission

Adults £5.00
Concessions £4.00 (Over 60s, part-time and international students).
Free admission for under 18s, full-time UK students, staff of UK universities, registered unwaged.
Free admission on Mondays from 10am to 2pm (excluding public holidays).
Disabled visitors may bring a helper free.

How To Get There

The nearest underground stations are Charing Cross (Northern, Bakerloo and Jubilee Lines), Temple (District and Circle Lines — not open on Sundays) and Covent Garden (Piccadilly Line).
Any bus to Aldwych.

Access for the Disabled

There is level access to most parts of the gallery with a lift to all floors. There is no level access to Gallery One. One bookable car parking space is available. Please telephone 0044 (0)20 7848 2531.

Gallery Shop

Open every day 10am – 5.30pm.
The merchandise is inspired by the collection of artworks displayed in the Courtauld Institute Gallery. Over 800 different book titles in stock, covering a wide range of periods and styles as well as design and critical theory.

Gallery Café

Open every day 10am – 5.30pm.
Good food at reasonable prices.

Lucas Cranach the Elder

Adam and Eve 1526

Courtauld Institute Gallery

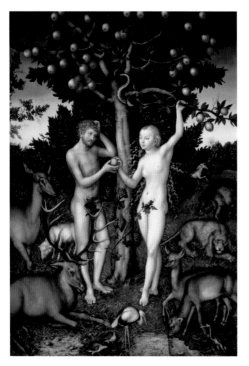

In 1504 Lucas Cranach travelled to Wittenberg from Vienna in order to take up the post of court painter to Duke Frederick the Wise. Thirteen years later Martin Luther catapulted the town to prominence when he nailed his 95 theses to the door of Wittenberg Palace church. Consequently Cranach found himself present at the birth of the movement later known as the Reformation — at the epicentre of events which would change Europe forever. A close friend of Luther, he naturally became the favoured portraitist for the circle which gathered around the reforming monk at this pivotal moment. But he was not content merely to provide artistic services, he was also an activist involving himself in designing propaganda sheets, underwriting the costs of publishing Luther's translation of the Bible and setting up a printing press in his house for this purpose.

However, his association with Luther did not stop him from accepting commissions from prominent members of the Church of Rome. His work was in demand and according to surviving tax records, from 1528 only one other citizen in Wittenberg was paying more tax. Much of his fortune was accumulated as a result of his celebrated working speed, producing many versions of the same subject or theme. Adam and Eve was one such theme and it had the added attraction of being sanctioned by Luther as a worthy subject.

It is noticeable that Cranach's nudes are a long way from the Italianate Renaissance ideal. They represent a model of beauty which is perhaps more familiar to the modern eye — Eve is slim with small breasts; Adam also has a natural, life-like build.

Here, the first pair of human beings stand either side of the Tree of Knowledge amidst the verdant pastures and luxuriant woodland of the Garden of Eden, surrounded by a most beautifully realised selection of beasts — two different types of deer, a lion, a sheep, a boar, a horse, and in the foreground, an out-of-scale stork, a pair of partridge and a heron. All is set against a perfect evening sky, the horizon alight with the last colours from the day's sun. But alas, we know that this paradise will soon be denied to our common ancestors for ever.

The tree is heavy with ripe fruit which forms a pleasing decorative effect against the surrounding foliage. From its crown slithers the serpent which has tempted Eve to take a forbidden apple. She hands it to a decidedly bewildered Adam who scratches his head in puzzlement. We are witnessing the very last moments of their blissful innocence and Man's subsequent fall from Grace. But around the base of the tree a vine has taken root and is sinuously winding up the trunk, echoing the attitude of the snake above. We notice, however, that two vinous tendrils have grown with coy precision to shield us from the sight of both male and female genital areas. The vine is a reference to the Eucharist through which Man can find redemption.

Contemporary Works

1525	Correggio: *Venus with Mercury and Cupid (The School of Love)*; London, National Gallery
1526	Albrecht Dürer: *The Four Apostles*; Munich
1526	Titian: *Madonna with Members of the Pesaro Family*; Venice

Lucas Cranach the Elder

1472	Born in Kronach.
1501 or 2	He is working in Vienna.
1504	Cranach is appointed court artist to the Elector of Saxony, Duke Frederick the Wise at Wittenberg.
1508	Duke Frederick grants him a coat of arms featuring a winged serpent, a device he now uses as his signature. Travels to the Netherlands on behalf of the duke.
1519	Designs the earliest surviving propaganda sheet in support of Reformation theology.
1520	Cranach engraves portraits of his friend Martin Luther.
1522	Illustrates the Book of Revelation in the first edition of Luther's translation of the New Testament. Cranach partly underwrites the publication of Luther's translation.
1523	Cranach installs a printing press in his house.
1524	Prints part of Luther's translation of the Old Testament.
1528	Cranach has become one of the wealthiest citizens in Wittenberg according to tax records.
1547	With the capture of Duke John Frederick by the forces of Charles V, Cranach loses his position as court painter.
1550	Decides to join the duke in captivity in Augsberg. Continues to paint.
1552	Moves to live with his daughter and son-in-law in Weimar.
1553	Dies at Weimar.

Pieter Bruegel the Elder

Landscape with the Flight into Egypt   1563

Courtauld Institute Gallery

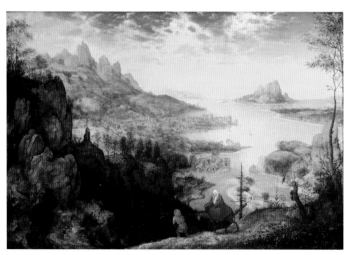

In 1559 Margaret of Parma, the illegitimate daughter of Emperor Charles V, became Regent of the Netherlands, one of the most important of the vast Habsburg possessions. She appointed as President of the Council of State, effectively her Prime Minister, a French-born diplomat and prelate, Antoine Perranot Granvelle, who had served King Philip II of Spain for many years. He was created Archbishop of Malines in 1560 and became a cardinal a year later. However, his policies created unrest and hostility and in 1564, on the advice of Philip II he retired but later resumed his career, becoming Viceroy of Naples and Chief Minister of Spain.

In 1563 Pieter Bruegel married Mayken (or Maria) Coecke, the daughter of Pieter Coecke van Aelst, in whose studio he had spent several years learning his trade as a painter. The marriage took place in Brussels and in the same year Bruegel moved from Antwerp to that city. Shortly after his arrival he painted *Landscape with the Flight into Egypt* for Cardinal Granvelle.

In common with many of his other compositions, this small landscape emphasises the dominant role of nature in the lives of contemporary men and women. The ragged, deeply indented coastline of an estuary or large lake stretches away into the distance. Settlements cling to the shore beneath improbably craggy mountains. This imaginary, composite landscape had its genesis in Bruegel's visit to Italy, via France and Switzerland between 1551 and 1554, but those unstable crags also betray the influence of Joachim Patinir, the Antwerp artist who, at the beginning of the sixteenth century had been the first painter to elevate landscape into a subject in its own right, no longer subordinate to the religious narrative taking place within the picture. The elevated viewpoint and the banded aerial perspective (whereby distance is suggested by the use of three zones of differing colour — brown in the foreground, blue-green for the middle distance and greyish blue for the background) are also derived from Patinir. But in Bruegel's hands the landscape becomes much more believable, the perspective more precise, creating a more credible depth beneath a beautifully luminous sky.

The Holy Family struggles to make progress in the midst of this magnificent but dauntingly mountainous setting. The red cloak of the Virgin, just off centre but aligned with castle, town and lowest point of the horizon, immediately catches our attention. Within its folds she swathes the Christ child. Joseph is straining to keep the recalcitrant donkey moving forward. They are dwarfed by the magnitude of the panorama which surrounds them and the dangers to come are all too apparent for they are approaching a yawning chasm (seen in the lower left corner) spanned by a decidedly frail bridge. Other travellers linger by the bridge — perhaps natural hazards are not the only threat to their safety.

Contemporary Works

1560	Titian: *Rape of Europa*; Boston
1563	Paolo Veronese: *Wedding Feast at Cana*; Paris
1565	Jacopo Tintoretto: *Crucifixion*; Venice

Pieter Bruegel the Elder

1525/1530	Probably born in Breda.
Before 1550	Bruegel works in the studio of Pieter Coecke van Aelst in Antwerp.
1550	Moves to Mechelen where he enters the studio of Claude Dorizi and works on an altarpiece which is now lost.
1551	Travels to Italy.
1552	Leaves Rome for Calabria and possibly visits Palermo.
1553	Returns to Rome.
1554	Leaves Italy for the Netherlands.
1555	12 prints by Bruegel known as the Large Landscapes are published by Hieronymus Cock in Antwerp.
1559	Paints *Netherlandish Proverbs* and *Battle between Carnival and Lent*.
1562	Paints *Fall of the Rebel Angels* and the *Triumph of Death*.
1563	Marries Mayken (Maria?) Coecke, the daughter of Pieter Coecke in Brussels.
1565	Completed *The Seasons* — six pictures commissioned for the house of Nicolaas Jonghelinck in Antwerp. Five survive.
1569	Dies in Brussels.

Hilaire-Germain-Edgar Degas

Two Dancers on the Stage   1874

Courtauld Institute Gallery

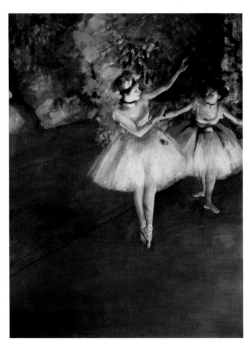

D egas sent work to all but one of the Impressionist group exhibitions
between 1874 and 1886. But although he was a radically innovative
painter in terms of his constant experimentation with new techniques
and media, as well as his strikingly original compositions, his work was
nevertheless grounded in a rigorously academic training, first under a
pupil of Ingres, then at the École des Beaux-Arts. There followed a three-
year visit to Italy where he studied the Renaissance masters. Degas' work
is therefore distinguished from most of the Impressionists principally in
his emphasis on the importance of line and also (excepting his late work)
in his use of often quite subdued colour. Furthermore, he rarely painted
en plein air, preferring to paint in the studio from sketches done on the
spot. These distinctions did not go unnoticed by the critics who in
general spared Degas from much of the rough treatment handed out to
his colleagues in reviews of the early Impressionist exhibitions. As one
critic put it 'We do not know why Monsieur Degas has included himself
in the Impressionist fold. He has a distinct personality and stands apart in
this group of self-styled innovators.'

Two dancers from the corps de ballet are on stage. They are executing
set ballet positions — perhaps as part of a performance for they are lit by
the harsh limelight emanating from the stage rim. Degas has chosen to
place them off centre — the hand of one of the dancers has been cut off
by the right edge of the frame and a fragment of a third dancer's tutu can

be seen intruding from the left. In between and extending toward the viewer is an expanse of freely painted stage. It is as though one has been walking in the wings of the ballet (as Degas did) and very quickly glimpsed this scene as one passes. It is a snapshot, not a posed piece — because everyday life is not posed. Degas was interested in trying to portray things as the eye might actually perceive them, where the angle of view will, more often than not, preclude a perfect compositional arrangement. It is unsurprising that he, like many of his Impressionist colleagues, was interested in photography.

Degas painted over 600 ballet scenes, far more than any other subject, not all depicting a performance on stage. He roamed at will behind the scenes, like many wealthy male devotees, capturing the dancers at rest or practising in rehearsal rooms or parts of the labyrinthine back-stage areas.

The corps de ballet was made up of poor working class girls. Degas refers to the low-born status of the two girls in this picture in a somewhat cruel way. Their facial features, with their upturned noses, reflect contemporary conceptions, associating the lower classes with certain facial characteristics. Notwithstanding his known interest in physiognomy one would like to think that Degas may have been undermining these ideas with his depiction of the elegant poses of the dancers, but bearing in mind his generally reactionary views, we cannot be sure that this was what he had in mind.

Contemporary Works

1873	Paul Cézanne: *Dr Gachet's House*; Paris
1874	James A. M. Whistler: *Nocturne in Blue and Gold (The Falling Rocket)*; Detroit
1874	Jean-Baptiste-Camille Corot: *Lady in Blue*; Paris

Edgar Degas

1834	Born in Paris, the eldest son of a banker.
1854	Instructed in the studio of Louis Lamothe who had been a pupil of Ingres.
1855	Attends the École des Beaux-Arts.
1856	Begins a lengthy visit to Italy where he stays with members of his extended family in Naples and Florence. He also visits Rome for long periods.
1859	Visits Siena and Pisa accompanied by Gustave Moreau. Then returns to Paris.
1862	Meets Manet while engaged in copying paintings in the Louvre.
1865	Exhibits the *Misfortunes of the City of Orléans* at the Salon.
1870	Degas enlists in the National Guard during the Franco-Prussian War.
1872	Travels to New Orleans where members of his family are cotton traders.
1874	Degas exhibits ten works at the independent show which later becomes known as the First Impressionist Exhibition.
1876	Shows 24 works at the Second Impressionist Exhibition.
1879	At the Fourth Impressionist Exhibition Degas has 20 paintings on show together with a number of decorated fans.
1881	At the Sixth Impressionist Exhibition his wax sculpture of a *Little Dancer aged Fourteen* causes uproar with critics who suggest that it ought to be in an anthropology museum rather that an art show.
1886	Increasingly at odds with many of his former Impressionist friends he sends only 10 works to the last group exhibition.
1894	The Dreyfus affair (Degas was fiercely anti-Dreyfusard) leads gradually to the loss of a number of friends.
1912	Enduring failing eyesight and poor health, no works are produced after this date.
1917	Dies in Paris (September).

Pierre-Auguste Renoir

La Loge (The Theatre Box) 1874

Courtauld Institute Gallery

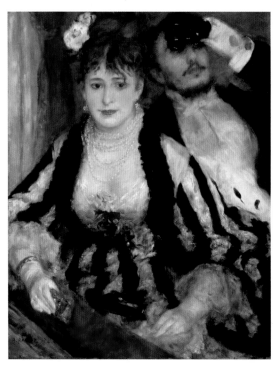

A man and a woman are occupying a box at the theatre but one feels that they are more intent on the social aspects of theatregoing than what is happening on stage. Certainly the man, training his opera glasses upwards, is absorbed in scanning the audience. Similarly, it seems that the rather glazed eyes of the woman are not fixed on the stage — she is really there 'to be seen'. The relationship between the two is not explicit and at least one reviewer drew the conclusion that she was a *cocotte*, a class of 'kept' women (whose status ranged from mistress to prostitute). It matters not — at this moment they inhabit Renoir's agreeable world of pleasure and sociable companionship.

The picture was exhibited at the First Impressionist Exhibition in 1874 and was one of the few paintings which were not subjected to derision by the critics. In fact it received some praise. This is probably because of its relatively 'finished' look in relation to much of the rest of the exhibition. Renoir was always able to produce elaborate set piece pictures at the same time as freer more 'impressionist' landscapes. In *La Loge* the woman's face has been finished to standards which would have pleased a conservative academician. In the rest of the picture there is a quite exceptional richness in the handling of the paint and the considerable attention to detail (the highlights on her necklace for instance) adds to the overall effect of opulence As in other large-scale set piece works of this period, Renoir creates a sort of nineteenth-century *sfumato*, deliberately blurring the edges between forms and then building up a frenzy of paint to produce a lavish and tactile rendition of the gown, which, with the face of Nini, is the principal subject of the picture. The stripes of the gown together with the evening wear of her companion give the composition an interesting black and white bias relieved by the leather and wood tones of the theatre box and the flowers, wonderfully painted by Renoir, placed in her décolletage.

Although the exhibition of the Société Anonyme Co-opérative d'Artistes-Peintres, Sculpteurs, Graveurs etc, to give it its correct title, was not a total failure in terms of sales, and even though the painting received praise, La Loge did not sell at its asking price of 500 francs but was sold later for 425 francs. Over a century later this picture has been hailed by one critic as Renoir's finest masterpiece. It has some tough competition but having seen it in the 'flesh' you may well consider this assessment to be no less that the truth.

Contemporary Works

1873	Jean-François Millet: *Spring*; Paris
1874	James Tissot: *The Ball on Shipboard*; London, Tate Britain.
1875	Gustave Caillebotte: *The Floor-Scrapers*; Paris

Pierre-Auguste Renoir

1841	Born in Limoges, the son of a tailor, the sixth of seven children.
1844	The family moves to Paris.
1854	Renoir is apprenticed to a porcelain painter.
1861	Studies at the studio of Charles Gleyre — meets Monet, Sisley and Bazille.
1862	Admitted to the École des Beaux-Arts.
1864	Shares a flat in the Batignolles area of northern Paris with Bazille.
1869	Works with Monet at La Grenouillère, a popular bathing place near Bougival just outside Paris. Their collaboration is a milestone in the creation of Impressionism.
1870	After France's declaration of war on Prussia, Renoir is drafted into the cavalry.
1871	After contracting dysentery he is demobilised in March.
1873	Exhibits at the Salon des Refusés.
1874	Renoir plays a central role in the organisation of the first group exhibition of the Société Anonyme Co-opérative d' Artistes-Peintres, Sculpteurs etc.
1876	Shows 15 paintings at the Second Impressionist Exhibition.
1877	Shows 21 paintings at the Third Impressionist Exhibition.
1879	Refuses to take part in the Fourth Impressionist Exhibition.
1880	Stays on the Île de Chatou, working on *The Boating Party*.
1881	Travels to Algeria. Whistler visits him at Chatou. Makes an extended tour of Italy.
1882	Visits Wagner in Palermo. Returns to France working with Cézanne at L'Estaque.
1885	Renoir's first son, Pierre is born to Aline Charigot, his long-term companion.
1886	Exhibits eight paintings at Les XX in Brussels and 38 paintings at a New York exhibition organised by Durand-Ruel.
1890	Marries Aline Charigot.
1892	Visits Madrid and Seville.
1894	On the death of Gustave Caillebotte, Renoir is named as his executor. Jean Renoir is born in Paris.
1898	Sells a Degas painting, a gift from Caillebotte's collection. This leads to a quarrel with Degas.
1900	Awarded the Chevalier de la Légion d'Honneur.
1904	One room in the Salon d'Automne is devoted to Renoir.
1907	Settles in Cagnes in the south of France. Suffers from severe rheumatism.
1919	Made a Commandeur de la Légion d'Honneur. Dies at Cagnes.

Édouard Manet

Courtauld Institute Gallery

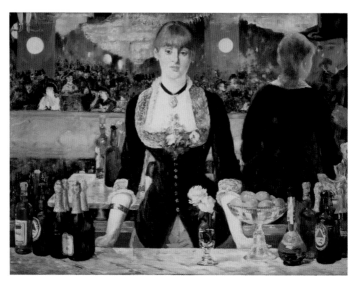

The Folies-Bergère was the largest, and one of the most fashionable places of entertainment in Paris. Reflected in the mirror of Manet's painting, behind the barmaid, one can see part of the cavernous interior — the chink of glasses, the music of a band and the roar of hundreds of conversations are almost audible; in the top left corner of the composition one can make out the feet of a trapeze artist perhaps about to swing our way. Arrayed in front of the *dame du comptoir*, on the marble topped bar is a beautifully painted still life — wine and beer bottles, Green Chartreuse, some oranges in a crystal dish and cut flowers in a glass — the last two splendidly offset against the black of her dress.

But the focus of the picture is the cashier herself, occupying her station behind one of the bars. Her gaze is unfocused and wistful. She seems to be somewhat detached, cocooned against the noisy sociability which surrounds her; she does not invite the attention of the next customer but will wearily fulfil her duties when asked. The Folies-Bergère was a venue at which fashionable society and the *demi-monde* mixed. Prostitutes thronged its public spaces and in such a milieu the status of the barmaid was often uncertain. It is possible that Manet is hinting at this potential availability, or at least to a certain ambivalence in his portrayal of this young woman (one of the real barmaids from the Folies-Bergère) surrounded as she is by other merchandise displayed at her counter.

The reflected images in the mirror are decidedly problematical and have triggered much comment. The barmaid is centrally placed and the reflection of the marble bar is parallel to the picture plane (meaning that the mirror is also parallel to the picture plane and that we are viewing the composition from a central vantage point). From this viewpoint the woman should in fact obscure her own reflection. But Manet has displaced her reflected image considerably to the right in a way that is consistent with the mirror being placed at an angle. Other anomalies are apparent. The placement of the bottles in the mirror is slightly different from that on the bar. Furthermore, the barmaid's reflection seems to show her in a different light from the woman facing us. She is not absorbed in her detached reverie but is leaning forward solicitously and engaging her customer who stands directly across the counter. This customer, who occupies the space between her and the corner of the picture, is far too near to the barmaid in the reflection. His reflected proximity would logically place him between us, the spectator and the bar. But there is perhaps a reason for his absence. Even though the barmaid is not engaging us directly as does Manet's favourite model Victorine in *Déjeuner sur l'herbe* and *Olympia*, she nevertheless gazes out of the picture into the space occupied by the viewer and by her next customer, and it seems that Manet may indeed wish to conflate the two in our minds — the viewer is the next customer and may be identified with the rather sketchily drawn gentleman.

All this compositional uncertainty leads us to believe that Manet is here challenging the accepted norms of representation and is deliberately provoking us to question pictorial reality. Indeed X-ray investigations reveal that Manet accentuated these anomalies as he worked on the painting, which was his last great work. It was accepted by the Salon in 1882 but a year later he was dead, probably as a result of gangrene brought about by syphilis.

Contemporary Works

1881	Pierre Puvis de Chavannes: *The Poor Fisherman*; Paris
1882	Max Liebermann: *Bleaching Linen on the Grass*; Cologne
1884	Georges-Pierre Seurat: *Bathers at Asnières*; London, National Gallery.

Édouard Manet

1832	Born in Paris, the son of a civil servant in the Ministry of Justice.
1850	Enters the studio of Thomas Couture, the academic history painter.
1856	Sets up his own studio.
1862	*Concert at the Tuileries Gardens* is painted in the open air.
1863	*Déjeuner sur l'herbe* is rejected by the Salon but causes a sensation when exhibited at the Salon des Refusés which is set up to exhibit the many rejections from the official Salon. Marries Suzanne Leenhoff, his piano teacher.
1865	*Olympia* causes another scandal when exhibited at the Salon. The brazen gaze of the naked woman causes particular offence. Saddened and frustrated by the reception of *Olympia*, Manet decides to visit Spain.
1867	In the face of public hostility, Émile Zola publishes an article praising Manet in the *Revue du XIX siècle*.
1870	Manet serves as a Lieutenant in the National Guard during the Franco-Prussian War and the Siege of Paris.
1872	Visits the Netherlands where he is influenced by the paintings of Frans Hals.
1874	Manet's friendship with Claude Monet grows closer and the two paint together on the banks of the Seine at Argenteuil.
1880	Holds a one-man exhibition at the premises of the periodical *La Vie Moderne*.
1882	Exhibits his last great work, *A Bar at the Folies-Bergère* at the Salon.
1883	In early April his left leg becomes gangrenous. This is amputated but he dies soon afterwards.

Camille Pissarro

The Quays at Rouen

Courtauld Institute Gallery

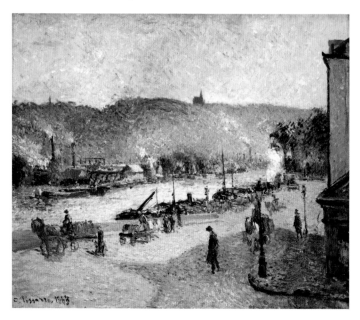

Pissarro was the only artist to take part in all eight Impressionist Exhibitions (though none of them bore the title which is now used). He fulfilled a pivotal role in the development of Impressionism and in the movements it later spawned, becoming something of a father figure and mentor to such artists as Cézanne, Gauguin and van Gogh, and enthusiastically supporting the aims of the Neo-Impressionists.

In the autumn of 1883 Pissarro took a room in Murer's Hotel in Rouen. For three months he worked on thirteen paintings of the city with the river Seine and the attendant commercial activities of the port as his principal motif. Thirteen years later he was back in the city to undertake one of the series of urban scenes which constituted much of Pissarro's output during the last ten years of his life. These series paintings amounted to some three hundred canvases made up of views from a single vantage point, usually a hotel room high above the chosen scene. In retrospect, the canvases painted in Rouen in 1883, which can be divided into three groups of subjects, can be seen as his first attempt to create a series of cityscapes.

In this picture, as in his later urban series, he uses a raised viewpoint partly it seems in order to distance the viewer from the panorama presented by the artist and to create the feeling that we are voyeurs, detached from the lives of those engaged in the day-to-day activities of the city — lives from which a brief moment has been captured and frozen on the canvas.

Pissarro constructed his pictures at this time using a heavy impasto — small dabs and dots of colour are built up, dab on dab, to produce a surface which almost seethes with colour. Small flecks of lighter paint across the surface help to give the impression of occluded sunlight. Two years after his stay in Rouen, Pissarro met Seurat and Signac, after which he adopted, for a while, a pointillist style. However, this picture already exhibits aspects of a nascent pointillism and it seems that Pissarro would have needed little encouragement from them to adapt to full blown Neo-Impressionism.

Contemporary Works

1882	William Powell Frith: *The Private View at the Royal Academy in 1881*; London
1883	Pierre-Auguste Renoir: *Dance at Bougival*; Boston
	Arnold Böcklin: *Ulysses and Calypso*; Basel
1884	Sir Edward Burne-Jones: *King Cophetua and the Beggar Maid*; London, Tate Britain.

Camille Pissarro

1830	Born on the West Indian island of St Thomas, then part of the Danish Virgin Islands, to a Jewish family.
1842	Sent to boarding school in Paris. His gifts as an artist are discovered and nurtured.
1847	Returns to St Thomas in order to go into the family business.
1852	Travels with the Danish artist Fritz Melbye to Venezuela where they establish a studio.
1855	Pissarro arrives in Paris.
1856	Works in the studio of Fritz Melbye's brother, Anton.
1859	Meets Monet while attending the Académie Suisse.
1860	Julie Vellay comes to live with the Pissarro family as a servant and Pissarro forms a liaison with her.
1861	Meets Cézanne and Guillaumin at the Académie Suisse.
1866	Meets Manet. Attends meetings at the Café Guerbois and at Bazille's studio with Monet, Renoir, Sisley and others.
1869	Moves to Louveciennes, just outside Paris, and begins to paint in an Impressionist style.
1870	With the outbreak of the Franco-Prussian war Pissarro flees advancing troops. Eventually arrives in London in December.
1871	Marries Julie at Croydon in June. Returns to France to find his house has been looted with the loss of over 1,000 paintings.
1872	Moves to Pontoise where he works with Cézanne who is deeply influenced by Pissarro.
1874	Shows five paintings at the First Impressionist Exhibition.
1876	Thirteen paintings by Pissarro are exhibited at the Second Impressionist Exhibition.
1877	Exhibits 22 paintings at the Third Impressionist Exhibition
1879	Works with Paul Gauguin.
1883	The dealer Durand-Ruel mounts an exhibition of Pissarro's work.
1884	Moves to Eragny-sur-Epte in Normandy.
1885	Pissarro is introduced to Signac and Seurat and adopts a pointillist style.
1888	Contracts an eye infection which causes him problems for the rest of his life.
1890	An operation is deemed necessary for his eye.
1892	Provides financial help for the families of detained anarchist activists. Visits London. Monet helps him to buy his house at Eragny.
1894	Visits Belgium where he stays with the Neo-Impressionist Théo van Rysselberghe.
1896	Paints series of paintings of the Bridges and Quays of Rouen.
1901	Paints series of views of Dieppe.
1903	Dies in Paris (November).

Claude Monet

Courtauld Institute Gallery

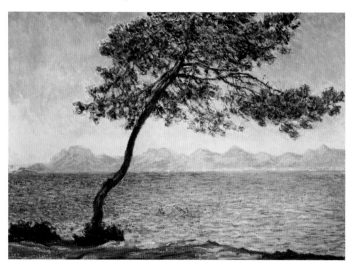

The 1880s saw Monet at the height of his powers — he was creating some of his finest and most satisfying compositions, this being a very good example. During the decade he made many painting trips to the coast — to various locations in Normandy and to Belle Île in Brittany where he captured the rugged beauty of the coastline of that region and relished the challenge of the rapidly changing light and weather. In 1884 he visited Bordighera on the Mediterranean near the border with Italy and in 1888 he returned to the Mediterranean, this time to Antibes. Here the challenge was different — how to capture the intense light and colour of the south.

The light seems to assail you from this canvas; the beauty of its colours besieges your eyes. The picture encapsulates the experience of the Mediterranean — Monet pins down the very essence of that special light using a palette which matches the dominant tones of the region — utilising colours which he had rarely used in his 'northern' work. 'It is so beautiful here,' Monet wrote, 'so bright, so full of light. One is afloat in blue air. It is awe inspiring.' The effect of shimmering light playing on a gently rippling sea is achieved by the application of a multitude of brushstrokes each loaded with subtly different colour. The sea is made up of juxtaposed strokes of dark and light blue, green, violet and white, all of which miraculously coalesce into as perfect an approximation of moving water as can be achieved in paint. It is typical of Monet that it all looks so effortless. But a recent X-ray examination has revealed that the work went through many metamorphoses before it arrived at this final perfection. In particular, the tree was moved somewhat to the left (its central position set against the sea and distant hills is reminiscent of Japanese prints reminding us that, like many of his Impressionist colleagues, Monet was an admirer of Japanese art).

It is in the 1880s that Monet started to use several canvases when painting at a particular site. He would change from one unfinished canvas to another as the quality of the light altered throughout the day, gradually building up finished pictures each reflecting particular conditions. This working method led to his creation of the great series paintings of the 1890s but his compulsive efforts to capture on canvas every conceivable light effect were a lifelong obsession. As Cézanne famously observed, Monet is 'only an eye, but God what an eye'.

Contemporary Works

1887	Émile Bernard: *Portrait of Père Tanguy*; Basel
1888	Vincent van Gogh: *Sunflowers*; London, National Gallery
	James Ensor: *The Entry of Christ into Brussels*; Antwerp

Claude Monet

1840	Born in Paris.
1845	Monet's family moves to Le Havre, his father joining a family grocery business.
1858	Meets Eugène Boudin and paints outdoors with him.
1857	Monet's mother dies but his aunt encourages his interest in painting.
1859	Enrols at the Académie Suisse in Paris where he meets Camille Pissarro.
1860	Called up for military service and posted to Algeria for a year.
1862	Discharged from the army due to illness. Meets the Dutch artist Johan Barthold Jongkind who is influential in directing Monet towards landscape painting. Enters the studio of Charles Gleyre in Paris where he meets Renoir and Sisley.
1867	Camille Doncieux, Monet's mistress gives birth to their first son.
1869	Monet and Renoir work together at La Grenouillère, a popular bathing place on the Seine, near Paris. Their paintings prove to be of great importance in the formation of Impressionism.
1870	Marries Camille. With the onset of the Franco-Prussian War they move to London.
1871	Monet's father dies leaving him a modest inheritance. Returns to France where the family rent a house at Argenteuil near Paris.
1873	The Société Anonyme Co-opérative d'Artistes-Peintres, Sculpteurs, Graveurs etc. is formed, being the nucleus of the group later labelled the Impressionists.
1874	The first group exhibition takes place. The critic Louis Leroy coins the word 'Impressionist' in a sarcastic review of Monet's *Impression, Sunrise*.
1876	Meets Ernest Hoschedé who commissions panels for his château.
1878	Monet's patron Ernest Hoschedé is declared bankrupt. The Hoschedé and Monet families set up house together at Véteuil.
1879	Camille dies.
1883	Monet, Alice Hoschedé (now his lover) and their eight children move to Giverny.
1890	Monet is able to purchase his house in Giverny.
1892	Following the death of Ernest Hoschedé, Monet and Alice are married.
1893	Buys more land to extend his garden at Giverny where he builds a 'Japanese' bridge over a pond and plants waterlilies.
1894	The Durand-Ruel Gallery exhibit Monet's series showing the façade of Rouen Cathedral seen under varying light conditions.
1904	Exhibition of paintings resulting from Monet's recent visits to London.
1908	Monet and Alice visit Venice.
1911	Alice dies.
1916	A large studio is completed at Giverny which Monet uses to work on his huge waterlily decorations which are designed to surround the viewer.
1918	Monet announces that he will donate his waterlily decorations to the state.
1926	Dies at Giverny.
1927	The waterlily decorations, installed in the Orangerie are opened to the public.

Paul Cézanne

The Lac d'Annecy   1896

Courtauld Institute Gallery

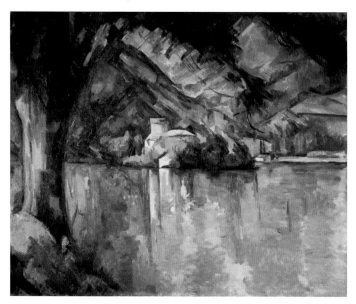

The Lac d'Annecy is situated in the Haute Savoie, in the approaches to the French Alps. Cézanne has chosen a view of the Château de Duingt from across the lake. The composition is framed and confined by a tree which is positioned close to the left edge of the canvas and whose branches intrude from the top edge. The tree seems to cast its shadow across the whole composition which is dominated by rich, but cool tones of blue and green.

The hill behind the château and the more distant hills are fashioned with blocks of colour, the principal blue tones broken by warmer areas of russet and ochre. Each of these blocks and strokes are composed using an immense variety of subtly different colour within the blue-green scheme. The effect is kaleidoscopic but at the same time calming and still.

This work forms part of an increasing trend in Cézanne's late output to reduce motifs to their essentials — small areas of colour are used as a 'shorthand' to accentuate the differing planes and facets of the landscape – a tendency which later culminated in the famous series of studies of Mont Sainte-Victoire. At that time he wrote to Émile Bernard that 'Nature must be dealt with in terms of cylinders, spheres and cones'. In this painting we can see the genesis of that approach (a decade or so before the groundbreaking movements of the early twentieth century changed everything) and the clear debt owed to Cézanne by both the Fauves and, in particular, the Cubists is very evident.

Not long before his death in 1906 Cézanne wrote to his son that '...the realisation of my sensations is always painful. I cannot attain the intensity that is unfolding before my senses. I have not the magnificent richness of colouring that animates nature'. Perhaps he came close to this impossible and frustrating quest in this work.

Contemporary Works

1895	Frederic, Lord Leighton: *Flaming June*; Ponce, Puerto Rico
1896	Paul Gauguin: *Scene from Tahitian Life*; St Petersburg
	Henri de Toulouse-Lautrec: *La Toilette*; Paris
1897	John William Waterhouse: *Hylas and the Nymphs*; Manchester

Paul Cézanne

1839	Born in Aix-en-Provence the son of a prominent businessman.
1852	At school, he meets Émile Zola who becomes a close friend.
1857	Enrols at the École Municipale du Dessin in Aix.
1859	Under pressure from his father he studies law at the University in Aix. His father buys an estate near Aix, the Jas de Bouffan, where Cézanne sets up a studio.
1861	Moves to Paris after abandoning university. Attends the Académie Suisse.
1862	After a period back in Aix Cézanne returns to Paris.
1863	Fails the entrance exam for the École des Beaux-Arts. Exhibits at the Salon des Refusés (in company with Manet and Pissarro).
1869	Meets Hortense Fiquet, a nineteen-year-old model who becomes his mistress.
1870	At the outbreak of the Franco-Prussian war he quits Paris for L'Estaque near Marseille.
1871	Returns to Paris after the fall of the Commune.
1872	Hortense gives birth to a son (Paul). Cézanne hides his son's existence from his father. Moves his family to Pontoise where he works outdoors with Pissarro who he thought of as his master.
1873	Stays with his family in Dr Gachet's house in Auvers-sue-Oise. Meets van Gogh.
1874	Exhibits at the First Impressionist Exhibition where his paintings come in for particular criticism from the press.
1877	Shows 16 works at the Third Impressionist Exhibition. The critics are again scornful and he resolves not to take part in further group shows.
1878	Moves to live in L'Estaque but makes annual trips to Paris.
1881	Works with Pissarro again in Pontoise.
1884	Monet and Renoir visit Cézanne at L'Estaque.
1886	Cézanne falls out with Zola after the publication of the latter's novel *L'Ouvre* in which Cézanne recognises himself as the main character, a failed artist. Marries Hortense in April. His father dies in October.
1890	Spends five months in Switzerland with his family.
1892	Buys a house near the forest of Fontainebleau.
1894	Visits Monet at Giverny where he meets Rodin and Georges Clemenceau.
1895	Ambroise Vollard shows 150 works by Cézanne.
1896	Spends two months at Taillores on the Lac d'Annecy.
1899	Sells the Jas de Bouffan and moves to a flat in Aix; his wife and son remain in Paris.
1901	Builds a studio at Les Lauves on a hill overlooking Aix.
1903	Exhibits seven pictures at the Vienna Secession.
1904	At the Salon d'Automne Cézanne's paintings fill a room.
1906	Dies at Aix-en-Provence (October).

Paul Gauguin

Courtauld Institute Gallery

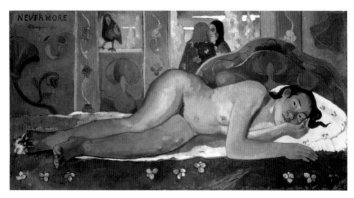

On 28 June 1895 Paul Gauguin boarded a train at the Gare de Lyon in Paris. A few days later he was on board ship, beginning his second voyage to Tahiti. He would not see France again. At the age of forty-nine he was already in very poor health suffering from the alcoholism and syphilis which would kill him within eight years. But, even though he was reportedly in tears when the time came to leave Paris, he was apparently leaving to 'be able to end my days free and at peace with no thought for tomorrow and without having to battle endlessly against idiots'.

Unfortunately, on arrival in Tahiti, his health robbed him of the chance to find this sought after peace of mind. Nevertheless, during this second stay in Tahiti, despite his growing depression, which culminated in a failed attempt at suicide, Gauguin produced some of his most evocative paintings. *Nevermore* is one such picture.

A naked Tahitian girl lies full length on a bed; her head framed by a lemon-yellow pillow. She is Pahura, Gauguin's young *vahiné* or mistress. The walls are richly decorated and among the motifs employed by the artist we can identify two fairly explicit phallic references in the vegetative forms beneath the bird and above the girl's shoulder.

The somewhat comical bird in the window is supposed to be a raven but has turned out to look more like a guillemot. Gauguin admitted in a letter to his agent in Paris that the bird was badly painted '… but no matter, I think it's a good canvas.' Even though Gauguin denied it, the title of the picture, painted by the artist at the top left of the canvas, cannot escape inevitable association with Edgar Allan Poe's poem *The Raven* in which the eponymous bird perches above the door uttering 'Nevermore'. Gauguin saw it more as a symbol of the devil. It matters not, its presence contributes to the general feeling of unease which pervades the picture.

This disquiet is amplified by the wistful, or perhaps fearful look on Pahura's face. She seems to be aware of the raven and perhaps she is also listening to the two other figures conversing in the background. Her melancholy demeanour may have something to do with the loss of a baby daughter which had been born a year or so before this picture was painted but who had died soon after birth. Pahura and the baby appear in an earlier painting, *The Child of God* which shows the young mother, just after the birth, with a *tupapau* (a spirit of the dead) about to take the baby away.

Contemporary Works

1897	Camille Pissarro: *Boulevard Montmartre*; *Afternoon Sunshine*; St Petersburg
	Félix Vallotton: *The Spring*; Geneva
1898	Henry Ossawa Tanner: *The Annunciation*; Philadelphia
	Gustav Klimt: *Pallas Athene*; Vienna

Paul Gauguin

1848	Born in Paris. After the revolution of this year his father decides to move with his family to Peru. His father dies before arrival in Lima.
1854	Gauguin's family return to France to enable his mother to claim a legacy.
1865	At the age of 17 Gauguin enlists in the Merchant Navy.
1867	Gauguin's mother dies leaving her children under the guardianship of the financier, photographer and art collector, Gustave Arosa.
1871	Gauguin learns of his mother's death.
1872	Returns to France where Arosa has arranged a position for Gauguin in the Paris Stock Exchange. Becomes an enthusiastic amateur painter.
1873	Marries a young Danish woman, Mette-Sophie Gad.
1874	Visits the First Impressionist Exhibition. Later meets Camille Pissarro who becomes his mentor.
1876	Exhibits a landscape at the Salon.
1881	Gauguin, Pissarro and Cézanne paint together in Pontoise. Degas purchases some of his paintings.
1882	The French stock market crashes and Gauguin loses his job.
1883	Deciding to make a living through his art, Gauguin moves with his wife and five children from Paris to Rouen.
1884	Mette and the children leave for Copenhagen where they live with her parents. Gauguin eventually follows.
1885	Gauguin works as a salesman in Copenhagen but in June he returns to Paris.
1886	Paints in the Breton village of Pont-Aven for five months.
1887	Leaves Paris for Panama and Martinique. Becomes ill and returns to Paris.
1888	Leaves Paris in February for Pont-Aven where he renews a friendship with Émile Bernard and meets Paul Sérusier. In October Gauguin joins Vincent van Gogh in Arles, sharing a tiny apartment. This disastrous episode ends two months later when van Gogh severs part of his left ear and Gauguin flees back to Paris.
1889	Returns to Pont-Aven. Exhibits in Paris at the Café Volpini with Bernard and others. Returns to Brittany, basing himself at Le Pouldu.
1891	After a successful auction of paintings to raise money, Gauguin travels to Tahiti but does not find the paradise he is looking for.
1893	Returns to Paris where an exhibition of his Tahitian work, mounted by Durand-Ruel, elicits a muted response.
1895	Deeply depressed by his lack of success, Gauguin leaves France to return to French Polynesia.
1897	Hearing of the death of his daughter Aline, Gauguin attempts suicide.
1899	Lack of money forces him to take various jobs, one as a journalist writing for a local satirical paper, *Les Guêpes* (The Wasps).
1901	Leaves Tahiti for Hiva Oa in the Marquesas, seeking a world unspoilt by European influence. He paints with renewed enthusiasm after two barren years.
1903	Dies at Atuona, Marquesas Islands.

Henri de Toulouse-Lautrec

In the Private Room at the Rat Mort   1899

Courtauld Institute Gallery

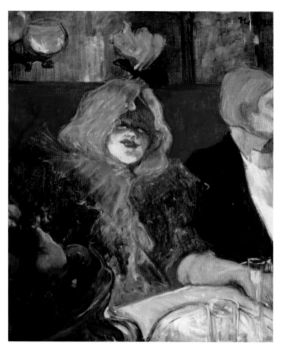

Paris in the Belle Époque was a city at ease with the demi-monde, the decadent underworld of brothels, bars and café-concerts — where prostitutes, dancers, writers and artists of every description mixed with the penniless and the bourgeois, and where *cocottes* and perhaps even the famous courtesans known as the *grandes horizontales* could be seen on the arms of 'respectable' gentlemen. No part of Paris was more associated with this world of hedonistic excess than Montmartre and Pigalle where highlife and lowlife came together in a heady mix of sex, absinthe, music and art.

And no artist is more associated with the bars and brothels of Montmartre during this period than Henri de Toulouse-Lautrec. An aristocrat of impeccable lineage, Lautrec's forebears, in their efforts to preserve the purity of their line by intermarriage, probably contributed to the congenital skeletal weaknesses which resulted in his stunted growth. Unable to take part in the outdoor life which his father considered suitable to his station, Henri was rejected by one parent but received lifelong support from his mother who nurtured his artistic talent — a talent which required stimulation and instruction in the studio of an established artist. And so Lautrec found himself in the City of Lights and very soon in Montmartre (where the action was).

He became besotted with the area and especially with its women. His bodily deformities did not impair his healthy sexual appetite and he could not have been better placed to assuage these desires. Some of the brothels in Montmartre were splendidly appointed and Lautrec became such a devotee that he occasionally left his studio and took up residence for a month or so (or even longer). Throughout his peregrinations he assiduously recorded the lives of the workers (usually female) and customers in this demi-mondaine entertainment hub.

The subject of this painting is Lucy Jourdain, a celebrated *cocotte* who is enjoying dinner at the renowned Rat Mort, a café-restaurant in the rue Pigalle. We have no way of identifying her escort as the picture frame has cut through his face (a device much used by Degas — an obvious influence on Lautrec) consigning him to perpetual anonymity, a state which no doubt suited the gentleman concerned. Lucy's red lipstick and somewhat over-the-top outfit would have been a sure sign to contemporaries regarding the nature of their relationship. Be that as it may, judging by the half-empty champagne glass in front of her and her facial expression, Lucy is having a very good time and this ebullient mood is echoed in the bravura brushwork especially in the striking treatment of her gauzy dress and her extraordinary headgear (which seems to mirror the pear in the foreground). But in the midst of this gaiety Lautrec is unerring in his ability to capture the psychological undercurrent within a given situation and one senses that there are melancholy tensions beneath Lucy's smiling façade.

Contemporary Works

1899	Thomas Eakins: *The Wrestlers*; Columbus, Ohio
	Vilhelm Hammershøi: *Interior*, London, National Gallery
1900	Édouard Vuillard: *Still Life with Candlestick*; Edinburgh

Henri de Toulouse-Lautrec

1864	Born Henri-Marie-Raymond de Toulouse-Lautrec-Monfa, the son of Comte Alphonse and Comtesse Adèle at Albi. He is a direct descendant of the medieval counts of Toulouse who ruled large parts of the Languedoc until 1271.
1878	Henri, who suffers from extremely fragile bones, breaks his left thigh.
1879	Breaks his right thigh. These incidents leave him with atrophied legs.
1882	Moves to Paris, accompanied by his mother. Studies under Léon Bonnat and then with Fernand Cormon who specialises in vast biblical canvases.
1884	Sets up his own studio in rue Lepic, Montmartre.
1886	Meets van Gogh at Cormon's studio.
1888	Eleven of his paintings are exhibited at Les XX in Brussels. Theo van Gogh takes some of his pictures to exhibit at the Boussod, Valadon & Cie Gallery.
1889	At the grand opening of the Moulin Rouge, Lautrec's *At the Fernando Circus* is hung prominently in the entrance hall.
1891	Designs his first poster for the Moulin Rouge which revolutionises poster design and brings him instant popular fame.
1892	Commissioned to paint sixteen canvases for the reception room at one of his favourite brothels.
1896	Collaborates with Vuillard and Bonnard on set designs for Alfred Jarry's play *Ubu Roi*.
1898	Lautrec's health begins to deteriorate and his output declines.
1899	Ravaged by alcoholism, his family consign him to a clinic for detoxification. After his discharge he lives with a friend Paul Viaud who chaperones him.
1900	Lautrec's health deteriorates further with frequent attacks of amnesia.
1901	Leaves Paris for Arcachon where he suffers a stroke. He is taken to his mother's château in the Gironde, where he dies.

Dulwich Picture Gallery, founded under the terms of Sir Francis Bourgeois's will on his death in 1811, was England's first public art gallery. Sir Francis, who was an art dealer, had been contracted to amass a collection on behalf of the King of Poland who had then been unable to take delivery of his paintings because by the time Sir Francis had fulfilled his commission the kingdom of Poland had unfortunately ceased to exist. Sir Francis left his collection to Dulwich College even though he had no particular connection with the school, stipulating that the paintings should be made available for the 'inspection of the public'.

Another condition of the founder's will was that his friend Sir John Soane should be engaged to design the new building which would house his collection as well as a mausoleum for his remains. This building is probably the world's first purpose-built art gallery.

Further donations of paintings have necessitated extensions to Soane's original building but a refurbishment during 1999-2000 has reversed a number of changes in an effort to get back to Soane's initial concept.

Dulwich Picture Gallery

Gallery Road, Dulwich Village, London SE21 7AD
Tel: +44 (0)20 8693 5254
www.dulwichpicturegallery.org.uk

Opening Hours

Tuesday to Friday 10am – 5pm
Saturday, Sunday and Bank Holiday Mondays 11am – 5pm
Closed Monday except Bank Holidays. Also Closed New Year's Day, Good
Friday and 24 – 26 December

Admission

Adults £4.00, Senior Citizens £3.00
Unemployed, disabled, students and children are admitted free.

How To Get There

By train from Victoria Station to West Dulwich Station (the Orpington
line). The train leaves Victoria twice an hour (at 23 and 53 minutes past
the hour), Turn right out of West Dulwich station. Take the first left which
is Gallery Road. The gallery is along Gallery Road and on the right — a
fifteen-minute walk from the station.

Alternatively, from London Bridge Station to North Dulwich. There are
several trains an hour. Turn left out of North Dulwich Station and walk
through Dulwich Village to the gallery; a ten minute walk.

Access for the Disabled

Access for the disabled is good as the collection is displayed on the
ground floor. Two disabled parking spaces are available beside the gallery
(Gallery Road entrance.)

Gallery Shop

Dulwich Picture Gallery shop has a wide range of books and gifts, many
of which are based on the gallery's permanent collection and visiting
exhibitions.

Gallery Café

There is an excellent licensed restaurant overlooking landscaped
gardens.

Rembrandt

Dulwich Picture Gallery

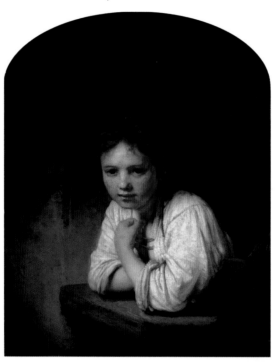

A young girl leans on something that looks like a stone pedestal but the exact nature of the space she inhabits is difficult to discern. The Dulwich Gallery have named this picture *Girl at a Window*, but it is exceedingly difficult to detect where this window might be. The stone object on which she leans may be part of a balcony but we really can't tell. Rembrandt's prime concern is to concentrate our attention on the subject of the painting, so he uses one of his favourite devices and dissolves the background into shadow and darkness while focusing his light source on the face, arms and upper body of the girl. In fact it is not easy to determine what sort of light could illuminate her face and her upper body as well as the wall next to the pedestal but at the same time fail to fall on the wall directly behind her head. But this is of no concern to him. It is better for his purposes that the young girl's face be lifted from the gloom by this peculiar radiance — a luminosity which seems almost to emanate from the girl, rather in the manner employed by his countryman Geertgen almost two centuries before in his enchanting *Nativity at Night* (see page 80).

She is of indeterminate age — her round face and rosy cheeks would seem to suggest that perhaps she has not yet left her childhood entirely behind. It looks as though her hair, full of reddish brown highlights, has been braided and it seems that the end of one braided strand is hanging on her shoulder. She may have a small hat on her head but it is difficult to make out its precise character against the darkness of the background. Her left hand strokes her neck and plays with the fastenings for her white linen blouse. She gazes intently out of the picture — her eyes engaging the viewer with a searching empathy. No painter can better construct this intense rapport between the subject of a painting and the viewer than Rembrandt. He seems to imbue the very paint with humanity in a way that is impossible to understand.

Contemporary Works

1644	Diego Velázquez: *Don Diego de Acedo*; Madrid
1645	Claude Lorrain: *Landscape with Cephalus and Procris reunited by Diana*; London, National Gallery
	Salvator Rosa: *Self Portrait*; London, National Gallery

Rembrandt

1606	Rembrandt Harmensz van Rijn is born in July, the son of a miller in Leiden.
1620	He enrols at Leiden University at the age of fourteen.
1622	Starts a three-year apprenticeship with the painter Jacob Isaacz van Swanenburgh.
1625	He spends about six months in Amsterdam studying with Pieter Lastman. Then returns to Leiden to establish himself as an independent artist.
1628	Rembrandt takes on his first pupil — the 14-year-old Gerrit Dou.
1630	Rembrandt's father dies.
1631	Moves to Amsterdam where he lives with the art dealer Hendrick van Uylenburgh.
1634	Marries Saskia van Uylenburgh, Hendrick's niece.
1635	Rents a house in Amsterdam.
1639	Now an acclaimed artist, Rembrandt buys the house next door to Hendrick van Uylenburgh for 13,000 guilders.
1641	Rembrandt and Saskia's son Titus is born; they have already lost three earlier children in infancy.
1642	Rembrandt finishes *The Night Watch*. Saskia dies of tuberculosis. Geertje Dircz is employed as a nurse for Titus. She soon becomes Rembrandt's mistress.
c1647	A new servant, Hendrickje Stoffels is employed and replaces Geertje as Rembrandt's mistress.
1649	Geertje sues Rembrandt for breach of promise and is awarded an annual allowance of 200 guilders.
1650	Rembrandt instigates legal proceedings which end with Geertje being committed to a house of correction in Gouda.
1654	Hendrickje gives birth out of wedlock to a daughter, Cornelia.
1656	Rembrandt declares himself insolvent. An inventory of his belongings and art collection is made.
1658	After the auction of his collection and house he moves to rented accommodation.
1660	Becomes an employee of a business in the joint names of Hendrickje and Titus.
1663	Hendrickje dies.
1668	Titus marries in February but dies in September leaving a pregnant wife.
1669	Titus' daughter Titia is born. Rembrandt dies and is buried in a rented grave in the Westerkirk.

Canaletto

Dulwich Picture Gallery

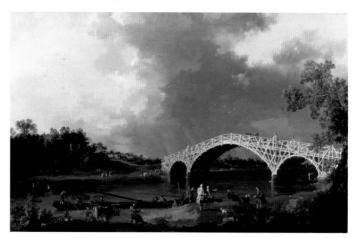

In October 1740, the Holy Roman Emperor Charles VI committed that most egregious dynastic sin and died without having produced a male heir. He had made provision for his daughter Maria Theresa to inherit the various Habsburg kingdoms and duchies spread over much of Europe but the question of the election of a new Holy Roman Emperor — a Habsburg title since the fifteenth century, but only open to male candidates — remained open. Prussia, a parvenu European military power saw its opportunity for expansion and in December 1740 invaded the Habsburg province of Silesia thereby igniting a sporadic conflict known as the War of the Austrian Succession.

One of the myriad consequences of this action was that the number of English gentlemen travelling to Europe on the Grand Tour diminished very considerably. And this in turn (an example perhaps of chaos theory in an historical context) led to a severe diminution in commissions for one Giovanni Antonio Canal, known as Canaletto, whose chief source of income had been the production of Venetian scenes for these gentlemen, who cherished them as up-market souvenirs of their travels.

In 1746 Canaletto decided that he could wait no longer for the political situation to improve and, taking matters into his own hands, he moved to England where he was soon introduced to a number of aristocratic and other well-connected patrons. Towards the end of his stay in England, one such client, a Whig member of parliament, Thomas Hollis, commissioned this picture.

Old Walton Bridge was not so old in 1754, it had only been in place for four years and it appears in this beautiful little picture in all its gleaming novelty, its pristine white paint picked out against a threatening storm cloud by the waning evening light of an English summer. In the foreground, in a suitably central position and wearing a fetching primrose coat stands Thomas Hollis. Nearby, sitting on a stool we can see Canaletto presumably busy making preparatory sketches for this work.

When seen from a usual viewing distance the picture seems to sparkle: as one draws nearer it is clear how this has been achieved. At every opportunity, wherever the raking light within the picture falls on objects in its path, Canaletto has made liberal use of gold, silver and white highlights, animating the surface of the picture with a subtle richness and an enhanced sense of clarity. He has faithfully reproduced here the singular quality of northern light (so different from the hard brilliance of his Venetian views) which is perhaps at its best after rainfall and at either end of the day.

Contemporary Works

1752	Giambattista Tiepolo: *The Marriage of Frederick Barbarossa and Beatrice of Burgundy*; Würzburg
1755	François Boucher: *Landscape with a Watermill*; London, National Gallery
1756	Thomas Gainsborough: *The Painter's Daughters chasing a Butterfly*; London, National Gallery

Canaletto

1697	Giovanni Antonio Canal is born in Venice, the son of Bernado Canal, a painter of theatrical scenery.
1716	Works in Venice painting scenery with his father and uncle for Vivaldi operas.
1719	Travels to Rome with his father to paint opera sets.
1720	Joins the Venetian painters' guild.
1725	His first documented paintings of Venetian views are produced and Canaletto almost immediately builds a formidable reputation producing works mostly for English patrons as mementos of the Grand Tour.
1735	An album of 14 views of Venice, after Canaletto paintings, is published – all are in the collection of Joseph Smith a banker and resident of Venice who acts as intermediary between Canaletto and his English customers.
1740	The outbreak of the War of the Austrian Succession reduces the flow of English tourists to Venice. Canaletto concentrates on drawing and etching.
1746	As a result of a marked decline in commissions because of the war he moves to England.
1750	Visits Venice.
1751	Returns to London.
1756	He is permanently resident again in Venice.
1766	Canaletto's last dated work bears an inscription stating that at the age of 68 he had painted it without the aid of spectacles.
1768	Dies in Venice.

The Estorick Collection of Modern Italian Art opened in London in 1998 housed in a Grade II listed Georgian building. The collection, built up by Eric Estorick and his wife Salome after the Second World War, has a core of Futurist works, as well as figurative art and sculpture dating from 1890 to the 1950s.

Estorick Collection

39a Canonbury Square, London N1 2AN
Tel: +44 (0)20 7704 9522
www.estorickcollection.com

Opening Hours

Wednesday to Saturday 11am – 6pm
Sunday 12noon – 5pm
Closed Monday and Tuesday. Also closed throughout the Christmas and New Year holiday.

Admission

Adults £3.50
Concessions £2.50
Free admission for school children and students with valid NUS ID card.

How To Get There

The nearest underground station is Highbury and Islington (Victoria Line).
Also, Silverlink Metro to Highbury and Islington Station.
Buses: the 271 takes you to the door. The 4,19,30,43 go to Upper Street or Canonbury Lane.

Access for the Disabled

Wheelchair access to Galleries 1–4, café, shop and toilets only. Limited car parking for orange badge holders, please telephone in advance.

Gallery Shop

The shop offers a range of postcards, catalogues and posters relating to the permanent collection and temporary exhibitions.

Gallery Café

A licensed Italian café has outdoor seating in a landscaped garden, offering light lunches with daily specials, cakes and pastries.

Giacomo Balla

The Hand of the Violinist   1912

Estorick Collection

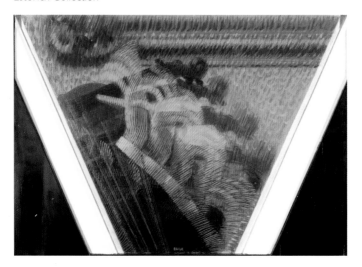

In 1910, together with several other Italian artists, Giacomo Balla signed two Futurist manifestos. Futurism was the creation of the poet Filippo Marinetti who, the previous year, had published the first of a number of manifestos in the French newspaper *le Figaro*. The movement wanted to set Italy free from the suffocating burden of its artistic past and glorified all things modern — powerful cars were a particular favourite; as Marinetti famously quipped, 'a roaring motorcar, which runs like a machine-gun, is more beautiful than the Winged Victory of Samothrace'.

Movement and speed were central to the Futurist creed and in this picture Balla, whilst not choosing a subject which was symbolic of modernity, is nevertheless exploring how he can depict the speed with which the musician's hand and bow move across the strings of his instrument. It was painted during a visit to Germany in order to complete a commission for murals at the home of a former pupil, Grete Löwenstein. Her husband, Arthur, was an amateur violinist and he became the model for this composition.

Balla, like his fellow Futurists and other contemporary artists, (such as Marcel Duchamp whose famous *Nude Descending a Staircase* was painted in the same year as this picture) was fascinated by recent photographic experiments which were trying, in one way or another, to isolate the constituent elements of human and animal movement. Étienne-Jules Marey was one such photographer who produced sequential photographs which strove to freeze each instance of movement. Balla would have seen his work at the Exposition Universelle when he visited Paris in 1900. He also knew of the photography of Eadweard Muybridge and his countryman Anton Giulio Bragaglia.

Balla has used these influences and fused them with the divisionist techniques of the French Neo-Impressionists (who he had seen during his

Paris visit) and their Italian followers.

The initial image of the violin is quite distinct at the top of the sequence, becoming less so until the outline of the neck is almost lost. The hand and finger movements form a marvellous composite image which again blurs to semi abstraction, each instance represented with lines of yellow paint. The cuff of the violinist morphs into a continuous outline as it follows the enclosed wrist in its passionate excursions. Here is a perfect example of the assertion, contained within the Technical Manifesto of 1910, that 'movement and light destroy the substance of objects'.

Contemporary Works

1912	Marcel Duchamp: *Nude Descending a Staircase No. 2*; Philadelphia
	Pablo Picasso: *Ma Jolie*; New York
	Lovis Corinth: *Self Portrait in White Smock*; Cologne
1913	Pierre Bonnard: *Dining Room in the Country*; Minneapolis

Giacomo Balla

1871	Born in Turin.
1895	Moves to Rome.
1900	Makes an extended visit to Paris where he works as an illustrator and where he sees Impressionist and Neo-Impressionist work.
1901	Returns to Rome.
1909	Balla's painting *Street Lamp* already exhibits aspects of proto 'Futurist' style.
1910	Signs the Manifesto of Futurist Painting (February) and the Technical Manifesto of Futurist Painting (April).
1912	Decorates the house of Arthur and Grete Löwenstein in Düsseldorf.
1913	His painting *Speed of Car + Light + Noise* is the climax of his attempts to represent speed. It is essentially abstract.
1917	Designs stage sets for Stravinsky's *Feu d'artifice*.
1920-40	Works in a variety of divisionist and geometrical styles but is primarily interested in the decorative arts.
1958	Dies in Rome.

Visitors to London may not be familiar with Kenwood and the Iveagh bequest which it contains. But it is a house and collection not to be missed. It must be admitted that it is not easy to get to but a visit will most definitely repay the effort. Set in splendid grounds beside Hampstead Heath, the outstanding Neo-Classical house holds one of the most important collections of paintings ever given to the nation.

The house was remodelled by Robert Adam from 1764 to 1779 for the great judge, Lord Mansfield. The richly decorated library is one of his masterpieces. Kenwood remained in the family until 1925. When developers tried to buy the estate, the house and grounds were saved by a brewing magnate, the first Earl of Iveagh. In 1927, when the earl died, he bequeathed the Kenwood Estate to the nation together with part of his collection of pictures.

Kenwood House

Hampstead Lane, London, NW3
Tel: +44 (0)20 8348 1286

Opening Hours

1 April – 31 October; every day 10am – 5pm
1 November – 31 March; every day 10am – 4pm
Wednesdays and Fridays; the house opens at 10.30am
24 – 26 December and 1 January; the house is closed

Admission

Free

How To Get There

The nearest underground stations: Hampstead (Northern Line, Edgware branch) (1 mile); Archway or Golders Green (both Northern Line, High Barnet branch and Edgware branch respectively), then catch the 210 bus. The journey from central London requires some planning but it is worth it.

Access for the Disabled

Wheelchairs and shooting sticks are available. The ground floor, which contains all of the principal paintings is level throughout. There is an easy staircase to the upper floors for ambulant disabled visitors, with good banisters. Chairs provided.

Shop

The shop sells a good range of books and gifts.

Café

The Brew House Café is open all year serving delicious home-made food throughout the day.

Aelbert Cuyp

View of Dordrecht c1655

Kenwood House

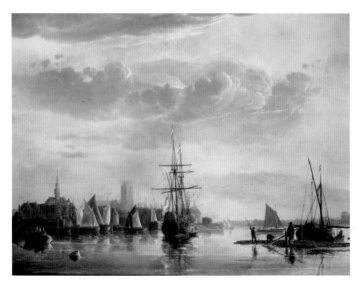

Aelbert Cuyp was born in Dordrecht and apart from a number of journeys up the Rhine, one of which took him into Germany, he seems to have been more than content to stay put. Cuyp's parochial proclivities, producing pictures almost exclusively for local patrons meant that his art was almost unknown outside Dordrecht. After his marriage to a wealthy widow he became prominent in civic affairs — responsibilities that took up so much of his time that his artistic output dwindled to virtually nothing.

Despite this anonymity he was enthusiastically championed by British connoisseurs and artists (including Gainsborough) in the late eighteenth and nineteenth centuries and he was called the 'Dutch Claude'. As a result, there are more examples of his work in Britain than anywhere else.

This picture is one of twenty-five views of his home town painted by Cuyp. However, it is evident that the true subjects of the painting are the sky and the river.

A ship stands off the port, forming a central fulcrum for the composition. To the right Cuyp portrays the Dutch waterworld of the Rhine delta. An unusual vignette occupies this lower quarter of the composition — loggers are engaged in guiding their floating cargo on the very last stage of their long journey from the German forests. Dordrecht was their terminus — the timber trade was a staple industry for the town.

To the left is the old town dependent on waterborne trade, but increasingly losing out to competition from Amsterdam and Rotterdam. The imposing tower of the Grote Kerk, the 'signature' edifice of the skyline is bathed in a golden evening light flooding in from the sun which is setting just outside the bounds of the picture. But the massive tower is dwarfed beneath the infinite sky to which Cuyp has devoted over three-quarters of the picture. A bank of cloud is suspended above the town, its westernmost edge touched by the fast departing rays of the sun. The glassy water is slightly disturbed by a very light breeze. It is the sort of evening which one might well remember for years — the sort of evening which might enter one's personal lexicon of jewelled moments.

Contemporary Works

1655	Rembrandt: *The Flayed Ox*; Paris
1656	Bartolomé Esteban Murillo: *Vision of St Anthony of Padua*; Seville Cathedral
	Diego Velázquez: *Las meninas*; Madrid

Aelbert Cuyp

1620	The son of a painter, he is baptised in Dordrecht.
1639	First signed and dated works.
1651 or 2	Travelled up the Rhine into Germany. Many of the sketches he made during this journey were used as the basis for later works.
1658	Marries Cornelia Boschman, a wealthy widow. Cuyp's artistic output dwindles after his marriage as his other responsibilities increase.
1672	Becomes an elder of the Reformed Church.
1673	Appointed as a member of the High Court of South Holland.
1691	Dies in Dordrecht.

Rembrandt

Self Portrait with Two Circles c1665

Kenwood House

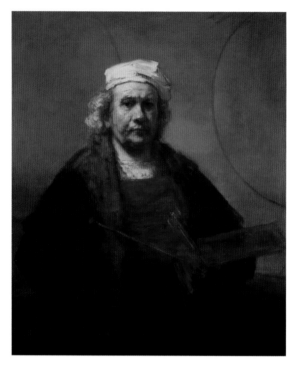

This is one of the most extraordinary examples from the greatest series of self portraits ever painted — perhaps the crowning achievement of one of the most celebrated artists of the European tradition.

An encounter with this painting is a spiritual experience; to engage with those eyes is somehow to share in the common experience of humanity; they are full of sympathy and melancholy, resignation, serenity and love. Of course they had seen the vicissitudes of life — fame, bankruptcy and the death of two wives; they will eventually weep for the loss of his beloved son. They also provide the conduit, perhaps a little disturbingly, for a two-way process, for while your gaze plays on the features of his profoundly sympathetic face, Rembrandt's eyes constantly draw you back and seem to reciprocate your search for the soul within. As one stands in front of this two-dimensional object (a lifeless concoction of paint and canvas) one wonders at the marvellous alchemy fired by Rembrandt's genius and asks oneself if this is the closest it is possible to get to the essence of an individual from a distant age.

The face is painted with unsurpassed skill — when inspected at close range the flecks and blobs of pigment have been applied quite liberally to form a fairly heavy impasto. But as you draw away the features come to life — the bulbous nose, the slight moustache, the single line etched across the brow. The rest of the picture is much less finished with some elements, like the painter's brushes, palette and hand being represented by no more than a few strokes of paint. His white cap, in complete contrast to the head upon which it sits, has been dashed off in a similarly free style.

And what are we to make of the two arcs painted on the flat surface behind Rembrandt? There has been much scholarly debate about the significance of these circles but no one has come up with a definitive hypothesis. They may symbolise eternity and perfection but the theory which attracts the greatest number of adherents is that they are a symbol, or rather evidence, of artistic skill, in that to draw a perfect circle freehand was traditionally thought to be the ultimate test of draughtsmanship.

Rembrandt's bankruptcy in 1656 did not spell the end of his reputation although a commission from the Stadhuis of Amsterdam was returned to him shortly after its installation in 1662. Recent research has exploded the myth of the forgotten artist. Indeed in 1667, two years before Rembrandt's death and at about the same time as this portrait was painted, he received a visit from Cosimo de' Medici (later the Grand Duke of Tuscany) who was passing through the Netherlands on his Grand Tour. Apparently Cosimo met a great many artists whilst in the Netherlands but in his journal only three were described as 'famoso', one of these being Rembrandt.

There may be a link between Rembrandt's fame and the fact that he produced so many self portraits. It seems that there was a considerable contemporary market for self portraits of famous artists — they were collectable because they were both a representation of a famous person and an example of the reason for that fame.

This picture certainly deserves veneration — it is undoubtedly one of the greatest pictorial treasures in London and its presence alone requires one to make the pilgrimage to Hampstead.

Contemporary Works

1664	Jan Steen: *Celebrating the Birth*; London, Wallace Collection
1665	Bartolomé Esteban Murillo: *The Infant St John with the lamb*; London, National Gallery
1666	Jan Vermeer: *The Letter*; Amsterdam
	Claude Lorrain: *Morning*; St Petersburg

Rembrandt

See Page 39

Thomas Gainsborough

Mary, Countess Howe

c1764

Kenwood House

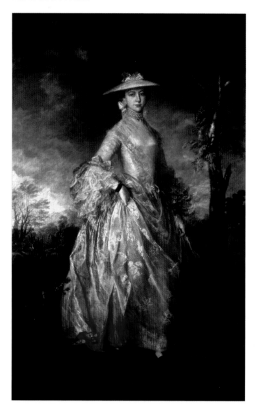

M ary Hartopp married Richard Howe, the second son of Viscount
Howe in February 1758. A few months later Richard's older brother
was killed in action while serving in North America and Richard inherited
the viscountcy. After many years in the Navy, in 1763 he was rewarded
for distinguished service with the position of Commissioner of the
Admiralty. In December of that year the couple were in Bath to see if the
waters might cure Richard's gout, and Gainsborough, who had moved to
Bath from East Anglia in 1759, was commissioned to paint two full-length
portraits of the couple. If one was being punctilious this painting should
really be called 'Lady Howe' as she did not become a countess until 1782
when her husband was created Earl Howe (after his relief of Gibraltar
which had been besieged by French and Spanish forces). In 1794 his
victory over the French fleet in the North Sea made him a naval hero
only to be surpassed by Nelson himself.

However, back in 1764 there is no doubt who Gainsborough was taken
with. He seems to have quickly captured Mary's likeness but X-radiography
reveals that he went to endless trouble to perfect his depiction of her dress.
By contrast, the companion portrait of her husband is a fairly standard affair,

somewhat wooden and conventional. One is tempted to surmise that perhaps Gainsborough's fussing over her costume might have constituted a strategy to necessitate further sittings. Frankly, looking at this icon of femininity, one is tempted to ask what male would not have done the same. Of course there is absolutely no evidence for this although it has been postulated that the presence of a stump emanating in a very particular way from the silver birch tree on the right might signify a level of appreciation in the painter which surpassed the merely cerebral.

Lady Howe was evidently an enchantingly beautiful woman but also a commanding presence. Her strikingly direct gaze is most unusual in terms of contemporary female portraits (another example being the portrait of Nelly O'Brien by Reynolds in the Wallace Collection, see page 232) and it confirms her manifest self assurance. She was clearly determined to be painted clad in the very latest fashion, augmented by an array of accessories the most interesting of which is the fine straw hat, probably imported from Italy. Her elegant neck is encased in a choker made from five rows of pearls. But apart from the lady herself, the star of the show is that magnificent confection of pink silk offset by the grey gauze and lace of her pinafore, fichu and ruffles. Gainsborough's handling of these transparent materials is a *tour de force* as is his very skilful rendition of silk — you can almost hear it rustle. And perhaps to emphasise the precious vulnerability of this very expensive outfit, he has introduced a thistle which, blown by the wind, might just snag the dress as Lady Howe passes.

Gainsborough has created a landscape which perfectly complements her clothes and her character. She confidently glides through the country, her smart black shoes betraying no sign of contact with the earth over which she seems to float, completely at ease on her own and in need of no escort. Storm clouds are gathering — clouds which echo the grey of her sleeve ruffles and pinafore, and which are shot through with a sunset pink that resonates with her gorgeous silk dress. All this contributes to what Whistler would have called a symphony in pink and grey.

Contemporary Works

1764	Joshua Reynolds: *Nelly O'Brien*; London, Wallace Collection
1765	François Boucher: *Rest on a Journey*; Boston
	Jean-Honoré Fragonard: *Le petit parc*; London, Wallace Collection

Thomas Gainsborough

1727	Born in Sudbury, Suffolk.
1733	Gainsborough's father, a clothier, is declared bankrupt.
c1740	Trains in London with a French artist named Gravelot. Possibly works with Francis Hayman decorating supper-boxes at Vauxhall pleasure gardens.
1746	Marries Margaret Burr (July).
1748	His father dies and he returns to Sudbury.
1752	Moves to Ipswich.
1759	Finds it difficult to make a living in Ipswich and consequently moves to Bath.
1768	Founder member of the Royal Academy.
1774	Gainsborough moves with his family to London.
1784	Quarrels with the Royal Academy over the issue of where to hang some of his portraits of royalty.
1788	Dies in London.

The National Gallery houses the national collection of Western European painting: over 2,300 pictures dating from about 1250 to 1900. It is one of the greatest collections of European painting in the world and arguably the most well balanced with something to suit everyone's enthusiasm.

In April 1824 the House of Commons agreed to pay £57,000 for the picture collection of the banker John Julius Angerstein. The thirty-eight pictures were intended to form the core of a new national collection. Until a gallery building was constructed, the pictures were displayed at Angerstein's house in Pall Mall. Eventually, in 1831, a site in Trafalgar Square was chosen for the construction of a purpose-built gallery. Regular extensions in 1876, 1907, 1975 and 1991 (with the opening of the Sainsbury Wing) have kept pace with the expansion of the collection.

National Gallery

Trafalgar Square, London WC2N 5DN
Tel: +44 (0)20 7747 2885
www.nationalgallery.org.uk

Opening Hours

Every day 10am – 6pm (Wednesdays until 9pm)
Closed 1 January and 24 – 26 December

Admission

Free

How To Get There

The nearest underground stations are Charing Cross (Northern and Bakerloo Lines) and Leicester Square (Northern and Piccadilly Lines). Trafalgar Square is a hub for many bus routes — 3, 6, 9, 11, 12, 13, 15, 23, 24, 29, 53, 77A, 88, 91, 139, 159, 176, 453.

Access for the Disabled

The Getty Entrance offers street-level access from Trafalgar Square. A platform lift gives access to Level 0 for the café, shop etc, and a large lift with low-level controls gives access to the paintings on Level 2.
The Sainsbury Wing also has a street-level entrance from Trafalgar Square. Large lifts with low-level controls give access to all levels.

Gallery Shops

There are three shops in the National Gallery. The largest is in the Sainsbury Wing which has an extensive bookshop as well as a range of jewellery, gifts, postcards and posters. The shop near the main entrance to the gallery offers guidebooks and postcards. The newest shop is by the Sir Paul Getty entrance selling art magazines and periodicals, as well as a range of guidebooks, gifts and postcards.

Gallery Restaurant and Café

Crivelli's Garden Restaurant on Level 1 of the Sainsbury Wing has a panoramic view of Trafalgar Square. Open daily 10am – 5.45pm (Wednesdays 8.30pm). The National Gallery Café on Level 0 of the main building caters for all visitor needs, whether it is a cup of coffee, lunch or afternoon tea. Open daily 10am – 5.30pm (Wednesdays 8.30pm).

Duccio di Buoninsegna

National Gallery

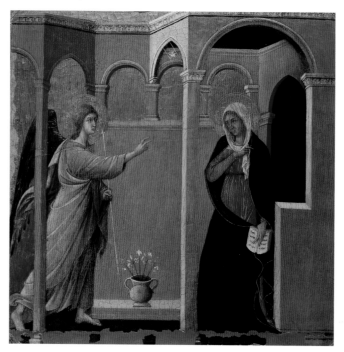

On 9 June 1311 a great procession made its way through the streets of Siena to the fine new cathedral, completed only about forty years before.

> ... the Bishop ordered a great and devout company of priests and brothers with a solemn procession, accompanied by the Signori of the Nine and all the officials of the Commune, and all the populace and all of the most worthy were in order ... with lights lit in their hands, and then behind were women and children with much devotion ... making procession around the Campo, as was the custom, sounding all the bells in glory out of devotion...

The reason for all this pomp and the focal point of the grand parade was a huge new altarpiece produced in the workshop of Duccio di Buoninsegna which was being ceremonially carried to the Duomo for its installation. The altarpiece was in the form of a polyptych with a huge central panel facing the congregation, depicting a Madonna and Child enthroned in majesty surrounded by saints and angels (known as a *Maestà*). Above this panel were two tiers of smaller panels, probably a dozen in all. This ensemble rested on a box-like structure known as a predella upon which were painted scenes from the life of the Virgin commencing with this *Annunciation* placed on the extreme left. But this was not all — the structure was double sided, with a further set of paintings on the reverse only visible to the clergy.

All in all the polyptych measured about five metres in height.

This magnificent assemblage remained in place at the high altar for two centuries until it was removed to make way for a new altar in 1506. In 1771 it was dismantled, the two faces being sawn apart; most of the panels can still be seen at the museum attached to Siena Cathedral, but some smaller panels were sold, three of them eventually finding their way to the National Gallery.

Duccio could not have completed every part of the *Maestà* (as the whole polyptych has become known). But scholars are fairly certain that the *Annunciation* is by his hand, based on infra-red evidence which reveals the underdrawing.

The scene is depicted with great simplicity and the architectural setting (some sort of loggia perhaps), which the painter is struggling to use in order to create a semblance of three-dimensional space, does not detract from the psychological tension between Mary and the divine messenger, even though it helps to set the Virgin apart. The Archangel Gabriel enters from the left as he almost always does in western art. (Interestingly, this is usually reversed in the Byzantine tradition of eastern Europe.) He holds a staff which confers on him his singular status and he is shown blessing Mary as he utters the words 'Hail, thou that art highly favoured, the Lord is with thee; blessed art thou among women'.

Mary shrinks back, shocked by the magnitude of these words. But perhaps she has had some presentiment of this meeting for Duccio, in line with tradition, has placed a book in her left hand which she has presumably been reading. It is inscribed in Latin with Isaiah's prophecy 'Behold a Virgin shall conceive and bear a son'.

Framed in an arch in the centre of the picture, a tiny dove, symbolising the holy spirit, descends from Heaven, guided towards Mary as though on rails by two thin white lines, presumably thoughtfully provided by the paternal part of the Trinity. In the space between the angel and the Virgin stands a vase of lilies reminding us of Mary's purity.

Contemporary Works

c1290	Cimabue: *Madonna Enthroned*; Florence
	Pietro Cavallini: *The Last Judgement*; Rome
c1310	Giotto: *Madonna Enthroned*; Florence

Duccio di Buoninsegna

1278	First recorded as painting 12 coffers for the Commune of Siena.
1285	Duccio agrees to paint a Madonna and Child with Angels (*Maestà*) commissioned by Società di S Maria Virginis, now known as the Rucellai Madonna.
1302	Duccio is paid for an untraced *Maestà* to be installed in the Palazzo Publico in Siena.
1311	A huge *Maestà* five metres high, painted by Duccio is ceremonially installed in Siena Cathedral.
1318 or 19	Duccio dies before 3 August 1319.

Unknown

The Wilton Diptych   1395-99

National Gallery

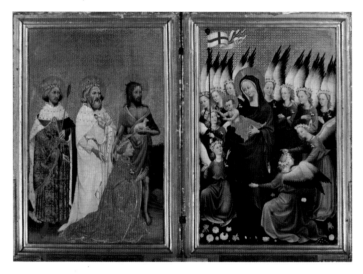

The Wilton Diptych was a travelling altarpiece which could be closed like a book, commissioned by King Richard II of England for use during the constant peregrinations which characterised the life of medieval kings.

The exterior of the left wing is fairly well preserved and depicts a white hart, Richard's personal emblem, lying in a verdant pasture strewn with rosemary (one of the emblems of Richard's first wife, Anne of Bohemia). The other exterior half — the back when closed — is badly damaged which is unsurprising considering its usage. The main elements are nevertheless legible showing a heraldic device including the royal arms of England and France impaled (halved vertically) with the supposed arms of Edward the Confessor.

The act of opening the diptych must have been a wondrous experience, for the interior presents us with a scene of transcendent beauty. The background of both wings has been decorated with exquisitely stippled and tooled gilding. The left wing depicts the king kneeling in an act of homage facing the infant Christ held by his mother and surrounded by angels.

As intercessors between the earthly king and this celestial realm Richard has engaged the services of a saintly triumvirate who are shown presenting their protégé to the heavenly duo. St John the Baptist, holding his lamb and clad in animal skins stands to one side of the king and extends his hand behind Richard's back in a paternal gesture of support. Richard was born on the feast day of Christ's Baptism and the Baptist was the king's patron saint. Next to St John stands Edward the Confessor holding a ring — which Edward was said to have given to a penurious pilgrim who turned out to be St John the Evangelist. Edward, the last Anglo-Saxon king, was canonised in 1161 and Richard was an enthusiastic devotee of his cult impaling the royal arms with the mythical arms of Edward (as shown on the exterior).

The third saint, standing on the extreme left, dressed in an eye-catching blue robe with exquisite gold patterning is St Edmund, last king of East Anglia who was martyred by the Danes in the ninth century when he refused to renounce his Christian beliefs; he is shown holding the arrow which killed him. He later became one of the patron saints of England.

And it seems that the presence of the two English patron saints is the link which connects the two halves of the diptych. One of the angels closest to the Christ child is holding a banner. We now recognise this as the flag of St George and of England but in the fourteenth century it was also a symbol of the Resurrection. The banner is in fact flying in this dual capacity. Very recently, during cleaning, it was discovered that the tiny orb which surmounts the banner containes a minuscule scene depicting a green island surrounded by sea. Scholars have linked this with a lost altarpiece, once in Rome which showed Richard offering an orb symbolising England to the Virgin. Descriptions of this altarpiece mention an inscription which translates as 'This is your dowry O Holy Virgin, therefore rule over it O Mary'. It seems that in the Wilton Diptych Richard may be in the process of a very similar transaction. His hands are not held as in prayer but have perhaps just released the banner which has been presented to the Virgin. The Christ Child has accepted the gift on her behalf, and given it to the angel who now holds it and who looks directly at the infant Jesus as he blesses the king. Richard will soon receive the banner back and will then hold his realm under the feudal protection of the Virgin.

Nothing is left to chance in underlining the royal status of the only mortal personage represented in the picture. The diptych is stuffed with royal emblems. Richard adopted the white hart as his personal device and here he wears a jewelled badge in the form of a white hart with a gold crown around its neck. It reappears as the principal motif in his brocaded robe which is beautifully rendered by the artist. But it does not end there, Richard has persuaded the eleven angels assembled in heaven to sport his badge much as the logos of sponsors appear on football shirts.

Richard wears another royal device around his neck in the form of a golden collar of broomcods. The seed pods of the broom plant (*planta genista*), had been used as emblems by both the Plantagenets, and the French royal family. Richard married his second wife, the seven-year-old daughter of the King of France, in 1396 after the death of Anne, and it was at this time that he adopted this emblem. The white harts decorating Richard's cloak are surrounded by garlands of broomcods and, needless to say, his angelic cheerleaders are also wearing similar collars.

All in all, no expense has been spared. Consummate workmanship combined with the finest materials — gold and ultramarine, used in abundance for the Virgin's cloak and those of her angelic retinue — have together conspired to bring into being a most exquisite object no doubt playing a small part in bolstering Richard's highly elevated view of his own royal status — his soaring arrogance was certainly a contributory factor in the political crisis culminating in his deposition in 1399.

Contemporary Works

c1399	Lorenzo Monaco: *Agony in the Garden*; Florence
1399	Melchior Broederlam: *Wings of the Retable of Champrnol*; Dijon

Masaccio

National Gallery

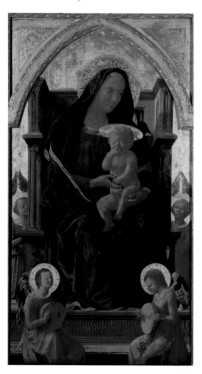

The *Virgin and Child* is a fragment of an altarpiece which was commissioned for the church of Santa Maria del Carmine in Pisa. Masaccio received a final payment for the work in December 1426. The altarpiece was dispersed in the late sixteenth century when structural alterations were carried out in the church. A probable reconstruction of the polyptych places the National Gallery portion in a central position — further fragments now displayed in other museums have been identified. A small strip is missing from the bottom of the panel.

Masaccio's heavy boned Virgin is perhaps not the most gracious example of the genre — art historians speak of monumentality and there is no doubt that this term fits the bill, but others might see her as somewhat lumpen. Nevertheless, Masaccio's principal aim of creating volume has been triumphantly realised. By using precise linear perspective and lighting the picture from one source he creates a believable space in which the Virgin and Christ child sit flanked by attendant angels, two of which sit on a step at the feet of the Madonna playing lutes. These angelic instruments are exercises in foreshortening and they also show how Masaccio has used his light source emanating from the top left of the composition to increase the illusion of three-dimensional space; the front of one lute receives direct light, the other is shaded. This same light, and the shadows which it creates, adds solidity to all the figures in the painting, especially that of the infant

Christ — the shadows helping to give three-dimensional form to his naked body. Christ is shown eating grapes, the red juice of which is a reference to the blood that is destined to flow from his body on the cross.

The throne is a reminder that Masaccio shared an interest in antique remains with his friend, the architect Brunelleschi. Of course the renewed interest at this time in the remains of the Roman world was a key influence on the course of early Renaissance art in Italy. But, in line with his Italian contemporaries, he was using egg tempera as a medium to bind his pigments when painting on panel. This has badly degraded over time revealing some of the greenish underpainting especially in the face of the Virgin. It would be some time before Italy adopted the superior oil-based technique which at this moment was being used in the Low Countries by such artists as Robert Campin.

However, Masaccio's mastery of perspective and his use of lighting effects build on the work of earlier masters to break free of the two dimensions of the picture plane and create some of western art's earliest naturalistic paintings.

Contemporary Works

1423	Gentile da Fabriano: *Adoration of the Magi*; Florence
c1425	Robert Campin: *Nativity*; Dijon
1425	Fra Angelico: *Madonna and Child with Angels*; St Petersburg

Masaccio

1401	Born in San Giovanni Val d'Arno in Tuscany, between Florence and Arezzo.
1418	A document describes Masaccio as a painter.
1422	Enters the Florentine painters guild.
1426	Works in Pisa on the altarpiece in Santa Maria del Carmine.
1427	In January he is a witness to a legal document in Pisa. By July he has returned to Florence. In August Masaccio and Masolino begin painting the frescoes in the Brancacci Chapel in the church of S Maria del Carmine in Florence.
1428	Masaccio travels to Rome to work on an altarpiece for the church of S Maria Maggiore. Massacio dies in Rome.

Jan van Eyck

Portrait of a Man (Self Portrait?)   1433

National Gallery

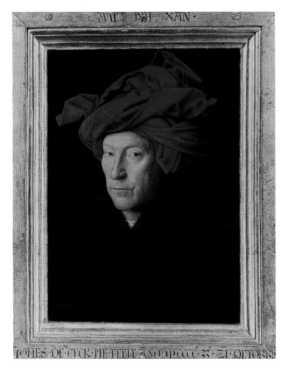

T he direct stare of the subject of this picture contrasts with the detached demeanour of many of van Eyck's sitters. Some scholars see this as evidence that the painting is a self portrait. However other portraits do exist by Jan where a similar direct gaze has been used, so why should this particular work be seen as a depiction of the artist?

Supporters of the theory would point to the *trompe l'oeil* inscriptions which look as if they have been carved into this rare example of a fifteenth-century original frame. The bottom edge is taken up with a Latin legend which translates as 'Jan van Eyck made me 1433 21 October'. Along the top the Flemish words *Als ich kan* are inscribed — 'As I can' in English. This seems to be a shortening of a Flemish proverb, 'As I can but not as I would (or wish)', and it may also be that the artist intended the phrase to be a pun on his name; the two personal pronouns, *ich* in Flemish, written partially in Greek as IXH, were to be interpreted as 'Eyck'. In any event the proverb implies some faux modesty on his part although it may not lead us any nearer to an interpretation of this picture as a self portrait. In fact the three words were something of a personal motto which were used on several other paintings.

The face of the sitter seems to materialise from the stygian depths of the very dark background. A light source plays on the face and headgear but does not penetrate elsewhere — our attention is thus fixed on the subject of the portrait and his extraordinary hat.

The wealthy and powerful denizens of the Netherlands at this time seem to have had a penchant for eye-catching hats. Giovanni Arnolfini (see page 64) chose an oversized hat for the famous double portrait. You might think that it was a courageous choice — the voluminous character of the hat over-accentuates his thin, angular, rat-like features. A similar hat appears in another van Eyck portrait, that of Baudouin de Lannoy and both van Eyck and his contemporary Robert Campin (probably to be identified with the painter known as the Master of Flémalle) painted other portraits of men with identical red turbans, albeit tied in a looser fashion. You can contrast van Eyck's and Campin's treatment of the subject as the latter's picture is also in the National Gallery. So red turbans seem to have been all the rage and van Eyck's representation of this particular example is a tour de force using the raking light to emphasise every fold and crease; the luminosity of the red pigment used for the turban also shows how he exploits the potential of oil paint to the full.

But it is the artist's treatment of the face which is of course the greatest marvel. He has delineated every individual stubble hair on the chin and those of us who shave can almost feel that stubble catch annoyingly on the fur collar. It also looks as though the sitter may have enjoyed one too many glasses of wine before his sittings because van Eyck has taken his passion for veracity to the extent of outlining the burst blood vessels in the subject's left eye.

The usual impassivity that one expects in a van Eyck portrait lends an air of inscrutability which compounds the mystery of who this is. Could this really be van Eyck? It would be nice to think so but of course we will never know.

Contemporary Works

1430	Robert Campin: *Portrait of a Man*; London, National Gallery
1433	Fra Angelico: *Linaiuoli Madonna*; Florence

Jan van Eyck

c1390-5	A birth date for Jan van Eyck is unknown but he was probably born about 1390 or perhaps a little later, almost certainly in the town of Maaseick.
1422-5	Jan, already a master, is recorded as court painter to John of Bavaria, Count of Holland working on decorative schemes for his palace in The Hague.
1425	On 19 May Jan is in Bruges where he enters the service of Philip the Good, Duke of Burgundy as painter and *valet de chambre*.
1426-7	Jan is in Lille, probably painting the walls of the ducal palace. He also seems to have undertaken two secret missions for the duke at this time.
1428-9	Jan is part of a Burgundian embassy which travels to Portugal in order to negotiate for the hand of Isabella, daughter of John I. Jan paints the Infanta's (untraced) portrait.
1431	Settles in Bruges where he works on completing the *Ghent Altarpiece*, left incomplete by his deceased brother Hubert.
1432	Jan buys a house in Bruges.
1434	Jan's first son is born. The Duke of Burgundy is his godfather.
1436	Duke Philip sends Jan on a secret mission to a 'distant land', possibly the Holy Land.
1441	Jan dies on 9 July in Bruges.

Jan van Eyck

National Gallery

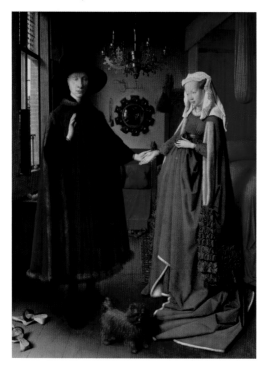

Giovanni Arnolfini was a successful merchant-financier from Lucca, a member of the Italian community resident in the Low Countries, which then formed part of the possessions of the Duke of Burgundy. He was engaged in the lucrative importation of luxury fabrics, in large part to satisfy the Duke of Burgundy's considerable appetite for such goods. His wife, Giovanna Cenami may have been born in Paris of Italian parentage. In this double portrait, Giovanni holds his wife's hand and at the same time raises his right hand in a gesture of affirmation.

Some commentators view this picture as nothing more than a portrait of a married couple in their bed chamber, but it is difficult to believe that it is merely a fifteenth century family snap. The analysis of the great art historian Erwin Panofsky is more convincing. He put forward the very credible hypothesis that the painting is in fact a record of a wedding ceremony. The fact that they are alone does not preclude this as a possible interpretation. It was not until the Council of Trent in 1563 that a priest was required to solemnise a wedding — before that date Canon Law permitted a couple to exchange vows between themselves in the presence of two witnesses. The two necessary persons are indeed in attendance for they can be seen reflected in the convex mirror which hangs on the wall.

Just above the mirror the painting has been signed in a most unusual way — the Latin inscription is translated as 'Jan van Eyck was here (or present)'.

This inscription is written in the elaborate script more typically to be found in court or legal documents and this has led some scholars to maintain that the artist has signed the painting in the capacity of a lawful witness. One of the two men reflected in the mirror would therefore be van Eyck himself.

If we are witnessing a wedding ceremony then most of the objects in the room take on a symbolic resonance. The elaborate chandelier contains a single candle which is burning even though it is daytime. This perhaps symbolises the presence of the Holy Spirit although it may also refer to the candle that was by tradition placed in the chamber of a newly married couple and was left burning until consummation. On the floor, in line with the chandelier, we can see a pair of red slippers and in the foreground a pair of clogs have been discarded; the couple have removed their footwear which may be an allusion to the hallowed ground upon which they stand at this moment. Against the back wall, a decorative statuette can be seen atop a chair or bench; this has been identified as St Margaret, the patron saint of women in childbirth. The 'spotless' mirror, in addition to its other pictorial roles can be seen as a symbol of the unblemished status of the bride. The little dog, so engagingly painted, is a symbol of marital fidelity.

Also symbolic and not to be taken too literally, is the swollen stomach of Giovanna. It was the norm during this period to represent women with an exaggeratedly rotund lower torso (van Eyck's depiction of a naked Eve in the Ghent Altarpiece shows her looking decidedly pregnant), and it was also the fashion for women to wear dresses with voluminous amounts of material gathered in front of their abdomen. However her pregnant stance serves as another reference to the consequence of most marriages.

Van Eyck's traditional identification as the inventor of oil painting stems from his fame. In fact the practice of using oil as the medium for binding pigment had been known for many years before van Eyck's lifetime. However it seems that knowledge of better quality oils and how to mix different oils became established in Flanders early in the fifteenth century and van Eyck was the supreme exponent of the new technique. This picture is a wonderful example of that superlative technique. A glance at any part of the relatively small panel will reveal instances of truly astonishing virtuosity — just a few examples can be cited; the depiction of light falling on the metal chandelier giving it real substance and weight; the miraculous rendition of the convex mirror including the ten surrounding miniature scenes from Christ's Passion; the extraordinary realisation of the long-haired coat of the little lapdog. One has to keep reminding oneself the this picture was painted in 1434. But even more amazing is the skill with which Jan suffuses the room with light. He deploys perspective with only partial success but his use of light to construct a credible space, surrounding and moulding the objects in the room is masterful.

Contemporary Works

1432	Fra Angelico: *Coronation of the Virgin*, Paris
1435	Stefan Lochner: *Last Judgement*, Cologne
	Rogier van der Weyden: *Descent from the Cross*, Madrid

Jan van Eyck

See Page 63

Pisanello

National Gallery

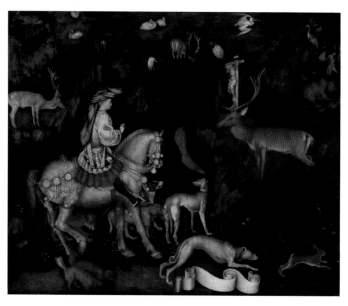

According to legend, a Roman general, while out hunting near Tivoli came across a stag with a crucifix growing between its antlers. The general was instantly converted to Christianity and when he was baptised he took the name of Eustachius. He became a martyr when he refused to sacrifice to the Roman gods and was consequently roasted to death with his unfortunate family inside a brass bull. He subsequently became a patron of hunters.

It is of course a mistake to see the advent of the early Italian Renaissance as an all-pervasive movement which changed the way artists worked overnight. In fact great painters such as Gentile da Fabriano and Pisanello were working in cities where interest in 'medieval', Arthurian chivalry existed at the same time as humanism was sweeping all before it in the Medici court in Florence. Indeed, it has been pointed out that, taking Italy as a whole, the figure of Lancelot was just as influential at this time as was Plato.

Pisanello is often described as working in the International Gothic style — this label being shorthand for the widespread practice of many artists in the late fourteenth and early fifteenth century of focusing on the naturalistic representation of, for example, the animals, plants and costume within a painting while remaining unconcerned with the spatial relationship between these elements in the composition as a whole. Realism was confined to detail, naturalism did not extend to the representation of space or volume; the use of extravagant materials underlined the refined and courtly nature of those who commissioned these works. If one wanted an exemplar of this style then *The Vision of Saint Eustace* has all the right qualifications.

Untroubled by the exigencies of perspective (unlike his contemporaries in Tuscany), Pisanello instead creates a beautifully decorative piece. The meeting between Saint Eustace and the stag takes place in a dark forest. But they are certainly not alone. The forest teems with beasts and birds each one represented with great charm — one of the hounds can be seen sniffing around a greyhound — another greyhound has launched itself in pursuit of a rabbit or hare.

In his lifetime, Pisanello was famous not only as a painter but also as a designer of medals. The particular type of personal commemorative medal in which he specialised (almost always showing the sitter in profile) seems to have been invented by him. And in this picture we can see that the artist has favoured the use of profiles in the depiction of almost all of his menagerie as well as St Eustace.

But the detail which gives me most pleasure is the sumptuously decorated harnesses and accoutrements of St Eustace's horse. Pisanello has built up each stud and fastening using some form of plaster or gesso so that it stands out from the panel in 3D. He has then finished each stud with real gold. So here naturalistic detail and lavish decoration find a home together in the work of an innovative and original artist.

Contemporary Works

1448	Rogier van der Weyden: *Last Judgment Altarpiece*; Beaune
1451	Piero della Francesca: *Portrait of Sigismondo Malatesta*; Paris
	Stefan Lochner: *Virgin of the Rose Bower*; Cologne

Pisanello

1395	The probable date of Pisanello's birth either in Pisa or Verona.
c1415-22	Works with Gentile da Fabriano at the Palazzo Ducale in Venice.
1422	He is in Mantua working for the Gonzaga family.
1424	Pisanello is documented as being in Verona and he may also have painted some frescoes in Pavia.
1424-6	Painted the *Annunciation* in S. Fermo in Verona.
1427	Gentile da Fabriano dies bequeathing his brushes and other equipment to Pisanello.
1431-2	Pisanello completes frescoes started by Gentile in S. Giovanni in Laterano in Rome but which had been left incomplete at his death.
1433-8	Living in Verona with his wife and daughter.
1438	Pisanello is in Ferrara when the Byzantine emperor John VIII Palaeologus visits the city for an ecumenical council. He later strikes a medal to commemorate the event.
1440	He is in Milan.
1441	Returns to Ferrara.
1447	Probably the year he paints the frescoes of *War* and *Chivalry* in the Palazzo Ducale in Mantua.
1448	Arrives in Naples.
1449	Last documented reference to Pisanello in Naples.

Piero della Francesca

National Gallery

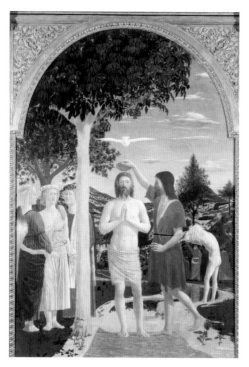

This panel was probably commissioned as an altarpiece for a chapel dedicated to John the Baptist by the Abbey of Borgo Sansepolcro perhaps in the mid-1450s. Borgo Sansepolcro was the birthplace of the artist and it seems very probable that the town which appears in the middle distance in this picture (just to the left of Christ's hip) is in fact a representation of Piero's birthplace set in the landscape of eastern Tuscany. The stream (hardly a river) in which the baptism is taking place beautifully reflects the surrounding landscape. In the extreme foreground Piero has tried to represent that point at which the optical properties of water change from reflection to translucence and we see the river bed. One has to say that this has not really come off.

Here we are privy to the moment at which John baptises Christ with a few drops of (Tuscan) water. The head of Jesus occupies the very centre of the composition; John's simple receptacle is precisely positioned directly above Christ's head and the dove hovers in the stillness exactly in line with this central vertical axis while at the same time marking the horizontal transition between the upper lunette shape and the main rectangular body of the picture. This is a direct pictorial realisation of the description in Mark's Gospel where we are told that the Holy Spirit, in the form of a dove, appeared over Christ's head during the baptism. Three angels witness the event impassively, their statuesque poses reminiscent of classical representations of the Three Graces, while other players in the drama including the next candidate for baptism are oblivious to the solemnity of the occasion. Near the right-hand edge of the picture, in the middle distance, we see one of Piero's trademark funny hats adorning a priest-like figure, a member of a group which seems to be proceeding away from the scene.

Like all of Piero's work, *The Baptism of Christ* is suffused with an enigmatic stillness and a cool luminosity. It is this austere gravity coupled with the obvious mathematical precision of his compositions (stemming from a pursuit of the secrets of mathematical perspective which led Piero to publish a number of treatises on the subject) which appeal to the modern eye.

Contemporary Works

c1450	Jean Fouquet: *Étienne Chevalier and St Stephen*; Berlin
c1455	Enguerrand Quarton: *Pièta of Villeneuve-lès-Avignon*; Paris
1450's	Paolo Uccello: *Battle of San Romano*; London, National Gallery

Piero della Francesca

c1418	Born in Borgo Sansepolcro, near Arezzo in eastern Tuscany.
1439 – 40	Piero works with Domenico Veneziano in Florence on frescoes for the church of Sant' Egidio which are now lost. While in Florence he witnesses a visit by the Byzantine emperor John VIII Paleologus.
1442	He is back in Borgo Sansepolcro, where he is a candidate for a position on the Town Council.
1445	A contract is signed commissioning Piero to produce a polyptych of the *Madonna della Misericordia* for the Compagnia della Misericordia in Borgo.
1449-51	Works for Sigismondo Malatesta in Rimini and the Este family in Ferrara.
1452	Piero begins the fresco cycle of the *Legend of the True Cross* in the church of San Francesco in Arezzo.
1458-9	Piero is in Rome working on frescoes (now lost) in the Vatican but is also engaged in *The Resurrection* and the unfinished *Madonna della Misericordia*, both in Borgo.
1460-1470	Works in Borgo, Arezzo and Perugia.
1469	Stays in Urbino with Giovanni Santi, the father of Raphael.
1474-8	He is again in Urbino working for Federico da Montefeltro.
After 1478	Spends most of his time in Borgo Sansepolcro; it is at this time that he produces his treatises on perspective.
1492	Dies and is buried at Borgo Sansepolcro.

Paolo Uccello

National Gallery

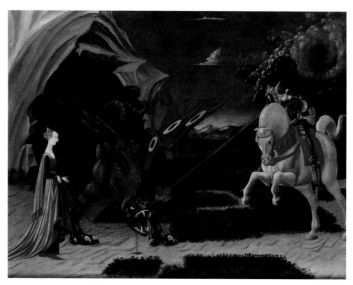

In his *Lives of the Artists*, the sixteenth-century painter, commentator, and biographer Giorgio Vasari gives us a rather bleak portrayal of Paolo Uccello as a monomaniac, so obsessed with his studies of the finer points of linear perspective that, in Vasari's opinion, other aspects of his art suffered. 'Such details may be attractive and ingenious' Vasari writes 'but anyone who studies them excessively is … choking his mind with difficult problems … turning a fertile and spontaneous talent into something sterile.' This is a little uncharitable but Uccello does betray an undeniable propensity to labour the point.

A good example of this tendency can be seen in this picture — the peculiar patches of vegetation conveniently forming regular mat-like structures (looking as if they have been laid on top of the bed rock rather than growing from it) the better to illustrate and reinforce the receding lines of perspective.

But there is much more to Uccello than this. His early training in the workshop of the great Florentine sculptor Lorenzo Ghiberti grounded him in the mannered and refined tradition of the prevailing Late Gothic style and despite his later fascination with Alberti's theories on perspective, his personal style remained a mix of Late Gothic charm and Early Renaissance rigour. This picture is a delightful evocation of the famous legend with Uccello conflating two incidents from the story of St George as told in the *Golden Legend*.

The three central characters inhabit a somewhat arid dreamworld. Behind the dragon and his erstwhile prey there is a gaping cave — presumably the monster's lair — looking rather as if it has been constructed from papier-mâché. To the right, the saint, clad in the armour of a medieval knight and riding his white horse (which looks as if it might be more at home in the nursery) is seen at the moment when his exceptionally elongated and elegant lance has wounded the dragon in the head. Blood flows from the dragon's maw, its head forced downwards as if in obeisance to its conqueror. It seems that this direct hit is as much the result of divine intervention as chivalric valour for an improbable confection of cloud resembling a stratospheric ammonite has aligned itself on the axis of the saintly lance, presumably to enhance the power and accuracy of its thrust.

However, placed to the left of the dragon (resplendent with RAF-style roundels decorating its wings) a young maiden already seems to have the fearsome beast under control, having it leashed with a chain. This part of the painting refers to one version of the legend which tells us that rather than killing the dragon, George merely subdues it. The woman, who is in fact a princess, hailing from a nearby town, the subject to a reign of terror by the beast, had experienced the extreme misfortune of having drawn a fatal lot dooming her to be the dragon's next square meal. Thanks to George's knightly charge she is now able to lead the pacified brute triumphantly into the town.

Contemporary Works

1459	Andrea Mantegna: *San Zeno Altarpiece*; Verona
c1460	Rogier van der Weyden: *Portrait of Francesco d'Este*; New York
1465	Alesso Baldovinetti: *Portrait of a Lady in Yellow*; London, National Gallery

Paolo Uccello

c1397	Born Paolo di Dono in Florence, the son of a barber-surgeon, but becomes known as Uccello, according to Vasari, because of his love of birds.
c1412	Probable date of his apprenticeship to Lorenzo Ghiberti.
1414	Joins the Compagnia di S Luca, the artists guild.
1416	Leaves Ghiberti's workshop.
1425	Uccello is in Venice, working in S Marco as a mosaicist.
1430s	Works on frescoes in the cloisters of S Maria Novella in Florence.
1445	Uccello visits Padua.
1450s	Produces three paintings showing different stages of the Battle of San Romano, decorations for the new Palazzo Medici in Florence.
1465	Working in Urbino.
1467	Returns to Florence.
1475	Dies in Florence.

Andrea Mantegna

Agony in the Garden

National Gallery

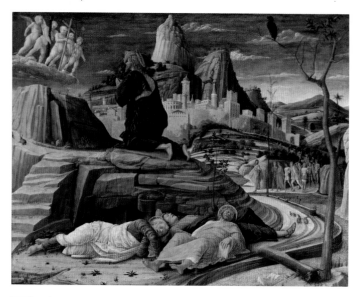

The drama occurs within sight of the walls of a most extraordinary city — Jerusalem has been transformed into a pink fairytale confection but, being Mantegna, it is a confection with a very hard edge. The architecture of the city is a composite of Roman and Renaissance styles featuring a structure which is similar to the Colosseum in Rome and another which bears a strong likeness to the campanile of S. Marco in Venice. Some of the towers look decidedly Tuscan. The walls have obviously been subject to attack for patches of different coloured stone betray the rebuilt stretches.

Linearity is central to Mantegna's style and here, heavily striated rock forms the stage upon which the inexorable events of the night before Christ's crucifixion take place. It is difficult to understand how the three apostles sprawled in the foreground could possibly fall asleep on such terrain. But they will soon be awakened from their fitful slumbers for Judas is fast approaching from the direction of Jerusalem accompanied by the troops who will very shortly take Jesus away. Christ is still engaged in prayer, kneeling at a rough outcrop which doubles as a makeshift altar, asking to be spared from his fate. But his prayers have been answered by the appearance of five implacable cherubs (standing on a cloud of such solidity that only Mantegna could have been its author) who present him with the gruesome instruments of his imminent torture and death — the column used to secure Jesus during the Flagellation, the cross upon which he will be crucified, the sponge which was dipped in vinegar and offered to him and the lance which was used to pierce his side. To ram the message home, a vulture waits expectantly, perched on the dead branch of a tree which itself looks as though it might soon share the fate of the Saviour.

At the margins, Mantegna has introduced two charming vignettes — egrets are standing in the (rather two-dimensional) shallow stream and rabbits are frolicking nearby. Of course, this being the fifteenth century, these representations of wildlife are there for a symbolic purpose — the rabbits, exposed on the arid path leading to Jesus may represent those future followers of Christ who will put their faith in his message; the white egrets in the water are a reference to the purification which follows baptism. But they also provide a welcome instance of softness within the harsh landscape of Mantegna's unforgiving rocks.

Mantegna's characteristic style was highly influential. And this painting exhibits all of the skills for which he earned so much respect from his contemporaries — a confident use of perspective, a style renowned for its clarity and a firm grasp of composition.

Contemporary Works

1457	Piero della Francesca: *The Flagellation*; Urbino
c1460	Dieric Bouts: *Mater Dolorosa*; Chicago
1461	Benozzo Gozzoli: *Journey of the Magi*; Florence

Andrea Mantegna

1431	Probable date of birth.
before 1443	Mantegna is adopted by the painter Francesco Squarcione.
1448	He is commissioned to take part in the decoration of the Ovetari chapel in Padua. He is successful in legal action to gain his independence from his adoptive father.
1449	Works briefly in Ferrara.
1453	Marries Nicolosia, the daughter of the Venetian painter Jacopo Bellini. He becomes solely responsible for the completion of the Ovetari chapel.
1456	Ludovico Gonzaga, Marquess of Mantua invites Mantegna to enter his service but Mantegna is commissioned to paint an altarpiece by the abbot of the St Zeno monastery in Verona.
1460	Mantegna settles permanently in Mantua as court painter to Ludovico.
1466	Visits Florence.
1467	Mantegna is in Pisa.
1478	Ludovico Gonzaga dies. His heir, Federico continues to retain Mantegna at the Mantuan court and to hold him in great esteem.
1483	Lorenzo de Medici, the Magnificent, calls on Mantegna in order to express his admiration for the painter's work.
1484	Federico Gonzaga dies and is succeeded by his son Francesco.
1488	Mantegna is in Rome working for Pope Innocent VIII on the decoration of a papal chapel in the Vatican.
1490	Returns to Mantua.
1492	Francesco Gonzaga transfers ownership of some woodland to Mantegna in payment for the *Triumph of Caesar* series and the decoration in the Camera degli Sposi.
1504	Mantegna makes a will in which he leaves a great deal of money for the decoration of his personal memorial chapel in Mantua.
1506	Mantegna dies on 13 September in Mantua.

Giovanni Bellini

Agony in the Garden 1465-70

National Gallery

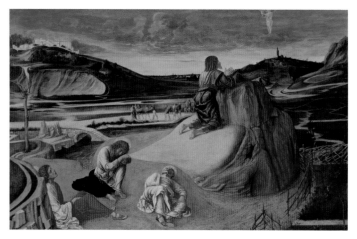

Giovanni Bellini was the rock upon which the great flowering of sixteenth century Venetian art was built. His interest in the primacy of colour and light became the touchstone of the great Venetian masters of the following generations.

Throughout his long life he was remarkably open to new ideas. Even though it is thought that he only left Venice and its environs once — on a visit to Pesaro, not too far along the coast to the south — as an inhabitant of the greatest trading city in the western Mediterranean, he had no need to travel as these novel influences were all around him. The arrival of Antonello da Messina in Venice, not long after this painting was completed cemented Bellini's interest in the use of oil paint. He also seems to have been aware of the work of Piero della Francesca.

In this relatively early picture one can detect the influence of Netherlandish art but also (perhaps pulling in the opposite direction) that of his brother-in-law Andrea Mantegna. The peculiar outcrop upon which Christ kneels in prayer, the striated rocky land around it, the skeletal tree and the canalised edges of the brook are all reminiscent of Mantegna's treatment of the same subject which hangs nearby in the National Gallery (see page 72). But here, some of Mantegna's edgy severity has been softened — instead of his brother-in-law's fantasy city clinging to hills which look as if they have been designed for the indoor set of an early Hollywood film, Bellini's background conforms more with reality.

His northern Italian hills are bathed in the most beautiful early morning light. Scholars have deduced that it is the first sunrise in all Italian art and it must still rate as one of the most wonderful examples from Italy or any other centre of western art. A rosy-apricot glow from the rising sun, still below the horizon, creates silhouettes of the trees in the valley and highlights the buildings of the two hill towns which, being higher, can already feel the first almost imperceptible warmth of the new morning.

Below, the biblical drama unfolds. Christ, knowing the torments that await him, is engaged in fervent prayer, asking that 'this cup pass from me'. The response is the appearance of an angel sent to strengthen his resolve. After the Last Supper he had led his disciples to Gethsemane, just outside Jerusalem across a brook called Kidron, and there he had asked his followers to wait while he prayed, selecting his three closest disciples to accompany him. Peter, John and James, unable to resist their extreme fatigue are seen sleeping while, not far away we can see that the arrival of Judas and his squad of soldiers is imminent. Soon they will pass over the rather picturesque bridge spanning the Kidron brook and they will make their arrest, sparking the Passion of Christ.

Contemporary Works

1464	Rogier van der Weyden: *Crucifixion*, Madrid
1469	Piero del Pollaiuolo: *Madonna and Child*; St Petersburg
	Joos van Ghent: *Altarpiece of the Crucifixion*; Ghent

Giovanni Bellini

1431-6?	Born in Venice, the son of the painter Jacopo Bellini.
1453	Giovanni's sister Nicolosia marries Andrea Mantegna.
1459	By this date he has his own house in Venice and is probably working as an independent artist although still helping his father and brother Gentile with some commissions.
1474	Bellini's Portrait of Jörg Fugger is painted using oil as a medium.
1475	Antonello da Messina visits Venice, influencing Bellini especially in regard to his use of oil paint.
1470s	Probably travels to Pesaro in connection with a commission, the only journey he ever makes outside the Veneto.
1479	Starts work on a series of scenes from Venetian history in the Doge's Palace. Continued to contribute to this cycle (now destroyed) for four decades.
1506	Dürer is in Venice and writes that Giovanni Bellini is the only Venetian artist to treat him in a friendly manner.
1516	Dies in Venice.

Antonello da Messina

St Jerome in his Study c1475

National Gallery

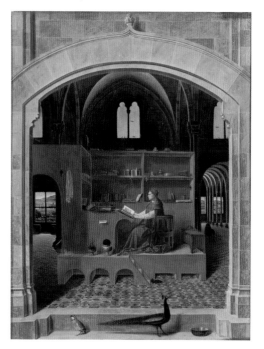

Antonello is traditionally given credit for the introduction into Italy of painting with oil glazes, a technique perfected by Jan van Eyck, where thin translucent layers of oil paint are painstakingly built up enabling the artist unparalleled scope for the depiction and modulation of detail. There is no independent evidence for this and there is some scepticism among scholars, but whatever the truth may be, this picture shows only too well why this notion should have been accepted. It is every inch an Eyckian work revelling in the meticulous, finely focused representation of every last detail from each individual floor tile to an ornithologically precise portrayal of a partridge, a recondite symbol of truth but so accurate that Audubon would have been proud of it. Antonello has also employed here the so-called 'empirical' method of perspective used in the Netherlands — only in later works did he adopt the Italian system based on mathematical exactitude. It may even be the case that this composition is partly based on one wing of a triptych by van Eyck (now lost but known to have been painted for an Italian client) which depicted the same saint in his library.

How these strong northern traits came to be so wonderfully employed by an artist who spent most of his life in Sicily is a mystery. But large slices of his life are undocumented — it may be that he saw some Netherlandish works in Naples, or in Milan when he travelled in northern Italy, but this does not necessarily explain how he acquired such mastery in a technique which was new to Italy. When he visited Venice in 1475-6 he seems to have had a considerable influence on such artists as Giovanni Bellini but his visits to mainland Italy also had their effect on Antonello whose later works exhibit more Italianate influences especially from Piero della Francesca, producing a fusion of north and south.

Here we see St Jerome at work in his carrel (a wooden study usually constructed in a cloister), spied through a Late Gothic opening, surrounded by his books and a variety of other beautifully realised objects, many of them replete with symbolism, illuminated by the light flooding past the viewer into the hallowed space. And what a mysterious edifice this sanctuary is, full of shadows but with views out onto a bucolic idyll — birds can be seen through the clerestory wheeling in the evening sky; framed in the window to the left a boat glides past on the still waters of a peaceful river.

After spending a number of years in the Syrian desert devoted to the ascetic life (as one did in the 370s AD), Jerome became secretary to Pope Damasus who asked him to translate the Bible from Greek into Latin. He devoted the rest of his life to the task and this is how Antonello has chosen to show him, as a scholar, and one of the four 'doctors' of the Latin Church, intent on his studies. Two of his attributes appear nearby — although the office of cardinal did not exist during Jerome's life he is often shown in cardinal's apparel and Antonello has placed his cardinal's hat on the shelf behind him. In the shadows of the colonnade, there lurks a rather incongruous lion who co-stars with Jerome in many paintings by numerous artists. Often these show the saint during his time in the desert when he took pity on the beast and bravely extracted a thorn from its paw thereby earning the lion's eternal gratitude.

Contemporary Works	
c1472	Leonardo da Vinci: *Annunciation*; Florence
1475	Antonio and Piero del Pollaiuolo: *Martyrdom of St Sebastian*; London, National Gallery.
1476	Hugo van der Goes: *Portinari Altarpiece*; Florence

Antonello da Messina	
c1430	Born in Messina, Sicily, then part of the Kingdom of Naples, the son of a stone-mason.
1457	Antonello is recorded as having his own workshop in Messina.
1460	He returns to Sicily after a long visit to mainland Italy. The destination(s) of that visit are unknown.
1475	Travels to Venice.
1476	He may have visited Milan (the Duke was interested in acquiring his services) but by September he is known to have been back in Messina.
1479	Dies in Messina (February).

Hans Memling

National Gallery

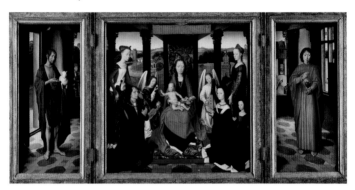

Sir John Donne was a Welsh knight who accompanied King Edward IV to the Low Countries on a number of occasions in the 1470s. Presumably this work was commissioned during one of these visits. The small size of the triptych would suggest that it was intended as a portable altarpiece which could be used as a focus for his devotions during his travels.

The wings show Sir John's two name saints. To the left St John the Baptist holds a charmingly cute Lamb of God. Behind the Baptist, half hidden behind an Italianate pillar, a man looks on — perhaps fearful of gatecrashing such an august assembly but nevertheless wanting to see more. St John the Evangelist appears in the right wing holding his chalice complete with emergent snake (when challenged to drink poison he is reputed to have made the sign of the cross over the receptacle thereby turning the poison into a serpent).

The central panel is a little more crowded. The Virgin sits on her throne backed by gorgeous damask. On her lap the Christ child is diverted by an angel. Everyone else looks as though they are lost in meditation or prayer. Kneeling to the Virgin's right we see Sir John, hands together at his devotions. He is presented by St Catherine who holds the sword with which she was beheaded. Facing him, his wife and eldest child are presented by St Barbara, a possibly mythical saint who was locked in a tower by her pagan father. Memling has integrated her tower into the landscape and on the other side of Mary, near to St Catherine, he has also depicted a mill wheel which is a reference to the instrument of Catherine's (unsuccessful) torture before her decapitation.

In common with many of his other triptychs the same background scene of bucolic peace seems to extend across all three sections. A good number of his works found their way to Italy where these exquisite background landscapes influenced such painters as Perugino and through him Raphael.

A marvellous serenity pervades every corner of this picture. All is still and contemplative. An ideal and flawless utopia is presented to us — a setting suitable for the heavenly personages who are attendant to the needs of the

Virgin and her child. The symmetry of the composition lends further gravitas to the hushed atmosphere.

Contemporary Works

c1478	Sandro Botticelli: *Primavera*; Florence
c1480	Giovanni Bellini: *St Francis in Ecstacy*; New York
	Domenico Ghirlandaio: *An Old Man and his Grandson*; Paris
	Hugo van der Goes: *Dormition of the Virgin*; Bruges

Hans Memling

1430-40	Born in Seligenstandt in Germany.
1465	Becomes a citizen of Bruges.
1474	Admitted to the Confraternity of Our Lady in the Snow in Bruges, all members of which were either wealthy or aristocratic.
1479	Completes his largest commission, *The Mystic Marriage of St Catherine*, for the hospital of St Jan in Bruges.
1481	Memling, together with over 200 other citizens of Bruges, is repaid money lent to support war against France. He is one of the wealthiest citizens in the town.
1487	Memling's wife dies.
1489	He completes the *Shrine of St Ursula* — a Gothic reliquary made of carved wood with eight paintings decorating the sides.
1491	Memling receives a commission for a triptych for Lübeck Cathedral in Germany.
1492	Completes a commission for a large altarpiece (most of which is now lost) for the abbey of Nájera in Spain.
1494	Dies in Bruges (11 August).

Geertgen tot Sint Jans

Nativity at Night

c1480-90

National Gallery

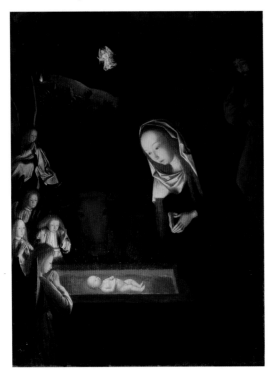

This exquisite Nativity illustrates one of the visions experienced by St Bridget of Sweden in which she is said to have been the recipient of descriptions of the Nativity, relayed by none other than the Virgin herself. The salient point about these Marian descriptions is that the naked Christ child became a source of light — a light so intense that it eclipsed all others.

Geertgen has reproduced this miraculous concept with consummate skill. The initial focus of our attention is the Christ child lying in his manger glowing with a divine energy which illuminates the face of his mother — a face full of peace and tenderness but also infused with a sweet melancholia. This is indeed a deeply moving depiction of the Madonna —she is a young mother intent on the wellbeing of her new arrival but at the same time she is the instrument of God and a realisation of the fate of her child may already be stirring within her.

The radiance of Christ also shines on a small assembly of angels who gather in awe at the head of the manger. Above the hillside a similarly radiant angel brings the news to a group of shepherds, some of whom are huddled round a fire which provides another point of light. Otherwise, on this black night even the stars have been outshone by the arrival of the Light of the World.

Joseph lurks in the shadows, cast in his usual walk-on part, a mere consort to the semi-divine Mary, just making up the numbers, not even awarded a front seat at the manger like the ox and ass who loom out of the murk to gaze in wonderment at the neon Christ.

Very few pictures by Geertgen survive and no documentary evidence relating to his life survives. He seems to have been influenced by Hugo van der Goes, the painter of the *Portinari Altarpiece*, that pinnacle of the northern Renaissance, now in the Uffizi in Florence. Indeed, the *Night Nativity* may be based on a lost work by Hugo. Be that as it may, Geertgen has created here a little masterpiece which triumphantly takes up the challenges associated with the portrayal of a strong light source and its concomitant shadows, the same challenges which fascinated Caravaggio and Rembrandt, a century and more later.

Contemporary Works

1482	Pietro Perugino: *Jesus handing the Keys to St Peter*, Rome
c1484	Sandro Botticelli: *The Birth of Venus*, Florence
c1489	Carlo Crivelli: *The Vision of the Blessed Gabriele*, London, National Gallery

Geertgen tot Sint Jans

As there is no primary evidence relating to Geertgen's life it is impossible to construct a chronology for him.

The principal source of information about him is Karel van Mander's *Schilderboek*, a collection of (often inaccurate) biographies about Netherlandish artists published in 1604. From this we know that he lived in Haarlem and that his name (which can be translated as Little Gerard of the Brethren of Saint John) derives from the fact that he lived at the Commandery of the Knights of St John in Haarlem. He seems to have been active for about twenty years.

| 1484-94 | Geertgen paints the *Lamentation* — the right wing and only surviving section of a triptych for the high altar of the Commandery church in Haarlem. |

Sandro Botticelli

National Gallery

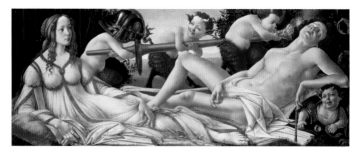

This picture was probably painted to celebrate a marriage, indeed its shape may point to its origins as part of a wedding chest (*cassone*). The subject was also appropriate for a Florentine wedding of the period; Venus, the goddess of Love gazes in a somewhat detached way in the general direction of her lover Mars, the god of War. It appears that Mars may have recently sampled the delights offered by the love goddess for he seems to be in the throes of post-coital slumber and of course the fact that his virility has been temporarily conquered by love would no doubt have been the source of comment and bawdy humour at the wedding celebrations.

Whether or not it was commissioned for a wedding, there are clues within the picture which may help to identify who commissioned the work. Mars, as he sleeps, is blissfully unaware of the wasps which can be seen buzzing around his head. They may symbolise the sting — the negative consequences — of desire but they might also be seen as a visual pun on the name of a very influential Florentine family, the Vespucci (the Italian word for wasps is *vespe*), who commissioned various works from Botticelli probably including the great *Primavera*. It is traditionally held that Simonetta Vespucci was the model for Venus in the *Primavera* as well as other works by Botticelli and the very beautiful features of both Venuses bear a strong resemblance to one another.

The presence of the baby satyrs could be interpreted as reinforcing the warning inherent in the presence of the wasps. The *satyrisci* (little satyrs) can be identified with *incubi* — bringers of nightmares, especially those of a sexual nature.

Botticelli was closely associated with humanist circles in Florence and is often seen as an archetypal Renaissance artist, primarily because of the classical subject matter of a small number of famous pictures of which *Venus and Mars* is one. But curiously, beyond the fact that the subject is drawn from pagan antiquity, Botticelli makes no further effort to emphasise the classical nature of the scene. Rather this picture, in common with other compositions such as the *Primavera* and the *Birth of Venus*, betrays an affinity with earlier styles which we might call Late Gothic in character. In particular, the sinuous contours of Mars and Venus together with the lack of depth in the composition are redolent of the more decorative priorities of the late thirteenth and early fourteenth century. In other respects Botticelli is keen to stress the contemporary — the hairstyle and gown worn by Venus reflect the fashion of the day and the armour and lance are Renaissance, not antique in provenance.

The advent of the hell-raising friar Girolamo Savonarola, who arrived in Florence not long after this painting was completed, proved to be a watershed for Botticelli as well as the whole city (the Medici were temporarily overthrown). We are told by the biographer and painter Giorgio Vasari that he became a committed adherent of the radical sect which surrounded Savonarola who railed against the worldliness of the ruling Florentine elite. Among his many targets Savonarola criticised the practice among artists of modelling holy personages on identifiable Florentines and in 1497 and 1498 he instigated the 'bonfires of the vanities' in which such diverse objects as dice, books, mirrors and paintings were burned. After this period of tumult a change can be seen in Botticelli's art — he returns exclusively to sacred subjects and becomes even more intent on following a retrospective path in which his later works lose the distinctive serenity of his mature period. No better example of this change exists than the *Mystic Nativity* also in the National Gallery.

Contemporary Works

1483	Luca Signorelli: *The Last Days of Moses*; Rome, Sistine Chapel
c1485	Hans Memling: *Madonna and Child with Angels*; Washington
	Gerard David: *Nativity*; New York

Sandro Botticelli

1444 or 5	Born in Florence.
1460s	Receives his initial training with Fra Filippo Lippi.
1470	First mentioned as an independent master.
1472	Enters the Compagnia di S Luca (the painters guild) in Florence.
1474	Works on a fresco in the cathedral at Pisa (destroyed in 1583).
1478	Paints *Primavera*, the first of his great mythological pictures.
1481	Botticelli travels to Rome where (together with Ghirlandaio, Perugino and Signorelli) he is employed by Pope Sixtus IV on the fresco decoration of the walls of the newly completed Sistine Chapel.
1482	Back in Florence, engaged in a number of commissions.
1484	Completes *Birth of Venus*.
1489	The Dominican friar Girolamo Savonarola arrives in Florence and denounces (among other things) the practice of painting images of holy personages in contemporary clothes. Botticelli becomes a devotee of the sect.
1498	Savonarola is burned at the stake for heresy.
1500	Completes the *Mystic Nativity*.
1510	Dies in Florence.

Carlo Crivelli

The Annunciation with St Emidius 1486

National Gallery

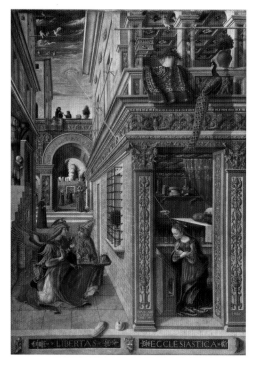

On 25 March 1482 the town of Ascoli Piceno was granted some rights of self government by the Pope. 25 March is also the Feast of the Annunciation and in carrying out his commission for the Franciscan church of the Annunciation, Carlo Crivelli has conflated the two events — one political and contemporary, the other religious.

The archangel finds himself in a street in Ascoli and, oddly, he is accompanied by the patron saint of the town, Saint Emidius, who seems to be intent on distracting heaven's emissary from his solemn task by engaging him in a discussion about the model of the town of Ascoli which identifies him and which he is carrying. This is indeed a very strange setting for the Annunciation — one of the protagonists is in a very public place separated from the other by a thick stone wall. Presumably the conversation is taking place through the window grille, not unlike the somewhat strained discourse between a visitor and an inmate in a prison.

In the background, on the bridge, a man is reading a message which has just been delivered by carrier pigeon. This is a reference to news of the papal grant which is arriving at the same time as the angelic Annunciation and is a parochial counterpart to the 'special delivery' which at this very moment is reaching its recipient via the dove of the Holy Spirit.

One feels that the action is taking place in a somewhat airless silence — the street is peopled, but not bustling, the inhabitants seem to be stilled —

caught in time as the news is dispensed. The townscape itself is represented in pristine condition, the streets are beautifully paved and the buildings are sumptuously decorated in Renaissance style. Every detail is rendered in Crivelli's trademark hard-edged clarity from the dovecote high above the street to the little child watching the proceedings from the top of the stairs and the peacock and eastern carpet adorning the loggia on the first floor of the Virgin's palazzo. Inside her room the Madonna is surrounded by the clutter of everyday life.

Crivelli does not let the architecture get in the way of his narrative — the shaft of light bearing the dove of the Holy Spirit enters the room via a very convenient hole cut in the solid wall. But, being Crivelli, he adds another characteristically quirky detail — the golden light or energy has left some sort of residual matter or reflection while passing through the masonry, imparting a golden efflorescence to the immediate surrounding of the cavity.

Crivelli's pictures are so appealing because of this quirkiness, this ability to surprise and amuse us with some unexpected detail.

Birdwatchers have invented a wonderful word — jizz — which they use to explain what it is about a bird which makes it quintessentially *that* bird rather than another similar type — its colour, shape, the way it flies and perches etc., all rolled into one. Well Crivelli has a very strong jizz — he is instantly recognisable and one always feels drawn to him when one glimpses his pictures for the first time.

Contemporary Works	
c1483-5	Leonardo da Vinci: *Virgin of the Rocks*; Paris
1487	Hans Memling: *Portrait of Martin van Nieuwenhove*; Bruges
	Sandro Botticelli: *Madonna of the Pomegranate*; Florence

Carlo Crivelli	
1430-35?	Born, probably in Venice.
1457	After legal action brought in Venice, Crivelli is imprisoned for six months and fined for adultery with a sailor's wife.
1465	He is recorded as living in the Venetian city of Zara on the Dalmatian coast (now Zadar, Croatia).
1468	Crivelli is working in Fermo in the Marches.
1478	He buys a house near the cathedral in Ascoli Piceno where he now seems to be based.
1486	Paints the *Annunciation*, now in the National Gallery, for the Annunziata church in Ascoli.
1490	Crivelli is knighted by Prince Ferrante of Capua.
1495	Dies in Ascoli Piceno (3 September).

Hieronymus Bosch

Christ Mocked (the Crowning with Thorns)   c1490-1500

National Gallery

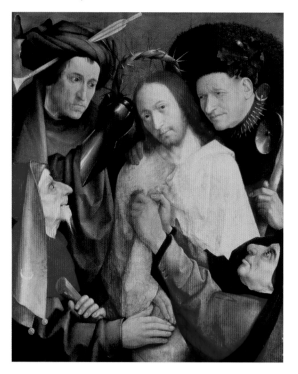

Before Jesus was taken to be crucified he was subjected to humiliating mockery by the soldiers of Pilate's palace. In the Gospel according to Matthew it states that '…they plaited a crown of thorns and put it on his head … and they kneeled down before him and mocked him, saying, Hail King of the Jews'.

In this painting Bosch has chosen to surround Christ with only four tormentors, each exhibiting his own special form of menace. He is the calm centre of the hatred swirling around him. His eyes hold us and then seem to penetrate us; they might be transmitting a gentle rebuke across the centuries. His four persecutors represent an evil and sinful world of which we are all part. The crown of thorns doubles as a halo but we know that very soon indeed the mailed fist will jam it mercilessly onto Christ's head provoking blood to flow.

In common with many of the artist's works, it is difficult to establish a clear iconography for this painting. It has been suggested that the four men surrounding Christ represent the four humours (or temperaments), with the two lower faces supposedly displaying sanguine and choleric characteristics, the two others revealing themselves as phlegmatic and melancholy. Or it might be that they are in some way diabolical mirror images of the four evangelists.

The curious red headdress of the man below and to the left of Christ sports an Islamic crescent, stigmatising him as a non-Christian. The two upper tormentors are military men as evinced by the elements of armour they wear. The crossbow bolt piercing the hat of the man in green is used (together with other variant implements such as knives) in other works by Bosch, but its exact meaning remains opaque. His opposite number wears a heavily spiked dog collar encircling his throat emphasising the bestial nature of the wearer.

A sprig of oak leaves with an acorn is attached to this man's hat (he is possibly a retainer wearing the leaves as a badge of loyalty). The wonderful facility with which this tromp l'oeil passage is painted makes these leaves one of the most extraordinary vignettes to be found in the National Gallery. The viewer sees that the cutting is a number of days old because the extremities of the leaves have begun to dry out and curl. And astonishingly, as the leaves curl away from the hat they seem to pierce the picture plane and invade our reality eliciting a momentary uncertainty as to whether it could be that someone has attached them to the painting.

Contemporary Works

1491	Carlo Crivelli: *The Virgin and Child with Saints Francis and Sebastian*; London, National Gallery
1495	Pietro Perugino: *St Sebastian*; St Petersburg
1498	Leonardo da Vinci: *Last Supper*; Milan

Hieronymus Bosch

About 1450	Born as Jeroen van Aken in 's Hertogenbosch in the central Netherlands.
1481	Marries Aleyt Goyarts van den Meervenne, whose dowry consisted of an estate near 's Hertogenbosch and other property. It is probable that Bosch did not need to support himself by painting.
1486 or 7	Jeronimus van Aken enters the Brotherhood of Our Lady in 's Hertogenbosch.
1488	Becomes a 'sworn' member of the Brotherhood, the only artist to be so honoured.
1488-90	Works on an altarpiece for the Brotherhood's chapel in the Cathedral of St John.
1504	Philip the Fair, Duke of Burgundy, orders the *Last Judgement* altarpiece from Bosch.
1516	Dies in 's Hertogenbosch.

Albrecht Dürer

St Jerome   c1495

National Gallery

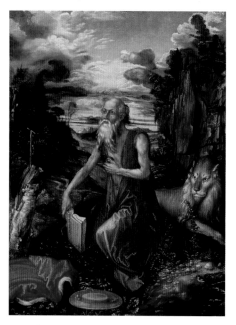

This picture, at only 23 centimetres high, is easy to miss. Make sure you don't for it is a little gem of a painting — bigger than a miniature, it nevertheless has that jewel-like quality which imbues the best work of miniaturists and illuminators. It dates from about the time of Dürer's return in 1495 from his first visit to Venice.

In 1494, despite his recent marriage, he left his wife to travel to northern Italy in search of the secrets of harmonious proportion and mathematical perspective which he believed the Italians could teach him. He found inspiration there in the work of Mantegna and Giovanni Bellini.

The influence of Venetian painting, and in particular Bellini (see page 74), can perhaps be seen in Dürer's sky. But other aspects of this painting remind us of the artist's more northerly roots. The beautifully painted sunset (or sunrise) spills a muted golden light over mountains (perhaps those he would have recently traversed) into a shallow valley, silhouetting a lifeless tree and imparting a honeyed tinge to some central clouds. However, framing this sky, and the saint, are two decidedly northern motifs — dense woodland to the left, pierced by a Germanic spired tower, and a jagged outcrop of sheer rock to the right. Arid, bolder-strewn terrain is shown in the middle distance, presumably Dürer's rather half-hearted reference to the Syrian desert where the saint spent many years as an ascetic hermit. Compared to the privations suffered by the real Jerome, this landscape seems to offer a more comfortable, if somewhat colder existence.

In the foreground, however, Saint Jerome has selected a conveniently lush patch of vegetation for his devotions. But we are a long way from the cultured, cosy confines of Jerome's study as depicted by Antonello da Messina (see page 76). His only apparel is a most impractical blue shift, very long but giving no cover to his arms and upper torso. He has discarded his cardinal's hat and ermine-lined robe and has fixed his crucifix to the torn stump of a birch tree (the bark of which is most precisely observed). He holds his Bible open with one hand while in the other hand he holds a stone with which he will beat his chest to prove his penitential credentials. Behind him his loyal lion, from whose paw he extracted a thorn, is his constant companion. It has been pointed out that this beast owes more to the lion of St Mark, emblem of Venice, than the study of a real one. But the artist has certainly observed at first hand the various plants which surround Jerome as well as the bullfinch and goldfinch (thought to nest in thorn bushes and therefore symbolising the Crown of Thorns) which flit by the stream, all of which have been represented in meticulous detail.

Contemporary Works

1492	Carlo Crivelli: *The Immaculate Conception*; London, National Gallery
1494	Vittore Carpaccio: *Miracle at Rialto*; Venice
1495	Andrea Mantegna: *Madonna of Victory*; Paris

Albrecht Dürer

1471	Born in Nuremberg, the son of a goldsmith.
1483	While apprenticed to his father he makes, at the age of 13 his famous self-portrait in silverpoint.
1486	After completing his apprenticeship with his father, the young Dürer enters the workshop of the painter Michael Wolgemut.
1489	Completes his apprenticeship with Wolgemut.
1492	Dürer is in Basel working on woodcuts for illustrations to Sebastian Brandt's book *Narrenschyff* (Ship of Fools).
1493	Leaves Basel for Strasbourg where he continued to produce woodcuts.
1494	Returns to Nuremberg in order to marry Agnes Frey but almost immediately after the wedding he travels to Venice.
1495	On his return to Nuremberg he establishes a workshop.
1496	Commissioned by the Elector of Saxony to paint his portrait and also two polyptychs for the palace church in Wittenberg.
1498	Dürer publishes an edition of *The Apocalypse* with fifteen full page woodcuts. The project is an immediate success and his fame spreads throughout Europe.
1505	Travels again to Italy, staying first in Padua and then to Venice.
1506	Dürer is feted by the German community. Completes an altarpiece for the German church in Venice. Travels to Bologna and possibly onward to Rome.
1507	Returns to Nuremberg.
1513	The engraving *The Knight, Death and the Devil* is completed.
1514	Dürer produces his masterpiece engraving *Melencolia*. His mother dies.
1515	The Holy Roman Emperor grants Dürer a pension of 100 florins as payment for a huge woodcut of *The Triumphal Arch of Maximilian I*.
1519	The Emperor Maximilian dies and with him goes Dürer's pension.
1520	Travels to Antwerp accompanied by his wife. Then to Malines where he meets the Governor of the Low Countries, Margaret of Austria. Attends the coronation of Emperor Charles V at Aachen. Charles reinstates Dürer's pension.
1521	Confined with illness at Antwerp for the winter. Travels back to Nuremberg.
1525	A treatise by Dürer on geometry is published.
1527	A treatise on fortifications is published by Dürer.
1528	Dürer dies in Nuremberg.

Piero di Cosimo

National Gallery

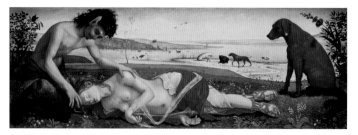

According to the artist and biographer Giorgio Vasari, Piero was an eccentric recluse who restricted his diet to hard-boiled eggs which he prepared in batches of fifty. It makes a good story but although Vasari was not the most reliable of biographers it seems likely that his account, at least in regard to his eccentric behaviour, contains more than a grain of truth. Certainly much of his output betrays his highly personal and idiosyncratic view of the world which endeared him centuries later to the Surrealists who saw him as a precursor of their own work.

Looking at this picture, you can see what they meant. There is a distinct air of incongruity, principally due to the presence of the large dog who has been given equal billing with the mythical protagonists. A satyr grieves over a dying or recently dead young woman, tenderly stroking her brow. The dog, gazing intently at the stricken girl, also seems to be mourning. The drama takes place on low-lying ground at the margins of an estuary or bay. Life goes on in the background — sailing vessels can be seen in the distance, more dogs roam nearby, a heron fishes by the shore.

It seems very likely that Piero is relating the story of Cephalus and Procris which appears in Ovid's *Metamorphoses*. Aurora, goddess of the dawn fell in love with the handsome Cephalus who rebuffed her advances, staying faithful to his wife Procris. Aurora, however, managed to plant the seeds of doubt in Cephalus' mind regarding the faithfulness of his wife and after a confrontation, Procris lived for some time in the countryside until they were eventually reconciled. But before long it was the turn of Procris to have her doubts about Cephalus (aided by some convoluted interaction between gods and satyrs). She decided to follow her husband on one of his hunting trips as she suspected him of having a liaison with a nymph. As Cephalus was resting he heard a noise and thinking he had discovered an animal he launched his magic unerring spear (given to him by Procris) which, true to its enchanted nature, found his intended target only too well. Procris dies in Cephalus' arms.

In Piero's composition Cephalus is nowhere to be seen. However scholars have pointed out that Ovid's tale formed the basis of a play (*Fabula di Cephalo*) written about 1480 in which a satyr figures prominently. Piero may have used this as his source rather than Ovid's original.

The shape of the piece means that it must have originally formed part of a *cassone* or perhaps a bench back (see Botticelli *Venus and Mars*, page 82), often presented to newly weds. If this is the case then Piero's beautiful painting would have provided a salutary reminder of the merits of fidelity.

Contemporary Works

c1490	Geertgen tot Sint Jans: *St John the Baptist in the Wilderness*; Berlin
c1496	Luca Signorelli: *The Adoration of the Shepherds*; London, National Gallery
1498	Albrecht Dürer: *The Four Horsemen of the Apocalypse* (Woodcut)

Piero di Cosimo

1461 or 2	Born in Florence, the son of a toolmaker.
1480	By this date Piero is apprenticed to Cosimo Rosselli from whom he took his name.
1481	When Rosselli is summoned to Rome Piero accompanies him.
1504	Piero enrols in the painters guild in Florence. He is also a member of the committee set up to select a site for Michelangelo's recently completed *David*.
1515	Piero is involved in preparing for the celebrations attendant on the visit of Pope Leo X to Florence.
c1521	Dies in Florence.

Leonardo da Vinci

The Virgin of the Rocks
Probably 1508

National Gallery

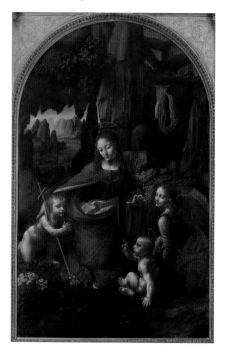

The first thing that one notes when viewing this picture is the very odd setting. The four faces seem to glow out of a dark and brooding landscape. The eponymous rocks are arranged like nothing in this world and the rock canopy does not obey any earthly laws of physics, otherwise it would surely endanger the continued existence of the sacred quartet. A break in this claustrophobic geology reveals a mountainous marine vista which, in a later century, might easily have found its way onto the cover of a science fiction novel set perhaps on a moon of one of the outer planets of the solar system. This other-worldly setting is no doubt a consciously non realistic backdrop for what is, after all, a gathering of holy and heavenly personages. But the rocks may also be a somewhat recondite reference to Mary's impregnable virginity.

The Virgin sits, probably with some discomfort, in the rocky wilderness; the infant St John is partially enfolded by her cloak as she extends a solicitous hand around his podgy shoulders. Another artist has added the Baptist's cross in an effort to dispel any confusion as to the identity of the two infants. The Christ child sits nearby supported by the archangel Uriel — a rare appearance for one of the lesser known celestial messengers.

This picture is one of two versions of the same composition, the other, earlier version being in the Louvre in Paris. Why were two paintings produced? Considerable documentation, generated by a very lengthy legal dispute, and the efforts of many eminent art historians have not produced a definitive answer. Suffice it to say that in 1483, Leonardo, together with Ambrogio and Evangelista de Predis were commissioned by the Confraternità dell' Immacolata Concezione in Milan to decorate and gild a recently finished wooden sculpted altarpiece and to paint panels which would be set into the frame. The central panel (now in the Louvre) and two separate images of angels (executed by the de Predis brothers) were probably completed in 1485 but the confraternity claimed that for some reason the commission had not been completed; the painters responded by maintaining that the central panel 'done in oils' was in fact worth more than the confraternity was willing to pay. The dispute was still in progress twenty-one years later when in 1506 arbitrators set a deadline of two years for the completion of the contract. The picture in the National Gallery is the product of this stipulation. The stylistic evidence appears to confirm that the Louvre version was fully completed in the 1480s so it is perhaps reasonable to surmise that the artists withheld this picture and possibly sold it, incorporating the London version into the altarpiece in 1508.

In any event the London version is essentially a replica of the Paris original (with some minor changes), and was most probably a collaboration between Leonardo and the de Predis brothers although the extent of Leonardo's participation is disputed. However, it seems likely that, at the very least, the faces of the Virgin and the angel are the work of the master and it is these two elements together with the strange and mysterious surroundings which confirm it as a profoundly satisfying work of art. As Lawrence Gowing points out 'the indisputable essence of great art is the mystery that is fated to remain unsolved'.

Contemporary Works

1507	Albrecht Dürer: *Adam and Eve*; Madrid
c1508	Raphael: *Madonna of the Pinks*; London, National Gallery
1510	Albrecht Altdorfer: *St George slaying the Dragon*; Munich

Leonardo da Vinci

1452	Born in Anchiano near Vinci, the illegitimate child of a notary, he was brought up in his paternal grandfather's household.
1472	By this date he is a member of the painters guild in Florence.
1476	Leonardo is recorded as apprenticed to Andrea Verrocchio. He is accused of sodomy but charges are not pressed.
1482	Moves to Milan where he enters the service of Ludovico Sforza.
1483	Commissioned to produce an altarpiece for the Confraternità dell' Immacolata Concezione in Milan.
1496	A procurator is appointed to adjudicate in the dispute between Leonardo and the Confraternità dell' Immacolata Concezione.
1497	He is nearing completion of the *Last Supper* in S Maria delle Grazie in Milan.
1499	Leaves Milan after a French army forces the fall of Ludovico Sforza.
1500	Returns to Florence via Mantua and Venice.
1503	Leonardo seems to have been employed by Machiavelli as a military engineer.
1506	Arbitrators instruct Leonardo to complete a second painting in order to settle the dispute with the Confraternità dell' Immacolata Concezione. Visits Milan.
1508	Returns to Milan, then under French occupation.
1513	Travels to Rome via Florence.
1516	Francis I invites Leonardo to France as 'first painter and engineer' to the King.
1517	By May he is resident at Amboise.
1519	Leonardo dies at Amboise.

Giorgione

The Sunset 1506-10

National Gallery

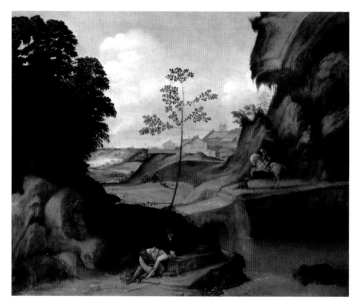

Mystery is the key 'Giorgionesque' word. We know very little about his short life and despite the furious endeavours of tribes of art historians it is impossible to agree on which paintings are certainly by him, outside a tiny core of perhaps six works. No signed and dated pictures by Giorgione have survived although two portraits carry inscriptions on their backs which are probably contemporary and which seem to confirm him as the artist. Only a handful of contemporary documents refer to him providing the barest biographical detail. But despite all this uncertainty Giorgione is universally regarded as the founder of the innovative Venetian style of painting in the sixteenth century, laying the foundations for Titian and greatly influencing many artists from later centuries such as Poussin.

The sense of mystery spills over into his paintings, for notwithstanding the efforts of those historians we are no nearer to a coherent interpretation of much of his output. Unlike his predecessors in Italy and Flanders Giorgione leaves very few keys which might enable us to unlock his inscrutable compositions. His paintings are not meant to be direct illustrations of biblical or other texts — he did not set out to make them explicit statements. Rather they should be seen as poetic inventions striving to evoke a mood.

The Sunset is not one of the paintings which make it into the charmed circle of works which all scholars agree are by Giorgione. But as Erika Langmuir points out in the *National Gallery Companion Guide*, the painting is so redolent of his style that in a way it does not matter. The picture was discovered in a villa just to the south of Venice in 1933; it was badly damaged and has been quite heavily restored.

In the foreground two travellers have stopped by a pool which seems to be inhabited by very strange creatures. Behind the pool a hermit can be made out and St George is busy dispatching a miniature dragon. It is known that the St George cameo is the product of a restorer working to cover a damaged area of paint with only the hint of a dragon's tail to go on. It is just possible that the travellers may be St Roch and his companion. St Roch cared for those afflicted with the plague but predictably became a victim himself. It is possible that the kneeling traveller is inspecting the ulcer that traditionally appears on the saint's leg. But it is impossible to know if this interpretation is valid or not.

What is so appealing about Giorgione is the enigmatic quality of his work and the mood of mystery he evokes. For me, he represents the genesis of a way of making art — a current which extends through Claude and Watteau to de Chirico and Magritte.

Contemporary Works

1506	Albrecht Dürer: *Feast of the Rose Garlands*; Prague
c1507	Giovanni Bellini: *The Assassination of St Peter Martyr*; London, National Gallery
c1510	Hans Baldung Grien: *Death and the Maiden*; Vienna

Giorgione

c1477 or 8	Probable birth date. Born in Castelfranco in the Veneto.
1506	A portrait known as *Laura* (now in Vienna) has an inscription on the back dating the work and naming Giorgione as the artist.
1507	In August Giorgione begins work on a painting for the audience chamber in the Doge's Palace in Venice.
1508	Completes the painting for the Doge's Palace and is paid for decorative frescoes adorning the façade of the German merchants' warehouse near the Rialto Bridge in Venice.
1510	In October Isabella d'Este wrote to her agent in Venice asking that he purchase a painting from Giorgione. The agent replied that he had recently died of plague.

Raphael

National Gallery

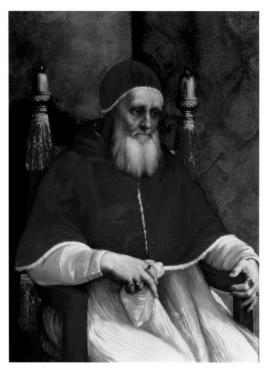

Julius appears as the quintessential worldly pope, hands encrusted with bejewelled rings. He has chosen to be portrayed sitting in a chair adorned not with any papal emblem, but with the acorn, his personal device, a reference to his family name della Rovere, meaning 'oak' in Italian. And indeed he really was the archetypal Renaissance pope, leading his troops in military action to re-establish papal control in central Italy but at the same time commissioning some of the greatest works of the Renaissance.

It was Julius II who had summoned Raphael to Rome three years or so before he sat for this portrait and set him to work on the decoration of the Vatican Palace. And, at the same time that Julius eased himself into his chair for Raphael to capture his likeness, Michelangelo was busy in another part of the Vatican complex putting the finishing touches to the Sistine ceiling while Bramante was working on the new St Peters.

Raphael has captured an extraordinary likeness of this remarkable man, its profound effect on near contemporary viewers attested by Vasari, the sixteenth-century artist, biographer and commentator, who reports that many were startled by such a lifelike image. There are some wonderful passages, particularly the use of light and shadow to define the undulations in the old man's face, in the modelling of the silk sleeves and in the foreshortening of Julius's left hand.

This picture was once thought to be a copy until, in 1970, scientific tests revealed that the motif of papal keys barely visible in the curtains behind Julius had once been painted gold. It became clear that this portrait was the original and that the artist had obviously changed his mind about the backcloth and had overpainted in green.

The picture can be fairly accurately dated by the presence of Julius's beard. In 1511 the papal city of Bologna was lost and Julius vowed to grow a beard as a mark of remorse. In March 1512 he shaved it off. The next year he was dead and Raphael's skills were at the disposal of a new pontiff.

Contemporary Works

1510	Albrecht Altdorfer: *Rest on the Flight into Egypt*; Berlin
1512	Michelangelo: Sistine Chapel ceiling completed; Rome
1514	Quentin Massys: *The Moneylender and his Wife*; Paris

Raphael

1483	Born in Urbino – his father Giovanni Santi was a painter at the Montefeltro court in Urbino.
1500?	He is probably a pupil of Perugino at about this time.
1504	Raphael moves to Florence. He becomes friendly with local artists, particularly Fra Bartolommeo and studies the work of Leonardo, Michelangelo and Donatello.
1508	Raphael is summoned to Rome to work for Pope Julius II primarily on the decoration of the Vatican Palace; first on the Stanza della Segnatura. Michelangelo is working on the Sistine ceiling at the time.
1512	Probable completion of the frescoes for the Stanza della Segnatura. Begins work on the Stanza d'Eliodoro. Also working on a number of commissions for altarpieces.
1514	Pope Leo X names Raphael as the architect of St Peter's in succession to Bramante who dies in April. Completes fresco decoration of the Stanza d'Eliodoro and starts on the Stanza dell'Incendio.
1515	Works on tapestry designs for the Sistine Chapel (Cartoons now in the V & A). Writes an open letter to the Pope appealing for an end to the destruction of archaeological remains.
1517	Starts work on his last altarpiece, *The Transfiguration* which is left unfinished at his death.
1518	Completes plans for a villa, to be sited just outside Rome, for Cardinal Giulio de' Medici.
1520	Dies in Rome (April) at the age of 37 at the height of his powers.

Jan Gossaert (Mabuse)

Adoration of the Kings   c1500-12

National Gallery

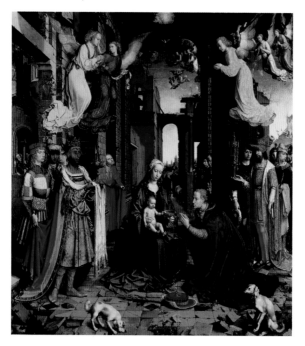

The three kings are attended by extensive retinues and are bedecked in fine silks, damasks and furs. They wear suitably outlandish and gorgeous headgear — a pointer to the fact that they hail from far flung destinations — incorporating crowns to confirm their status. Their gifts are proffered in intricately wrought monstrances of unimaginable cost. The Madonna, clothed in her usual ultramarine blue, is holding the Christ child, who has already received the gift of gold coins and a gold chalice from Caspar. We know who he is as his name is conveniently displayed on the chalice lid lying next to his peaked hat. Balthazar, on the left, is similarly identified by an inscription on his crown. The third king, Melchior, awaits his turn on the right. Joseph, clad in startling red and betraying his age by using a walking stick, appears from an arch behind the Virgin. The ox lurks in another opening and the ass grazes contentedly near the shepherds. Above this gathering of humanity the nine orders of angels hover, some garbed in peculiarly clashing colours, perhaps signifying their other-worldly provenance.

All this is taking place in a ruined structure of indeterminate use — weeds grow from the cracked and broken paving. This ravaged folly is symbolic of the 'old dispensation' before the arrival of Christ. The protagonists here assembled are witnesses at the beginning of a new world.

In the distance, glimpsed through the arch in the very centre of the composition, we can just see a fantastical 'ideal' city — all Late Gothic spires and crockets. This perhaps, is the new Jerusalem, now attainable since the birth of the Messiah — a parallel universe ushered in by squadrons of angels and finely accoutred kings.

Gossaert visited Italy in 1508, returning to the Netherlands the following year. It is not known if the *Adoration of the Kings* was completed before or after this journey but it betrays minimal overt influence from the south (unlike his later output) except perhaps a consummate understanding of perspective. Rather Gossaert seems to be following in the footsteps of Hugo van der Goes and other Netherlandish painters of the late fifteenth century. But the artist signals in other ways that he is aware of a wider artistic milieu – the dog in the right foreground is a straight quote from a Dürer engraving of about 1500.

The staggering richness of this picture and the clarity with which each minute constituent is represented does not detract from the overall impact of the composition but this is a picture which can entertain and inform the viewer for a prolonged period — a scan across the canvas will always reveal a new detail, a new marvel of flawless artistry.

Contemporary Works

c1505	Leonardo da Vinci: *Mona Lisa*; Paris
1510	Vittore Carpaccio: *Presentation of Christ in the Temple*; Venice
1513	Raphael: *Galatea*; Rome

Jan Gossaert also known as Mabuse

c1478	Born probably in Maubeuge in the southern Netherlandish province of Hainault, now in France.
1503	Becomes a master of the Guild of St Luke in Antwerp.
1507	It seems that Gossaert is part of the retinue of Philip of Burgundy, the illegitimate son of Philip the Good, Duke of Burgundy.
1508	Travels to Rome (via Verona and Florence) with Philip of Burgundy on a diplomatic mission to Pope Julius II.
1509	When the embassy returns to the Netherlands, Gossaert remains in Rome but returns a few months later.
1515	Philip of Burgundy commissions Gossaert together with Jacopo de' Barbari to undertake decorations for his castle on Walcheren Island.
1517	Philip of Burgundy becomes Bishop of Utrecht and Gossaert is engaged to produce mythological scenes for his residence.
1524	After the death of Philip of Burgundy Gossaert moves to Middelburg in Zeeland where he probably opens a workshop.
1532	Dies, probably in Antwerp

Titian

National Gallery

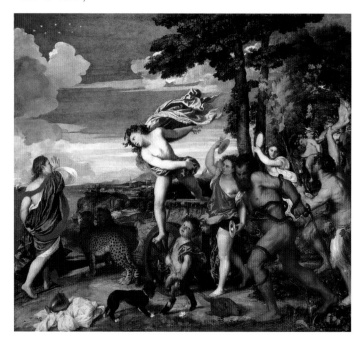

Glorious colour — this sums up the first impact of the picture. And it encapsulates the difference between the art of Venice and that of Florence. This picture could only have been made in one city in Renaissance Europe — Venice, and by one artist, the greatest of all Venetian painters, Titian.

One pigment in particular is used lavishly — the ultra-expensive ultramarine which Titian used in the coruscating sky and in Ariadne's drapery. This was an important commission and Titian's patron Alfonso d'Este, Duke of Ferrara, must have sanctioned the profligate use of such a precious substance in order to secure the best possible results. The painting was destined to hang in Alfonso's *studiolo* — a study where paintings, books and *objets d'art* were assembled for their owner's use and contemplation, where music could be played and poetry read in the company of scholars. One work, by Giovanni Bellini, had already been purchased for this room and other paintings had been commissioned from Fra Bartolommeo and Raphael, but they both died leaving only drawings. So Titian, who was already working on one picture, was asked to fill the gaps with another two — all illustrating bacchanalian subjects — and it seems that Titian may well have used Raphael's drawings as the basis for some parts of this picture.

Ariadne, the daughter of Minos, King of Crete, had assisted Theseus in his successful quest to kill the Minotaur deep within the labyrinth. She accompanied him when he left Crete but he showed his gratitude by abandoning her on the island of Naxos. There she was discovered by the god Bacchus (Dionysus). He was the focus of an earthy cult whose followers used wine to aid their entry into a trancelike state during which they would tear animals apart and eat their still warm flesh, believing that in so doing they were ingesting the god, thereby guaranteeing their eternal existence. Enraptured by Ariadne's beauty, Bacchus married her, gave her a seven-starred crown and ensure her immortality by converting the crown into a constellation after her death.

Ariadne is seen on the extreme left, her constellation already suspended in the azure sky above her, distracted from her distraught reverie at the swift exit of her treacherous lover (in the ship seen on the horizon) by the clamorous arrival of her next devotee, Bacchus. Titian has captured him in mid-air as he leaps from his leopard-drawn chariot, his sumptuous, silken cloak billowing behind him creating the most beautiful counterpoint with the perfect sky. The god is accompanied by his drunken, entranced entourage. One of his female retinue (a Maenad) is about to clash her cymbal; next to her a naked satyr-man is wreathed with snakes — symbolic of rebirth after death because snakes shed their skin. Behind him a similar satyr-like creature waves the dismembered leg of one of the group's bestial victims.

There had been no tradition of representing these bacchanalian subjects in paint before Titian but his evocation of a pre-classical Arcadia peopled by gods and mythical beings is compelling and magnificently painted.

Contemporary Works	
1521	Jan Gossaert: *Descent from the Cross*; St Petersburg
1523	Hans Holbein the Younger: *Erasmus of Rotterdam*; Paris
c1526	Jacopo Pontormo: *Deposition*; Florence

Titian	
1485-90	The date of Titian's birth in Pieve di Cadore is much disputed by scholars. Arrives in Venice as a child.
1508	According to Vasari, Titian works with Giorgione on exterior frescoes for the headquarters of the German merchants in Venice.
1516	Stays in Ferrara at the ducal castle for a month as the guest of the Duke of Ferrara. Meets Fra Bartolommeo.
1518	The huge, seven-metre tall *Assumption of the Virgin* is installed in the church of S Maria Gloriosa dei Frari in Venice.
1519	Titian is in Mantua.
1526	Completes another altarpiece for the Frari church in Venice.
1530	First meeting with the Holy Roman Emperor, Charles V. Titian's wife dies.
1533	Titian is created Count Palatine of the Golden Spur by Charles V.
1543	Titian is in Bologna where he paints a portrait of Pope Paul III.
1546	Visits Rome and meets Michelangelo. Paints *Pope Paul III with his Grandsons*.
1547	Charles V summons Titian to join him in Augsburg. Paints the equestrian portrait of *Charles V at the Battle of Mühlberg*. Charles' sister Queen Mary of Hungary, regent of the Netherlands, commissions large decorative paintings for her château in the Low Countries.
1548	Executes portraits of Ferdinand I, King of Bohemia and Hungary at Innsbruck.
1550	Travels again to Augsburg where he is commissioned by the future Philip II of Spain to paint a series of religious and erotic, classical subjects (*poesie*) to be sent at intervals from Venice to Spain.
1560's	His famous 'late' style is characterised by very loose handling of paint outlining forms which are dissolved by light.
1573	Commences his last masterpiece, the *Pietà*.
1576	Dies in Venice.

Correggio

National Gallery

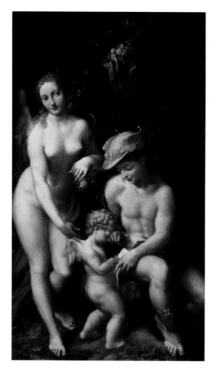

This painting was probably commissioned by Federigo II Gonzaga, Marquis of Mantua. He is known to have commissioned similar mythological scenes from Correggio, in particular an erotic series of the Loves of Jupiter, and although The *School of Love* is not recorded as part of the Gonzaga collection until 1627, over a century after its probable completion, it seems reasonable to assume that this collection was its original home.

Correggio here enables us to share in a private family moment. However this is no ordinary family; we are in the presence of gods but it seems even gods need to attend to family matters. Venus is standing naked, some pink drapery having just parted company from her heavenly form. She looks out at the viewer engaging us with a smile, gesturing to her son Cupid whose father Mercury, resplendent in gold helmet and matching grieves is teaching the winged infant to read.

Correggio, born Antonio Allegri, takes his name from his birthplace which is situated not far from Parma to the west and Mantua to the north. Very little is known about his short life but it seems certain that the many works by Mantegna in Mantua were the inspiration for his early style. Indeed, some scholars believe that Correggio may have had a hand in completing a number of Mantegna's later frescoes. Whether this is the case or not, and there is no doubt that Mantegna's influence is discernable in Correggio's large-scale fresco decorations, it is difficult to detect much of Mantegna in *The School of Love* which is nearer to the styles of Leonardo and Giorgione.

From about 1518 Correggio worked mainly in Parma which at the time was part of the Duchy of Milan. There is therefore a strong possibility that Correggio may have visited Milan and seen the work of Leonardo. The faint, enigmatic smile on the face of Venus is surely a quote from the great man and the soft modelling of the body contours of the divine threesome is derived from Leonardesque *sfumato*.

But Correggio is more than a mere follower. His synthesis of the art of Venice, Mantegna and Leonardo gives birth to the distinctive style which we can see here. The composition is complex, the execution masterful and there is a lightness of touch which is very distinctive. Indeed it is this delicacy which two centuries later inspired French Rococo painters such as Boucher and Fragonard who were able to study a number of works by Correggio in the royal collection.

Contemporary Works

1523	Titian: *Man with a Glove*; Paris
1526	Albrecht Dürer: *The Four Apostles*; Munich
1527	Hans Holbein the Younger: *Sir Thomas More*; New York

Correggio

? 1489	Born Antonio Allegri in Correggio a town about thirty miles from Parma.
1514	Receives a commission to paint organ shutters at an abbey near Mantua.
1515	Completes an altarpiece (*The Virgin of St. Francis*) for the church of S Francesco in Correggio.
1518-19	Most scholars postulate a journey to Rome at this time.
1522	Correggio completes frescoes in the dome of the church of S Giovanni Evangelista in Parma. Wins the commission to decorate the dome of Parma Cathedral.
1530	Completes the frescoes for the Cathedral dome.
1534	Dies in Correggio.

Hans Holbein the Younger

The Ambassadors (Jean de Dinteville and Georges de Selve) 1533

National Gallery

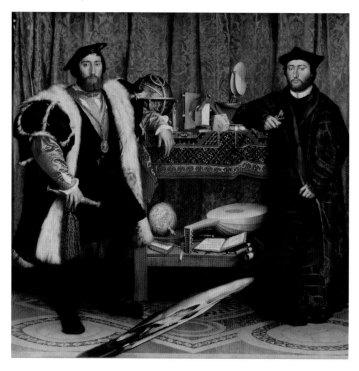

This large picture, painted on oak, depicts two life-size figures. Standing to the left is Jean de Dinteville, French ambassador to England; on the right is his friend Georges de Selve, Bishop of Lavaur who acted at various times as ambassador to a variety of European states. Holbein was probably commissioned to produce this wonderful piece to commemorate de Selve's visit to London in 1533, the date which also accompanies the artist's signature on the lower left.

Dinteville's right hand holds the sheath of his dagger which is inscribed with his age, 29, whilst the bishop rests his elbow on a book which reveals his age to be 25 by dint of a further inscription. From a twenty-first-century standpoint these two men have achieved considerable status at a surprisingly young age but one of the 'messages' implicit within the iconography of this composition is that life is short (as it so often was in the sixteenth century), that mortality could strike at any moment and that we should look to the church for hope of eternal life.

The mass of objects arrayed between the two friends point to the wide range of their interests. A celestial globe, other astronomical instruments, and a portable sundial are arranged on a Turkish carpet on the top shelf of the piece of furniture upon which they both lean. On the bottom shelf, there is a terrestrial globe, a lute with a broken string (a symbol of fragility), some flutes and two books. One of these is a treatise on Arithmetic and the other is a hymnal lying open and showing a composition by Martin Luther. Just visible at the extreme top left is a crucifix. Holbein is able to exhibit his unsurpassed skill in the flawless depiction of all these objects as well as the different textures of the sumptuous green wall-hanging in the background and the furs and silks clothing the two ambassadors. But, not satisfied with such tests of his powers, Holbein has created a very curious object for us to wonder at in the foreground. At first sight this seems to be some form of very large baguette which might have accidentally fallen to the ground. However, it soon becomes apparent that this is not a product of a French bakery but some form of painterly exposition. In fact it is a bizarrely elongated skull which when viewed from a point very close to the right hand edge of the picture (near de Selve's elbow) reveals itself in its correct proportions.

The presence of the skull is in the tradition of the *Vanitas* still life, much in favour at this time. Objects, such as hourglasses and butterflies, were selected to remind the viewer of the transience of life. But perhaps the distortion of the skull also serves to show the viewer that the reality of the picture is no more than an illusion and that the meanings inherent in it are just as important as the glossy depiction of the corporeal world.

Contemporary Works

1530	Lucas Cranach the Elder: *The Judgement of Paris*; Karlsruhe
c1532	Correggio: *Ganymede*; Vienna
c1535	Parmigianino: *Madonna with the Long Neck*; Florence

Hans Holbein the Younger

1497-8	Born in Augsburg. Date of birth uncertain. Holbein comes from a family of artists, his father and uncle were also accomplished painters.
1517	Holbein is working in Lucerne with his father and possibly visits Italy.
1519	He becomes a master in the Basel guild of painters.
1521	He is commissioned to paint murals on the theme of Justice for the Council Chamber at Basel.
1523	Paints several portraits of Erasmus, one now in the National Gallery, London.
1524	Visits France.
1526	Holbein leaves Basel and travels via Antwerp to London armed with a letter of introduction from Erasmus to Sir Thomas More.
1527	Paints a portrait of Sir Thomas More and other friends of Erasmus.
1528	Returns to Basel.
1530	Completes the murals in the Council Chamber at Basel.
1532	Returns to England where he finds that More was out of favour.
1533	Holbein gains the patronage of the Hanseatic merchants of the Steelyard and through them he probably meets Thomas Cromwell who may have been instrumental in obtaining for him the commission for *The Ambassadors*.
1536	First recorded as the king's painter. He is salaried but retains a private clientele.
1537	Paints a portrait of Jane Seymour.
1538	Commissioned to paint prospective brides for the king, including Christina of Denmark. Makes a brief visit to Basel while travelling for these commissions.
1543	Dies in London.

Hans Holbein the Younger

Christina of Denmark, Duchess of Milan   1538

National Gallery

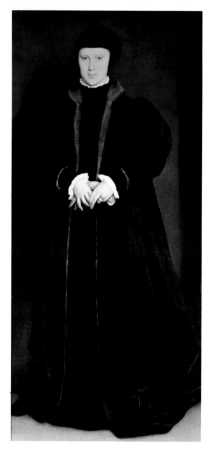

This is a remarkable painting for many reasons. It displays the usual array of Holbein's prodigious talents but it is also a fascinating historical document.

Christina was the daughter of King Christian of Denmark and at sixteen years of age she was already the widowed wife of the Duke of Milan. After his death she had lived in Brussels at the court of her aunt Mary of Hungary who was regent of the Netherlands, ruling this corner of the sprawling Habsburg possessions on behalf of her brother, the Holy Roman Emperor, Charles V. Across the North Sea, Henry VIII of England had just lost his third wife Jane Seymour after the birth of a son. Henry now eyed Christina as a candidate for his fourth queen. Holbein was therefore dispatched to Brussels in March 1538 and he was given a three-hour sitting in which to capture the spirit of the intended bride in one or more drawings. He then produced this full length portrait on his return to London.

How could Henry have turned her down? Looking at this portrait, she appears to have been just the sort of demure and submissive young woman Henry was looking for. Indeed it seems that Henry liked what he saw, but negotiations appear to have foundered, perhaps on the terms of the prospective financial settlement. Nevertheless, Henry kept the painting.

The eyes of the young duchess gaze out of the picture and engage the viewer head on. She stands against an unadorned background painted in the same shade of dark blue-green that Holbein used for *A Lady with a Squirrel and a Starling* also owned by the National Gallery and displayed nearby. It seems that Christina was proud of her slim feminine hands and the simplicity of her black widow's clothes concentrates our attention on her hands and on her face. But it is this very simplicity together with Holbein's unsurpassed skills as a portraitist which makes looking at this picture such a moving experience.

Contemporary Works

| 1534 | Corneille de Lyon: *Portrait of Pierre Aymeric*, Paris |
| 1538 | Titian: *Portrait of François I, King of France*, Paris |

Hans Holbein the Younger

See page 105

Bronzino

National Gallery

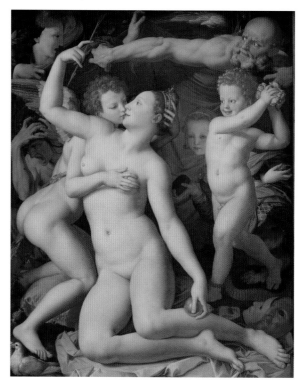

The picture was probably painted for Duke Cosimo de' Medici of Florence as a gift for the King of France, François I — it would certainly have been welcome as François was noted for his pursuit of women. The king and his courtiers would have been able to appreciate the eroticism of the piece safe in the knowledge that their attention could be explained by their presumed interest in its complex meaning.

Bronzino certainly packs the available space. His characters are set against an exquisitely painted satin backcloth for which the artist has used the extravagantly expensive ultramarine pigment. The flesh tones arrayed in front of this sumptuous cloth are somewhat cold as if Bronzino is deliberately invoking links with the marble of antique statuary. Every centimetre is given a lustrous finish; the effect is immensely pleasing as the eye passes over each area of fine detail discovering new delights as it goes. The piece is overtly erotic and Bronzino does not hold back. Even to the twenty-first-century viewer, a certain *frisson* accompanies the realisation that Cupid has parted two fingers in the hand which encompasses the breast of Venus so as to gently excite her nipple between them.

But what does it all mean? There is no definitive answer. The identity of the main protagonists is relatively clear but there is much learned debate concerning the identity of some of the other players. Venus, holding a golden apple, a reference to the Judgement of Paris, is incestuously embraced by her son Cupid (Eros, in his Greek form) who kneels on a large cushion covered in a beautiful pink silk. In the arcane world of allegory, this cushion is to be construed as a symbol of Lust. So, we are on safe ground to conclude that the picture is concerned with love, lust and pleasure, and the often malign consequences of this combination.

The naked child to the right of Venus is probably a personification of Foolish Pleasure who is about to release a handful of rose petals in the direction of Venus and Cupid. Behind him is a chilling depiction of Deceit whose pretty face, one realises with horror, is attached to a monstrous scaled body. In one hand she holds a sweet honeycomb but in the other is her scorpion's sting. The message is not too difficult — lustful activity may be pleasurable in the short term but may also result in less pleasing consequences. However, confusingly, there is another view, that the pretty face does not belong to Deceit but is Pleasure with the naked child as Folly.

In looking at the remaining peripheral figures, interpretations of meaning become even more uncertain. Directly above Pleasure, Father Time makes an appearance with his hourglass balanced rather incongruously on his right shoulder. He stretches an unnaturally long arm across most of the composition determinedly resisting the efforts of a mysterious personage inhabiting the upper left of the composition who seems to be trying to pull the backcloth over the whole scene. This mask-like apparition is probably Oblivion, for part of the head, and therefore those parts of the brain dealing with memory, are missing. Beneath Oblivion a screaming figure clutches its head. The presence of this figure is obscure; it may represent Jealousy or Despair. However, another theory proposes the figure as the personification of Syphilis which had recently arrived in Europe and was therefore a very powerful contemporary example of the down side of lust. If this interpretation is accepted then the tussle between Time and Oblivion might be seen as a reference to the fact that the most terrible symptoms of syphilis develop over considerable time.

This wonderful painting, so full of mystery and so finely wrought is a fitting testament to one of the most gifted artists of the Late Renaissance.

Contemporary Works	
1540	Hans Holbein the Younger: *Henry VIII*; Rome
1543	Lorenzo Lotto: *Husband and Wife*; St Petersburg
1546	Titian: Pope *Paul III and his Grandsons*; Naples

Bronzino	
1503	Born in Monticelli near Florence.
1520s	Works with the Florentine Mannerist Jacopo Pontormo on a number of commissions in and around Florence.
1530	Works in Pesaro.
1532	Returns to Florence where he paints a number of altarpieces.
1537	Bronzino becomes a member of the Compagnia di S Luca, the artists guild.
1539	Becomes court painter to Cosimo I, Duke of Florence, a post which he kept until his death. As well as executing portraits and frescos he also designs tapestries and writes poetry.
1545	Paints the *Lamentation*, a key Mannerist work.
1572	Dies in Florence.

Jacopo Tintoretto

St George and the Dragon

Perhaps 1560-80

National Gallery

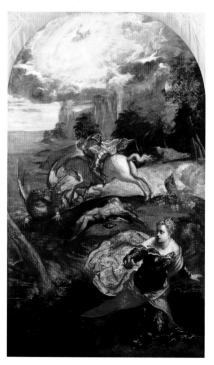

Very little detail has come down to us concerning Tintoretto's life. He may have spent some time in Titian's workshop, but quickly left — it is possible that he was expelled. He was reportedly unpopular with his fellow artists, being ruthless in the tactics he employed to obtain commissions.

It seems that he very rarely left Venice and all his major works are there. Much of his output is in the form of large-scale paintings commissioned as part of decorative schemes for churches, palaces and public institutions in the city. This picture is unusual in its comparatively small size — it was probably commissioned as an altarpiece for a private home. It is also a good example of how Tintoretto moulded his style to suit the commission or client. In contrast to the expansive and open technique employed in much of his work which allowed him to paint with great rapidity (for which he was censured by some contemporary commentators), here he has used a more meticulous approach leading to a much higher finish.

St George was a legendary entity supposedly born in Cappadocia (part of modern Turkey). Alternatively, his existence was a reality and he is not to be confused with the Cappadocian George — a cleric who espoused the Arian heresy. The choice is yours but there is no doubt that his cult grew in the Byzantine lands of the eastern Mediterranean in the sixth century.

Having become an officer in the Roman army, he was martyred in

Palestine during the persecutions of Christians during the reign of the Emperor Diocletian in the opening years of the fourth century. The story of his defeat of the dragon seems to have had its origins in the Greek myth of Perseus who rescues Andromeda from a sea monster and it is interesting that in this picture Tintoretto has placed the dragon directly, and somewhat precariously, on the sea shore. Be this as it may, for Christians, George's combat with the dragon is a simple story of good versus evil and when his cult spread to western Europe as a result of the crusades (his exploits appearing in the very popular *Golden Legend*) he became the quintessential embodiment of the Christian knight, adopted as the patron saint of Portugal and many European cities as well as England.

Here we see St George astride his white charger at the point of engagement with the awful monster, his whole weight concentrated behind the thrust of his lance. The fleeing princess runs toward us, naturally trying to put as much distance between herself and the dragon as possible, perhaps uncertain as to the eventual outcome of the encounter. Her curiously billowing cloak catches the viewer's eye and links with George's attire, both garments painted over a white ground in order to increase their luminosity.

Between them Tintoretto has introduced a novel, and somewhat grizzly, element into the traditional cast of characters — lying on the ground in a pose which echoes the crucified Christ we can see the cadaver of the dragon's last victim. Directly above St George, enclosed in a mandorla of glorious light which obscures much of the cloudy sky, God the Father looks down on the scene and blesses the actions of the intrepid warrior. A fairytale fortified town overlooks the scene, its walls seemingly useless in the face of the dragon's fearsome menace. Soon the town and its princess will be free of its threat thanks to the chivalrous saint's courage.

Contemporary Works	
1565	Pieter Bruegel the Elder: *The Return of the Hunters*; Vienna
1573	Paolo Veronese: *Christ in the House of Levi*; Venice
1577	El Greco: *The Assumption of the Virgin*; Chicago

Jacopo Tintoretto	
1519	Born in Venice, the son of a cloth-dyer, hence his nickname.
1539	After working for a very short time in Titian's workshop, Tintoretto is by this date working as an independent master.
1548	Produces *St Mark Rescuing the Slave* for the Scuola Grande di S Marco. This painting finally brings recognition in Venice for Tintoretto.
1551	Recorded as a member of the Accademia Pellegrina, a literary academy.
1564-88	Works on decorations for the meeting house of the Scuola Grande di S Rocco, his masterwork.
1565	Becomes a member of the confraternity of the Scuola Grande di S Rocco.
1577	After two fires, in 1574 and 1577, damage the Doge's Palace, Tintoretto is commissioned to contribute to the redecorations.
1580	Travels to Mantua regarding a commission for the Gonzaga family. This is his only recorded journey outside Venice.
1592	Again works on important commissions for the Doge's Palace.
1594	Dies in Venice.

El Greco

National Gallery

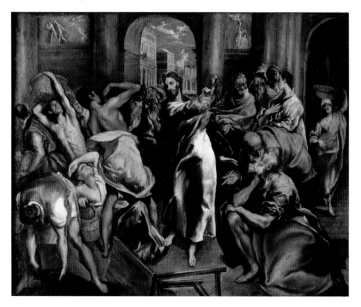

Born in Crete, then a Venetian possession, and trained in the Byzantine tradition of his native land, the natural destination for Domenikos Theotokopoulos when he decided to leave was Venice. Once there, it seems that this Cretan painter of icons may well have studied under the great Titian — quite a clash of cultures. The result was an intensely individualistic style which makes his paintings instantly recognisable — a sort of supercharged Mannerism overlaid with a personal spiritual passion.

In 1570 he left Venice for Rome where he seems to have courted controversy by joining in the debate about Michelangelo's *Last Judgement* in a particularly ham-fisted way. Some years later he reportedly said that Michelangelo 'was a good man but he did not know how to paint'. Opinions such as these were perhaps not best suited to win him many popularity contests in the Eternal City and it is possible that a certain antipathy towards him may have contributed to his decision to move on again, this time to Spain.

His first stop was Madrid, which he quickly left in favour of Toledo, the recently vacated capital, where he lived for the rest of his life. He was commissioned to produce two works for Philip II but he was left in no doubt that the second picture had not pleased the king. He nevertheless made a good living painting for religious and other patrons in Toledo where he apparently lived in some style, a proud and passionate presence, never afraid to seek legal redress should it become necessary. But it is not difficult to see how Philip, used to a more ordered and serene art, should have found El Greco's style to be so difficult to appreciate.

Here, Christ, dominating the centre of the composition, ploughs through the throng, lashing out, as we are told in St John's Gospel with his 'scourge of cords', throwing out of the temple 'the sheep and the oxen; and he poured out the changers money, and overthrew their tables'. To Christ's right, where he directs his fury, the traders recoil in terror, those near to him set in angular poses, preparing to protect themselves against the impact of his knotted whip. This clamorous confrontation is heightened by El Greco's use of colour. Christ's etiolated body is clothed in a striking crimson which immediately claims our attention. But his blue cloak chimes with other patches of blue encouraging our eye to wander over the painting restlessly, picking up areas of gold, yellow and green (set against the predominantly grey architecture) which seem to compound the compositional and narrative tension.

Above the crowded interior, on either side of the entrance to the temple, El Greco has depicted two Old Testament incidents as if in stone relief. The expulsion of Adam and Eve from the Garden of Eden on the left has been linked by theologians to this New Testament expulsion. To the right, Abraham can be seen at the very moment when he is about to sacrifice his son Isaac, a split second before Isaac is reprieved by divine intervention. Here too, a theological link is made between the intended sacrifice of Isaac, Christ's passion, and the mass of humanity, represented by the crowds in the temple, who will be saved by the sacrifice of the Messiah.

Contemporary Works

| 1595 | Caravaggio: *The Lute Player*, St Petersburg |
| 1602 | Annibale Carracci: *'Domine, Quo Vadis'*, London, National Gallery |

El Greco

1541	Born near Herakleion (then called Candia) in Crete, the son of a tax collector.
1563	It seems he has become a master painter by this date.
1568	He is recorded as being in Venice by this date. He visits Titian's studio (possibly studying under his guidance).
1570	Travels to Rome, visiting Parma, Verona and Florence on the way.
1572	Becomes a member of the Academy of St Luke in Rome. Opens a workshop.
1577	Travels to Madrid, probably in search of royal commissions for the decoration of the Escorial. Moves on to Toledo.
1581	Philip II commissions *The Martyrdom of St Maurice and the Theban Legion*.
1584	The *Martydom of St Maurice* is rejected by the king.
1588	Completes his masterpiece, the *Burial of Count Orgaz*.
1614	Dies in Toledo.

Caravaggio

National Gallery

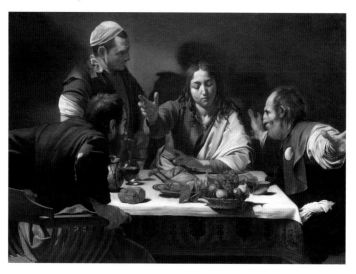

Caravaggio has here depicted the first appearance of Christ after his Resurrection. The story is told in St Luke's Gospel that on the same day Christ's tomb was found to be empty, two disciples were walking to Emmaus — about seven miles from Jerusalem — when they were joined by a stranger. Asking why they were in such low spirits they explained what had happened in the last few days. When they reached Emmaus the two disciples invited the stranger to eat with them. When the food was served it was their new friend who, in a parallel with the Last Supper 'took bread, blessed it and brake, and gave to them'. Then, in the words of Luke 'their eyes were opened and they knew him and he vanished out of their sight'.

Here we have that very moment of recognition with Christ blessing the bread and the two disciples reacting with incredulous surprise — the elbow of one juts towards the viewer as he strains to lift himself from his chair, the hand of the other extends through the picture plain encouraging us to believe that we too are participants in the miracle taking place before us — the first ever Mass.

The scene has been frozen as though Caravaggio might have used some decidedly twentieth-century technology such as a photographic flash. His famously theatrical lighting effects are used to instil his already dramatic compositions with even more punch. (These skills in lighting a scene may well have been learned from Leonardo and his Milanese followers for Caravaggio had had plenty of opportunity to study these artists during his early days in and around Milan). Everywhere he uses light to enhance the solidity and veracity of the people and objects in the scene before us.

There is no better example of still life than the food and tableware laid out on the white cloth. If we look at the glass carafe we notice that the light, whilst passing through the water within the carafe is focused at its base and then onto the tablecloth. This one passage is astonishing and yet every inch of the picture betrays the same 'high intensity' realisation of objects bathed in searching light; pinpoints of light stand out on the ripe white grapes, the blemishes on the skins of the apples are reproduced with just as much care as every other bravura passage. And Caravaggio uses the basket of fruit as another device to break the bounds between viewer and picture; the basket sits uneasily on the edge of the table and we ache to reach forward and place it more soundly on the table surface.

But Caravaggio's realism went further than his attention to detail. This new realism was shocking to many observers. He pulled no punches when it came to the representation of violence (possibly because he was so well acquainted with its consequences) and he painted the outcast and the peasant just as they were, not the sanitised versions which many of his ecclesiastical clients would have preferred. Caravaggio shows us the real thing; in this painting the sleeve of one disciple is torn and both have a generally dishevelled look. The innkeeper is equally proletarian. And, much more worrying, Christ has also been given the features of a real person rather than the usual Greco-roman facial stereotype, deriving from antique sculpture, which had been the norm for all Italian Renaissance painters. All this did not go down well with the artist's detractors who felt that these images demeaned the Christian story. But the fiery, violent and unpredictable Caravaggio always had just enough supportive patrons whose appreciation of his enormous talents outweighed their worries about some aspects of his art and his character.

Contemporary Works

1600	Guido Reni: *Assumption of the Virgin*; Pieve di Cento
c1600	El Greco: *Cardinal Fernando Niño de Guevara*; New York
1601	Annibale Carracci: *Triumph of Bacchus and Ariadne*; Rome

Caravaggio

1571	Born Michelangelo Merisi at Caravaggio, a small town close to Milan.
1577	Fermo Merisi, Michelangelo's father, dies of plague.
1584	Apprenticed to the painter Simone Peterzano in Milan.
1592	Probably resident and working in Rome.
c1596-7	Joins the household of Cardinal del Monte.
1599	Caravaggio receives his first public commission to paint canvases for the Contarelli Chapel in Rome. One is rejected but the *Calling of St Matthew* and the *Martyrdom of St Matthew* are received well.
1603	Caravaggio is imprisoned and later placed under house arrest as a result of a libel action brought by a rival artist.
1606	A disputed bet on a game of tennis leads to a brawl during which Caravaggio stabs and kills another man. He is forced to leave Rome and eventually stays in Naples for some time.
1607	Travels to Malta where he is welcomed, made a Knight of the Order of St John and receives several commissions.
1608	After assaulting a senior member of the Order, Caravaggio is again imprisoned but escapes and flees to Sicily, pursued by agents of the Knights, dashing off paintings as he travels.
1609	Returns to Naples in the autumn where, in a fight outside a tavern, he is seriously wounded, probably by agents of the Knights of St John.
1610	Talk of a pardon from Rome induces him to sail north from Naples. At Porto Ercole after yet another arrest, he dies of fever in a tavern.

Peter Paul Rubens

Autumn Landscape with a view of Het Steen in the Early Morning   1636

National Gallery

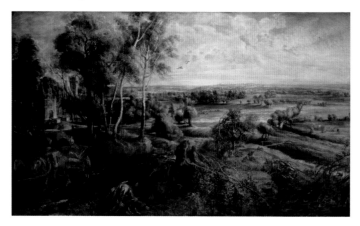

Much of Rubens' output — the biblical epics or the set piece classical allegories — are perhaps not to everyone's taste. But his landscapes are another matter. In the complete landscape canon, they are amongst the most beautiful. And *Autumn Landscape with a View of Het Steen* is one of his finest.

The quality of light and the type of plants in flower lead us to the conclusion that we are witnessing a beautiful early morning in autumn. It is one of those mornings when you feel glad to be alive. And this is the reason that Rubens bought the estate of Het Steen in 1635. In an amazingly full life he had travelled widely, amassed a fortune and taken on the role of diplomat. Now he wanted to gradually withdraw (with mixed success) from the cares of working to commission and travelling on diplomatic missions, and devote himself to his estate, to life with his second, very young wife Hélène Fourment, and to painting for his own pleasure. And often this meant painting landscapes.

The rising sun is making its appearance to the right of the picture and we are therefore looking due north across flat Flemish pasture and meadows with a town (probably Malines) in the distance. Yellow highlights on the foliage and trunks of the trees beautifully evoke the raking light of early morning. The manor house of Steen commands the left of the picture set amidst mature trees. In front of the house a prosperous family — presumably the Rubens family — are taking the morning air. In the foreground, the rhythm of rural life is under way; a cart leaves for market and a huntsman equipped with a fowling piece and accompanied by his retriever keeps low behind the cover of the brambles — man and dog forming a perfect vignette of expectant concentration; the object of their concerted attention, the covey of partridge feeding near the bridge over the stream, are oblivious to the impending danger. Nearby to the right goldfinches perch in a small tree.

In this picture, as in its companion, *Landscape with a Rainbow*, also in London, in the Wallace Collection, we gaze upon a perfect moment of bucolic grace where nature and man are bound together in a harmonious Eden.

Contemporary Works

1635	Diego Velázquez: *The Surrender of Breda*; Madrid
1636	Rembrandt: *The Blinding of Samson*; Frankfurt
	Nicolas Poussin: *The Triumph of Pan*; London, National Gallery
1637	Anthony van Dyck: *Prince Rupert, Count Palatine*; London, National Gallery.

Peter Paul Rubens

1577	Born in Siegen, Westphalia where his father is exiled from Antwerp having had an injudicious affair with the wife of William of Orange.
1578	The family moves to Cologne.
1588	After the death of Rubens' father, his mother returns with her family to Antwerp.
1598	Rubens becomes a master in the Antwerp Guild of St Luke.
1600	Travels to Italy where he joins the court of Vincenzo I Gonzaga, Duke of Mantua. Copies many Renaissance works in the duke's collection.
1602	Rubens is in Rome where he is commissioned to produce three paintings for the church of Santa Croce in Gerusalemme. Studies the work of Michelangelo and Raphael.
1603	The Duke of Mantua dispatches Rubens to Spain to deliver presents to Philip III. While there he paints an equestrian portrait for the king's minister the Duque de Lerma.
1604	Returns to Mantua.
1605-6	Rubens is in Genoa where he works on various commissions.
1606-8	Working in Rome again where he stays for a time with his brother. Completes a number of important commissions.
1608	Hearing of his mother's death, Rubens returns to Antwerp. Decides to remain in his home city where he soon receives the patronage of a circle of bourgeois collectors.
1609	Appointed court painter to Archdukes Albert and Isabella. Their connections with other European courts help to elevate and spread Rubens' already high reputation and he starts to receive commissions from all over Europe. Marries Isabella Brant.
1614	Completes the *Descent from the Cross* for Antwerp Cathedral.
1625	Rubens visits Paris on a diplomatic mission for Archduchess Isabella. Meets the Duke of Buckingham who commissions two portraits.
1626	His first wife Isabella dies.
1628	In his role as a diplomat Rubens visits Madrid in pursuit of a peace between Spain and England. While there he paints *Philip IV on Horseback*.
1629	He is in London pursuing his peace mission. Charles I commissions him to paint the ceiling of the Banqueting House. Philip IV appoints him as secretary of the Spanish privy council.
1630	Rubens receives a knighthood from Charles I. Marries the sixteen-year-old Hélène Fourment.
1631	Knighted by Philip IV.
1635	Rubens acquires the estate of Steen near Malines.
1636	Philip IV commissions the first of over 100 scenes from Ovid destined for the king's hunting lodge.
1640	Dies in Antwerp.

Anthony van Dyck

Equestrian Portrait of Charles I   c1637

National Gallery

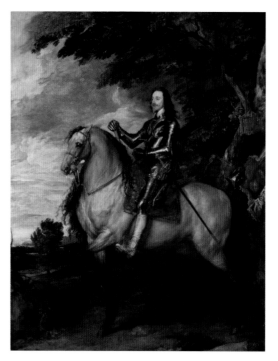

Charles I amassed a famously impressive collection of paintings in which Titian was particularly well represented. In Anthony van Dyck he found a soul mate who was equally devoted to the great Venetian having studied his work during a six-year stay in Italy in the 1620s. After van Dyck's return to his native Antwerp, where his services were very soon much in demand, Charles commissioned works from him and in 1632 he persuaded him to move to London. Van Dyck received a knighthood and embarked on a series of images of the king and the royal family of which this equestrian portrait is the most iconic.

By 1636 or 1637 when this picture was painted Charles was well on his way to his destiny as a royal martyr — or as a divisive and double dealing 'man of blood', depending on your point of view. He was nearing the end of an eleven-year period of personal rule, eschewing recourse to parliament which he saw as troublesome and impertinent. Only a few years later in 1642 he found himself at war with parliament — the most prosperous parts of his kingdom, including his capital, implacably opposed to his policies and his style of government. As the tragedy of civil war reached a climax, this singularly stupid monarch seemed to be incapable of grasping the fact that his power was now considerably proscribed — his persistent and ill-advised scheming sealed his fate and he was executed only twelve years after van Dyck's apotheosis of imperious monarchy.

This huge portrait reflects Charles's efforts to bolster his claims to absolute kingship. It is an icon proclaiming his divine right as king to exercise unbridled power. Its sheer size (over three and a half metres high) is designed to overawe the viewer — the sovereign's commanding presence sits astride his horse well above our eye line. The composition is a reiteration of the archetypal 'king as warrior' image but it also harks back to the equestrian portrait of the Emperor Charles V (now in Madrid) by that hero of both monarch and artist, Titian; and of course that reference could only strengthen, in the mind of the informed viewer, Charles' pretensions to emulate the absolute power of his namesake. Of course, the king's commander's baton and his armour would be in use only too soon — and through their use his pretensions to unqualified power would be dashed.

The mounted monarch is depicted in a autumnal landscape — a cloudy blue sky presides over a vista which disappears to a distant horizon. The king's head is set against dark clouds making sure that despite the size of the canvas this natural focal point draws the eye.

With this picture and many others depicting Charles, his family and the British aristocracy, van Dyck created a style which proved to be the model for the long tradition of portrait painting in the British Isles.

Contemporary Works

c1636	Peter Paul Rubens: *The Rainbow*; London, The Wallace Collection
1637	Nicolas Poussin: *Rape of the Sabine Women*; New York
1639	Claude Lorrain: *Seaport at Sunset*; Paris

Anthony van Dyck

1599	Born in Antwerp, the seventh child of a textile merchant.
1609	Becomes a pupil of the Dean of the Antwerp Guild of St Luke.
1617	His father becomes bankrupt.
1618	Registered as a master of the Guild of St Luke.
1618-16	He is working in Rubens' studio.
1620	Partly in order to avoid paying for his father's debts, van Dyck sets up his own independent studio in Antwerp, but later in the year he is in London.
1621	Van Dyck receives £100 from James I in recompense for 'special services'. In March he returns to Antwerp. In October he leaves for Genoa.
1622	He is in Rome. Then travels to Venice and Mantua, painting a number of portraits, some of travelling English aristocrats, as he went.
1623	Visits Turin, Florence and Bologna, then travels back to Rome where he paints more portraits. Meets Sir Kenelm Digby, a future English patron.
1624	He is in Palermo completing commissions from the Viceroy of Sicily.
1627	Returns to Antwerp where he paints religous subjects and portraits.
1630	Becomes painter to the court of Infanta Isabella in Brussels but remains resident in Antwerp.
1632	After spending the previous winter in The Hague, van Dyck travels to London receiving a knighthood from Charles I.
1634	In Antwerp attending to business and is elected Dean of the Guild of St Luke.
1635	Returns to England.
1637	Van Dyck is paid £1,200 by Charles I for 'certaine pictures'.
1639	Marries Mary Ruthven, a member of the queen's retinue.
1640	Visits Flanders; then travels to Paris in the hope of prestigious commissions for the Louvre.
1641	Dies in London eight days after his wife gives birth to their daughter Justiniana.

Diego Velázquez

The Toilet of Venus (*The Rokeby Venus*)   c1650

National Gallery

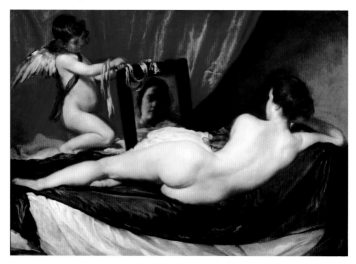

This is the most beguiling back in the history of western art — a masterpiece of sensuality emphasising the curve between a very slim waist and full hips. The flesh tones are perfectly offset against the black silk upon which she is reclining. All is realised with a very free style.

Venus gazes pensively at her reflection in a mirror supported by a very pudgy Cupid who one senses is only there to make up the numbers, as a token classical reference. Otherwise it would just be the two of us — Venus and her (male) admirer. The mirror is held at such an angle by the portly Cupid that the viewer, or should we say voyeur, can see the face of Venus staring back. Is there a hint of insouciance in her expression? Alas, it seems that the mirror may be made of inferior materials for the reflection is poorly defined, but as the viewer can see her face then she must be able to see the viewer so perhaps she is assessing the effect her body is having on her admirer.

Very probably completed during Velázquez's second stay in Rome — where he painted some of his most celebrated works — this is the first extant example of that extremely rare subject in Spanish art, the female nude. Influenced by the Venetian nudes of Titian and Giorgione, the painting is recorded in 1651 in the collection of the Marqués del Carpio y Heliche who was the son of the Spanish First Minister and later became the Viceroy of Naples. The status of the first owner is the key to the painting's existence for it is only someone of high rank who would have felt confident enough to face down the fierce disapproval of the Inquisition. Although the royal collection was replete with mythological nudes by Titian and others, it seems that the baleful influence of the Inquisition was responsible for the absence of any similar output by Spanish artists until Velázquez, and indeed continued to ensure that there were no further examples until Goya's *Naked Maja* well over a century later.

This most captivating of nudes is surely far more erotic than any number of full frontal rivals. Goya's *Naked Maja*, Manet's *Olympia* and Titian's *Venus of Urbino* will all have their champions but give me this muse every time.

Contemporary Works

1648	Adriaen van Ostade: *Winter View*, St Petersburg
	Claude Lorrain: *Seaport with the Embarkation of the Queen of Sheba*, London, National Gallery
1651	Nicolas Poussin: *The Finding of Moses*, London, National Gallery
	Salomon van Ruysdael: *Ferry Crossing the Environs of Arnhem*, St Petersburg

Diego Velázquez

1599	Born in Seville.
1610	Enters the studio of Francisco Pacheco.
1611	Signs an apprenticeship contract lasting for six years.
1617	Velázquez is licensed to work as an independent painter.
1618	He marries Pacheco's daughter Juana.
1623	Pacheco's good connections with the court result in a commission to paint a portrait of the king in Madrid. This is a great success and he immediately enters the service of Philip IV.
1628	Peter Paul Rubens arrives at the Spanish court representing Charles I of England on a diplomatic mission. He stays for many months and Velázquez is greatly influenced by him.
1629	The king gives him permission to visit Italy and provides him with letters of introduction. He visits Venice, Bologna and Rome.
1630	Velázquez is in Naples.
1631	Returns to Madrid.
1643	He is appointed Ayuda de Cámara.
1649	Velázquez visits Italy again in order to purchase works of art for the king and to contract painters to work on palace improvements. Visits Milan, Venice, Florence, Bologna and Parma and then stays in Rome.
1650	While in Rome he executes several influential works including the portrait of Innocent X which was greatly admired.
1651	Returns to Spain.
1656	Paints his masterpiece, *Las meninas*.
1658	Velázquez is granted the title Knight of Santiago.
1660	He is responsible for the organisation of the ceremonial meeting, on the Franco Spanish border, of Philip IV and Louis XIV during which the French king took the Infanta María Theresa as his bride. Velázquez becomes ill on his return to Madrid and dies.

Pieter de Hooch

National Gallery

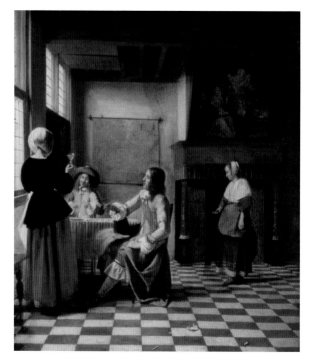

A woman stands with her back to us near a table raising a glass of wine. Two men, looking intently at her, are seated at the table which has been placed next to the window perhaps to make the most of the light which floods into the room from the large windows. Nearby, a maid is bringing some glowing coals into the room. De Hooch has used the raking golden light of evening to fill the room and make it a credible space. A combination of shadow and highlight effortlessly gives the objects and people in the room real volume and presence; the illusion of three-dimensional space is greatly enhanced by the way de Hooch has used the quintessentially Dutch chequered floor and the roof beams to show off his impressive mastery of perspective.

We know that de Hooch painted the architecture of the room first before starting on the figures. This is confirmed by infra-red photography but it is easy to see with the naked eye in some passages, in particular the pattern of the floor tiles can be seen through the fabric of the maid's skirt.

On the wall behind the two men hangs a map showing the seventeen provinces of the Netherlands. A painting has been placed above the fireplace but it is a little too large for its intended vantage point and so it seems that it has been wedged between the mantelpiece and the roof beams — slightly at an angle, the effect a little overbearing. The picture has been identified as the *Education of the Virgin* and its presence conveys a moralising lesson which contrasts with the leisured levity of the group gathered around the table. Perhaps the presence of shards from a broken pipe and a scrap of paper littering the floor is intended to reinforce this message.

In general de Hooch is not noted for heavy handed didactic symbolism but occasionally he employed the device (often used by others) of a picture within a picture to make a point. Of course, this was a favourite contrivance of the great Vermeer who almost certainly knew de Hooch during the years he lived in Vermeer's home town of Delft. Together they represented the apogee of the Delft School and after de Hooch left Delft in 1661 Vermeer refined de Hooch's twin stylistic canons — the use of naturalistic lighting effects together with a consummate command of perspective — to mould his own unsurpassed technique.

Contemporary Works

1656	Bartolomé Esteban Murillo: *St Ildefonsus receiving the Chasuble*; Madrid
c1657	Rembrandt: *Portrait of Titus, his son*; London, The Wallace Collection
c1660	Francisco de Zurbaran: *The Girlhood of the Virgin*; St Petersburg

Pieter de Hooch

1629	Born in Rotterdam, the son of a master bricklayer.
1652	After being apprenticed to Nicolaes Berchem de Hooch is by now working in Delft.
1653	He is noted as a painter and servant in the employment of a linen merchant Justus de la Grange.
1654	Marries Jannetje van der Burch in Rotterdam.
1655	Admitted to the Guild of St Luke in Delft.
1661	Settles in Amsterdam.
1684	At his death he is recorded as an inmate of the insane asylum.

Claude Lorrain

Landscape with Psyche outside the Palace of Cupid
(The Enchanted Castle) 1664

National Gallery

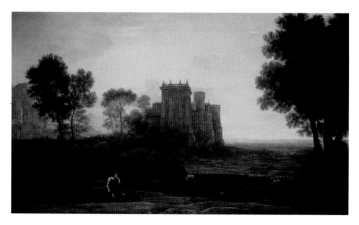

The story of Psyche is first told in *The Golden Ass*, by the philosopher and poet Apuleius who was born in North Africa in the second century AD. Psyche was a princess renowned for her beauty. As a result of the jealousy of his mother, Venus (Aphrodite), Psyche comes to the notice of the god Cupid who duly falls in love with the mortal princess. Cupid asks Zephyrus to transport Psyche to his palace and there he visits her at the dead of night, beguiling her with tenderness and charm but commanding her never to look on his face. Before light returns, Cupid leaves and thereafter he only visits Psyche at night making it impossible for her to discover who her lover is. This arrangement continues for some time but Psyche begins to fear that her suitor might be some sort of monster. Eventually her curiosity prevails and while her mysterious lover lies beside her sleeping she lights a lamp to find to her amazement that it is Cupid, his bow and arrows lying beside their bed. But at that moment a drop of hot oil from the lamp falls on Cupid and he wakes instantly. Reproaching Psyche for her lack of faith, he disappears and she is doomed to search the world for him. Eventually, Zeus takes pity on her and she is reunited with Cupid.

Claude has chosen to portray the moment when Psyche is abandoned by Cupid. She sits disconsolately on a rock outside his palace on a deserted shore. It is hard to think of another painting which is suffused with such delectable melancholy. The poignancy of Psyche's isolation is heightened by the extraordinary beauty of the landscape which is suffused with a sublime morning light. The rising sun strikes the castle's round tower. The rest of the castle is shrouded in shadow and appears to be totally deserted, adding to the feeling of loneliness. There is some activity out at sea and some deer graze nearby. Otherwise Psyche is alone, her solitude heightened by the gentle lapping of the sea on the shore.

This is a near perfect painting — an idealised landscape has been masterfully realised; but this is not all; the landscape forms a backdrop to a drama which has just reached a climax and Claude uses this to heighten our nostalgia for an unattainable Arcadian moment. We long to visit that place and to experience that very instant when the morning breeze begins to ruffle the sea and we long to gaze on that same mysterious castle.

Contemporary Works

1662	Johannes Vermeer: *View of Delft*; The Hague
1664	Frans Hals: *The Women Regents of the Old Men's Home in Haarlem*; Haarlem
	Jan Steen: *Celebrating the Birth*; London, The Wallace Collection

Claude Lorrain

1604-5	Born Claude Gellée in Chamagne, a small village near Nancy in the duchy of Lorraine. His date of birth remains a matter of debate despite his tomb in Rome being inscribed with the year 1600.
1617	He probably travels to Rome at about this time.
1618	Arrives in Naples on or after this date. He later studies painting under Agostino Tassi in Rome.
1625	Returns to Lorraine where he works on some frescoes for the Carmelite church in Nancy which are now destroyed.
1626-7	Returns to Rome, where he takes up permanent residence.
1633	Becomes a member of the Accademia di S Luca. His reputation grows.
1635 or 6	Prompted by the appearance of a number of forgeries, Claude begins his *Liber Veritatis* – a large book containing 195 drawings recording the great majority of his paintings before they left his studio.
1637	His fame results in a commission to paint Seaport (now in Alnwick Castle, Northumberland) for Pope Urban VIII.
1658	Claude becomes guardian of a young girl, Agnès who may have been his illegitimate daughter (he never married).
1662	Jean Gellée, a nephew, comes to Rome to live in the artist's household.
1679	Another nephew arrives to live with Claude.
1682	Dies in Rome.

Johannes Vermeer

A Young Woman standing at a Virginal   About 1670

National Gallery

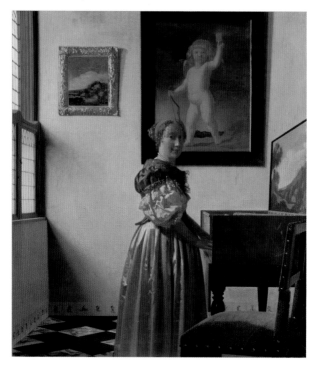

It is well known that Vermeer produced very few pictures. Out of a lifetime output of possibly fifty canvases (scholarly estimates vary between forty-three and sixty), perhaps only thirty-five survive. Today this scarcity enhances an inherent preciousness which is underpinned by Vermeer's extraordinary technique, but after his death the paucity of his output (much of which went to a single collector) contributed to two centuries of obscurity. Although it is not altogether true that he was totally forgotten, his posthumous reputation was certainly consigned to the shadows until 1866 when the French critic Théophile Thoré published a study which catapulted Vermeer towards stardom.

This picture is a superb example of the reasons for his fame. A young woman stands at the virginal, but it seems that her attention is elsewhere for she stares absentmindedly out of the picture towards the viewer. There is no doubt as to the reasons for her preoccupation — behind her a painting shows Cupid holding up a single card. His presence is a very obvious reference to affairs of the heart; his gesture with the card has been interpreted as symbolic of fidelity to a single loved one. The empty chair may possibly allude to the absent subject of her thoughts.

Vermeer has studied the fall of light from the window in minute detail; how it emphasises the intricate relief of the gilded frame surrounding the landscape painting on the back wall near to the window; how it highlights the upholstery studs which have been used to finish the blue chair; how it intensifies the lustre of the pearls which adorn the neck of the young woman, especially, of course, those nearest the window; how it accentuates the creases of her dress and intensifies the lustrous sheen of the satin. In order to record these minute details Vermeer almost certainly used the camera obscura which helped him to focus on the exact nature of the surface of velvet and satin and even the wall.

Vermeer's painstaking working methods, compounded by constant revisions, were the major reasons behind his pronounced lack of fecundity and this in turn contributed to his constant money problems which do not seem to have been eased by his income from his other businesses as an art dealer and also perhaps as a publican.

But these thorough and meticulous working methods were the key to the creation of a body of work which is now amongst the most admired in all Western art. Vermeer's harmonious but enigmatic compositions stir the soul and the intellect in equal measure. In this picture he has preserved the mysterious stillness and solemnity of a brief moment, a prosaic moment which has been so profoundly realised that it transcends its banal context.

Contemporary Works

1669	Rembrandt: *The Return of the Prodigal Son*: St Petersburg
1670	Bartolomé Esteban Murillo: *Christ healing the Paralytic at the Pool of Bethesda*; London, National Gallery
1672	Claude Lorrain: *Night*; St Petersburg

Johannes Vermeer

1632	Born in Delft.
1652	Vermeer inherits his father's property which included an inn.
1653	Marries (April) Catherina Bolnes, who is a Catholic, in spite of the initial opposition of his future mother-in-law. Vermeer seems to have converted to Catholicism possibly to mollify his wife's mother. In October he is admitted to the Delft Guild of St Luke as a master.
1662-3	Serves for the first time as *hoofdman* (headman) of the painters' guild.
1670-1	Serves again as *hoofdman*.
1672	Vermeer is summoned to The Hague in order to authenticate the attribution of paintings ascribed to Holbein, Raphael and Titian among others.
1675	Dies in Delft leaving eleven children.
1676	Catherina petitions for bankruptcy.

Meindert Hobbema

National Gallery

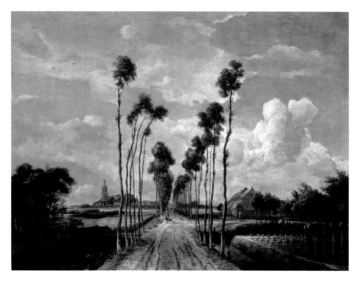

In 1668 Hobbema became a wine-gauger in Amsterdam. After this appointment his output as a painter is said to have declined. However, this painting, undoubtedly his masterpiece, is dated 1689.

The village of Middelharnis is situated on a small island in the mouth of the river Maas and apparently the view remains much the same today.

We are viewing the scene from the middle of a road which, unfettered by the constraints of any undulation (this being the Netherlands) continues, arrow-straight, to the village. An avenue of tall but heavily pruned trees accompanies the road and shepherds our eye down the central axis of the painting to its vanishing point very close to the horizontal centre of the composition. The dead-flat horizon provides a horizontal counterweight to the tree-lined road. It is a simple motif and yet it is curiously satisfying; once the eye has travelled the road it starts to roam beyond, looking left and right picking up the human presence within the landscape. On the lane that turns off to the right two people have stopped and are perhaps passing the time of day. In the foreground a man is staking trees in what looks like a tree nursery, the precise ranks of young saplings mirroring and continuing the mature avenue and contrasting with the trees growing on the opposite side of the avenue, left to grow naturally. Another man strolls towards us down the road with his dog, his place in the composition just enough off centre to avoid triteness.

It appears that the artist's first instinct was to include two trees on each side of the road in the foreground partially blocking off the distant vistas behind. But X-ray investigation has shown that these trees were overpainted at quite a late stage in the painting process. One can't help feeling that what we have is the best possible outcome.

Contemporary Works

1686	Luca Giordano: *Virgin of the Rosary*; Naples
1690	Godfried Schalcken: *Toilet of Venus, Daylight*; Kassel
1691	Godfrey Kneller: *Margaret Cecil, Countess of Ranelagh*; London, Royal Collection

Meindert Hobbema

1638	Born in Amsterdam the son of Lubbert Meyndertsz, he adopts the name Hobbema as a young man.
1653	He is taken into the care of an orphanage together with his brother and sister.
1655	Hobbema leaves the orphanage and probably in the same year enters the studio of Jacob van Ruisdael who was a great influence on his work.
1668	Marries Eeltje Pieters Vinck, the servant of an Amsterdam Burgomaster. (Ruisdael was a witness). He obtains a position as a wine-gauger with the Amsterdam Excise.
1704	His wife and two children die.
1709	Hobbema dies in Amsterdam.

Jean Siméon Chardin

The Young Schoolmistress 1736

National Gallery

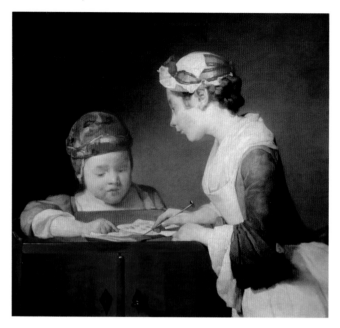

A girl, perhaps in her teens, is teaching a child to read. There might perhaps be a hiatus in the teaching process; a charged silence prevails — a quintessential element in many of Chardin's pictures. No background detail distracts us from the relationship between the two protagonists and Chardin has miraculously captured the look of intense (but nevertheless slightly baffled) concentration on the face of the child. Perhaps the child's mentor betrays a trace of irritation with the progress of her charge, but this is leavened with a stern but unmistakable sympathy.

Chardin came from a relatively modest background but his family were prosperous enough to enable him to study at the Académie Royale. He specialised as a still life painter for a number of years and had some success, becoming a member of the Académie Royale in September 1728. Not long before this picture was executed he also began to produce figure paintings, maintaining the small scale which he had generally favoured for his still life work. In his choice of subject and canvas size he was following in the footsteps of the great genre painters of the Dutch golden century, who were avidly collected in France during his lifetime. In particular, the way Chardin manages to fill such simple interiors with such charged atmosphere is reminiscent of Vermeer. However, he brings his own distinct French vision to this tradition; in his hands the prosaic pastimes and duties of everyday life attain a timeless, majestic quality.

The simplicity of Chardin's compositions also serves to highlight the fact that his work was considerably at odds with the prevailing Rococo court style epitomised by his contemporary, Boucher. However, this did not stop his genre scenes from becoming very popular at the Salon and from entering the collections of the wealthy and of royalty (including the Queen of Sweden and Louis XV). As his fame grew, a great many of his compositions were engraved, often accompanied by moralising verses, and in this way his work became available to the general public.

Contemporary Works

1735	Giambattista Tiepolo: *Jupiter and Danaë*; Stockholm
c1735	Canaletto: *The Feast Day of St Roch*; London, National Gallery
1740	William Hogarth: *Portrait of Captain Thomas Coram*; London, Foundling Hospital

Jean Siméon Chardin

1699	Born in Paris.
1728	Elected to the Académie Royale as a painter of 'animals and fruits'.
1731	Chardin's marriage is recorded.
1735	His first wife dies.
1739	*The Governess* is his first success at the Salon.
1744	Chardin marries again, this time to an affluent widow.
1764	He is commissioned to undertake some decorative work at the royal château of Choisy.
1779	Dies in Paris.

George Stubbs

National Gallery

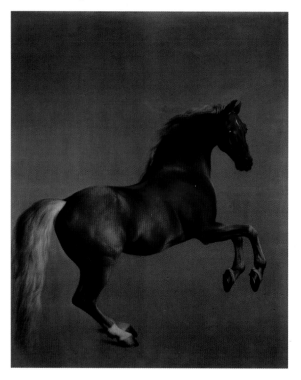

This astonishing canvas executed on a truly monumental scale dominates the room even though it is one of the largest rooms in the National Gallery and despite the fact that it contains some of the greatest and best loved works of British art. Standing in front of this magnificent beast makes you feel as though you are in the presence of a truly charismatic being. One is certainly in the presence of a great artist. Stubbs has infused life and character into every sinew and bone within the huge life-size frame of Whistlejacket; the horse exudes a visceral vigour as he rears above the viewer, his coat shining with good health, his mane and voluminous tail, the small white flash on his head and the white colouration of his near hind leg, all forming a foil to the even chestnut colour of the rest of his body. No landscape or extraneous decoration is allowed to impinge on our admiration of this beautiful animal; the neutral background, a most unusual device, seems perfect.

Of course Stubbs was by no means just a horse painter. He painted many compositions in which landscape and people are of more or equal importance to the animal, which is invariably present. And he painted many other types of animal, sometimes being employed by naturalists, such as Sir Joseph Banks, to create an accurate record of exotic species. But the horses painted by Stubbs are in a different league to anything produced by his contemporaries or indeed since. Naturally, all this was not achieved without an intimate knowledge of his subject matter. In the mid-1750s he worked for eighteen months with the corpses of horses supplied by local tanneries, studying their anatomy by carefully stripping away layers of muscle to gradually reveal the skeleton beneath, laboriously sketching each stage of the dissection. The results of these and subsequent studies were published as *The Anatomy of the Horse* in 1766 illustrated by eighteen plates engraved by Stubbs himself.

This portrait, for that is what it is, was commissioned by the 2nd Marquess of Rockingham who, in his desire to record the fine proportions of a favourite animal has given to us the image of the archetypal horse.

Contemporary Works

1762	Thomas Gainsborough: *The Painter's Daughters with a Cat*; London, National Gallery
1764	Joshua Reynolds: *Anne Dashwood as a Shepherdess*; New York
1765	François Boucher: *Landscape with a Young Fisherman and his Companions*; Manchester

George Stubbs

1724	Born in Liverpool.
c1741	Stubbs worked briefly copying paintings in the collection of the Earl of Derby. He soon left this job and taught himself to paint.
c1745	Moves to York and studies anatomy at the hospital there. Illustrates a medical treatise on midwifery, etching the plates himself.
1754	Visits Rome.
1756	It is at about this time that Stubbs begins to study the anatomy of the horse.
1758	Settles in London where he soon receives a large number of commissions from the many aristocrats who were keenly interested in breeding and racing horses.
1775	Starts to exhibit at the Royal Academy.
1777	Begins to publish engravings after his own works.
1781	He is elected an RA but as he fails to provide a diploma painting this honour is withdrawn.
1782	At the RA, Stubbs exhibits five works painted on ceramic plaques supplied by Wedgwood after discussions with Josiah Wedgwood.
1806	Dies in London.

Joseph Wright of Derby

An Experiment on a Bird in the Air Pump 1768

National Gallery

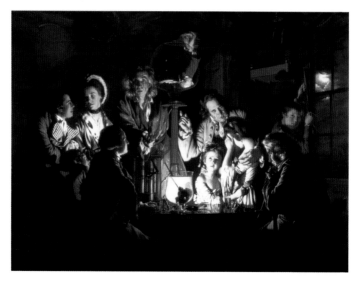

Joseph Wright, as his suffix tells us was born in Derby and spent much of his life there, excepting spells in Liverpool, London, Bath and Italy. Derbyshire was one of the principal centres of the early Industrial Revolution and Wright knew many of those who helped to shape it. Some years after completing this picture, he was commissioned to paint Richard Arkwright's likeness. Arkwright patented his water-frame, a machine for spinning cotton, in 1769 and installed a number of these machines in the first water-powered cotton mill, in Cromford, not far from Derby. Wright was also friendly with Erasmus Darwin and Josiah Wedgwood, two founder members of the influential Lunar Society, whose members (including James Watt and Matthew Boulton) met every month in Birmingham on the nearest Monday to the full moon, to discuss scientific matters and, most importantly, the practical application of science to manufacturing, medicine and education.

Trained as a portraitist, in the 1760s Wright began to paint dark candle-lit interiors and night scenes, influenced by the seventeenth-century Dutch followers of Caravaggio such as Rembrandt and Godfried Schalcken (who lived for a time in London in the 1690s). This stylistic direction combined with his interest in matters scientific spawned his famous scientific scenes in which striking lighting effects were used to heighten the drama.

At the centre of this composition are the two major players — the 'natural philosopher', or scientist as we would call him, and his victim, the cockatoo. The former, arrestingly God-like, engaging the viewer directly, exercises the power of life and death over the creature in the flask, which is close to the point of expiry, for the air pump on the table has produced a near vacuum inside the glass sphere. However, his left hand hovers near a valve at the top of the flask and, to the right, a boy is engaged in lowering a bird cage from its place near the ceiling; so we can expect that the valuable exotic bird will soon be reprieved.

Unaware of these preparations, two girls react to the experiment with understandable dismay while their father tries to offer a reasoned explanation (one senses without much success).

In the centre of the table, a skull is preserved in a milky solution contained within a large glass beaker behind which burns a candle, the source for the theatrical lighting. An older man stares at the skull and meditates on the transience of life and the certainty of eventual death. In the midst of the display of scientific enlightenment, this harks back to the 'vanitas' paintings of an earlier age but also chimes with the near death experience of the bird (beneath which the skull is exactly placed).

To the left a man is timing the experiment and a boy watches attentively. One could not so describe the couple behind the boy, who, far from being engrossed in the demonstration, only have eyes for each other; their future is ahead of them and they perhaps balance the older gentleman on the other side of the table in that their thoughts are most assuredly of life and love. They can be identified as Thomas Coltman and his future wife Mary and they married the year after this painting was completed. Wright was to paint them again in a double portrait two years after their marriage.

Contemporary Works

1765	Joshua Reynolds: *Lady Sarah Bunbury Sacrificing to the Graces*; Chicago
1769	Jean-Honoré Fragonard: *Portrait of the Abbé de Saint-Non*; Paris
1770	Francesco Guardi: *Venice: the Punta della Dogana with S Maria della Salute*; London, National Gallery

Joseph Wright of Derby

1734	Born in Derby, the son of a lawyer.
1751	Enters the London studio of Thomas Hudson, training as a portrait painter.
1753	Returns to Derby.
1756	Spends another year with Hudson.
1757	Returns again to Derby.
1768	Moves to Liverpool.
1773	Leaves Britain in October for Italy.
1774	Arrives in Rome in February. Travels to Naples and witnesses an eruption of Vesuvius in October.
1775	Returns to Britain, visiting Florence and Venice on the way. Bases himself in Bath.
1777	Settles permanently in Derby.
1781	Elected as an Associate of the Royal Academy.
1797	Dies in Derby.

Elizabeth Louise Vigée Le Brun

Self Portrait in a Straw Hat   After 1782

National Gallery

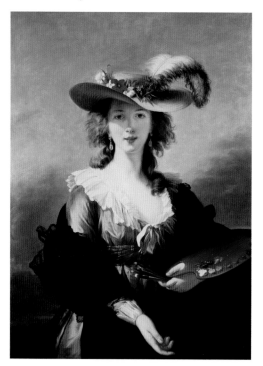

Elizabeth was taught to paint by her father Louis Vigée who was an artist specialising in portraiture using pastels as his medium. This enchanting self portrait was painted about three years after she was summoned to Versailles and commissioned to paint the likeness of the queen. All accounts of Elizabeth stress her charm and wit and these qualities endeared her to Marie Antoinette who made her painter to the queen. Their relationship quickly developed into a close friendship and Vigée Le Brun subsequently painted at least twenty-five portraits of the queen before the cataclysm of the revolution shattered their world in 1789. Elizabeth, so closely associated with the court, fled France in that year spending much of the next twenty-five years travelling around the capitals of Europe where she emulated the success she had experienced in France.

This picture exemplifies Vigée Le Brun's movement away from the conventions of Rococo artifice towards a simpler more natural look. She stands, holding the tools of her trade, in the open air engaging the viewer with a direct gaze. Sunlight falls from her right highlighting the pale delicate skin of her neck and breasts. She is wearing a wide-brimmed hat, which casts a shadow over much of her very pretty face, and which she has adorned with an arrangement of flowers and a large feather giving her a somewhat jaunty air; her hair is left unpowdered to emphasise the studiedly unaffected character of the composition.

The hat, which plays such a big part in the picture is there for reasons other than the purely decorative. Whilst visiting the Low Countries in 1782 she saw, and greatly admired, Rubens's *Portrait of Susanna Lunden* (known as *Le Chapeau de Paille,* and now also in the National Gallery). She was particularly inspired by the quality of light which Rubens had managed to capture and she determined that she would make a self portrait which would emulate his achievement. In this she has triumphantly succeeded. But she also made sure that she was wearing a real straw hat, and not a felt one which Susanna Lunden is wearing, despite the popular title of the Rubens painting.

Contemporary Works

1782	Joshua Reynolds: *Portrait of Colonel Banastre Tarleton*; London, National Gallery
1784	Johann Heinrich Fuseli: *Lady Macbeth Sleepwalking*; Paris
	Jaques-Louis David: *Oath of the Horatii*; Paris

Elizabeth Louise Vigée Le Brun

1755	Born in Paris: the daughter of Louis Vigée, a pastel portraitist. Taught to paint by her father and later Joseph Vernet.
1776	Marries Jean-Baptiste Le Brun, an art dealer.
1779	Summoned to Versailles and becomes painter to the queen.
1783	Vigée Le Brun becomes a member of the Académie Royale.
1789	After the outbreak of revolution she leaves France (October) and travels to Italy where she receives lucrative commissions at the courts of Turin, Rome and Naples.
1793 – 95	Takes up invitations to visit Vienna, then Prague and Dresden.
1795 – 1801	Lives in St Petersburg, Moscow and Berlin.
1802	Gains permission to return to Paris but dislikes life in Napoleonic France.
1803	Leaves for Britain where, like everywhere else, she is feted and much in demand as a portraitist, painting portraits of Lord Byron and the Prince of Wales.
1805	Returns to France: her output declines but she starts work on her memoirs — *Souvenirs de ma vie.*
1842	Dies in Paris.

Jacques-Louis David

National Gallery

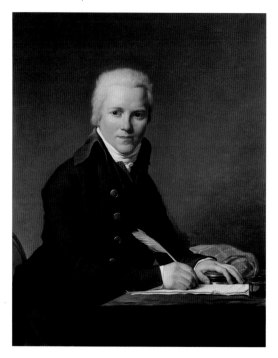

In 1790 David joined the Jacobin Club, the most radical of the political groupings which sprang up in the wake of the 1789 revolution. He became increasingly involved in political life and in 1792 he was elected as deputy for Paris in the National Convention where he chose to sit with the 'Mountain' (so called because they occupied the highest seats in the chamber) who were an extreme Jacobin faction led by Maximilien Robespierre. In 1793 David voted in favour of the execution of the king and he became a zealous supporter of the terror which ensued when Robespierre and his supporters gained control of the Committee of Public Safety and through it the governance of France.

During January 1794 David served as President of the Convention. One of his responsibilities was to sign arrest warrants and it seems that he was assiduous in undertaking these obligations. A few months later in July Robespierre was arrested at the Convention and executed the next day. David, so closely associated with Robespierre and with blood on his hands resulting from all those signatures, was now in grave danger. He was arrested and spent the rest of the year incarcerated (for most of the time in the Luxembourg Palace). He was arrested again in May 1795 and spent a further two months in prison, eventually being released due to ill health.

Shortly after this near miraculous escape from the guillotine he received a commission from two Dutch republicans who were in Paris to negotiate with the newly created Directory (now guiding France along a more moderate political path). Jacobus Blauw and Gaspar Mayer were the representatives of the Batavian Republic which had been set up after French military intervention in the Netherlands. The portrait of Gaspar Mayer also survives and is now in the Louvre. Interestingly Mayer never took delivery of the picture — he may have decided that owning a portrait by a disgraced Jacobin was not at the time a wise option.

Blauw was obviously made of sterner stuff. He was delighted by his likeness and wrote to David 'You have brought me to life again on the canvas; you have, in a way, immortalized me with your sublime brush'. As well as admiring David's art Blauw seems to have been in tune with his politics and this comes through in the portrait. His demeanour is one of determined and urgent conviction — one would not be surprised to find out that his pen had been captured at the very point of signing one of those warrants which caused David so many problems. His eyes are full of fervour and his expression is resolute although one feels that there is nevertheless a core of humanity within the politician.

It is a brilliantly observed portrait further enhanced by the care with which David has depicted such items as the brass buttons on Blauw's simple coat and the objects arrayed on the desk. All is set against the plain background which David favoured thereby concentrating our attention on the point of the painting — that stunning face.

Contemporary Works

1794	Francisco de Goya: *Interior of a Prison*; Barnard Castle
1795	Thomas Lawrence: *Portrait of Sarah Barrett-Moulton ('Pinkie')*; Los Angeles
1796	Benjamin West: *Death on a Pale Horse*; Detroit

Jacques-Louis David

1748	Born in Paris.
1757	David's father dies of wounds received in a pistol duel.
1765	Enters the studio of Joseph-Marie Vien.
1766	Enrols in the Académie Royale.
1774	After many attempts to win the Prix de Rome, David finally succeeds.
1775	Travels to Rome where he stays for five years.
1782	Marries Marguerite-Charlotte Pécoul.
1783	Becomes a full member of the Académie. Birth of his first child.
1784	Works on the *Oath of the Horatii* in Rome. The painting receives much praise.
1790	Joins the Jacobin Club.
1792	Elected to the National Convention attaching himself to the 'Mountain' faction.
1793	David votes in favour of the execution of Louis XVI. Serves a term as President of the Jacobin Club. Becomes a member of the Committee of General Security.
1794	Serves a short term as President of the Convention (Jan). Divorces his wife. Organises the Festival of the Supreme Being. After the fall of Robespierre, David is imprisoned.
1796	Re-marries his wife.
1799	Exhibits his *Sabine Women* in a room at the Louvre, charging for entry. The proceeds allow him to buy a country house.
1801	Completes *Bonaparte Crossing the St Bernard Pass*.
1804	Appointed First Painter to the emperor.
1807	Completes the *Coronation of the Emperor and Empress*.
1808	David is given a title and a coat of arms.
1816	After the fall of Napoleon, David is exiled as a regicide. Lives in Brussels.
1825	Dies in Brussels.

Caspar David Friedrich

National Gallery

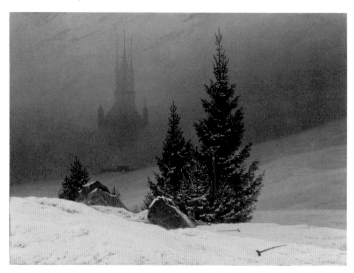

There are very few works by Caspar David Friedrich outside Germany or Eastern Europe so it is good to be able to see this small painting on the walls of the National Gallery.

Friedrich's landscapes were rarely a precise representation of an actual place; rather he utilised his many sketches of hills, streams or individual trees in different parts of Germany in the creation of a personal landscape. His paintings are effectively compilations — compositions emerged from his imagination and he would then use selected studies as building blocks or templates to put together the finished painting. But these ersatz scenes assumed a highly charged religious significance in keeping with a contemporary strand of Lutheran thought grounded in a philosophy which celebrated God through landscape.

There is no doubt about it, there are not many laughs to be gained from looking at paintings by Friedrich. But he is one of those artists who have a very personal voice. His paintings try to reveal the spirituality which he detected within Nature. And he chose to illustrate that spirituality by accentuating the superhuman scale and elemental power of Nature which usually dwarfs the human presence in most of his paintings. It is this emphasis on the disparity of natural forces, when juxtaposed with the human onlooker, which in large part produces the trademark melancholia and loneliness which suffuses his work.

In this picture we see that a crucifix has been erected in front of a fir tree. Other trees and a couple of rocks punctuate a snowy and otherwise featureless landscape. But looming out of the eerie half light of morning (or possibly evening) a curious Gothic structure rises, mirroring the shape of the large tree. For Friedrich, Gothic architecture was quintessentially German and there was also an equivalence between its natural construction (as he saw it) and the forms which appear in the forests of Germany. So this structure is there both as an emblem of faith and as a symbol of German nationalism.

On a cursory glance it is possible to miss the single man sitting in the snow. But there he is, his back propped against the central rock, praying before the crucifix. He has abandoned a pair of crutches in his eagerness to commune with God. This may at first appear to be a scene of utter despair but *Winter Landscape* should rather be seen as an image of hope in resurrection — an example of the solace to be gained from religious faith.

Contemporary Works

1809	Jacques-Louis David: *Sappho and Phaon*; St Petersburg
1811	Jean-Auguste-Dominique Ingres: *Jupiter and Thetis*; Aix-en-Provence
1812	Joseph Mallord William Turner: *Snowstorm: Hannibal and his Army Crossing the Alps*; London, Tate Britain

Caspar David Friedrich

1774	Born in Greifswald on the Baltic coast of Germany.
1794	Begins his studies at the Akademi for de Skønne Kunster in Copenhagen.
1798	Leaves Denmark and settles in Dresden where his output is predominantly drawing and sepia.
1805	He submits two drawings to the Weimarer Kunstfreunde and wins a prize.
1807	Friedrich begins painting in oils.
1813	Dresden is occupied by the French.
1814	After the liberation of Dresden, Friedrich takes part in a celebratory exhibition.
1823	The Norwegian painter Johann Christian Dahl takes up residence in part of Freidrich's house. They also exhibit together.
1824	Friedrich is appointed honorary professor at the Dresden Academy but fails to win a position as a landscape painting teacher. This failure was a great disappointment.
1835	He suffers a stroke which prevents him from painting.
1840	Dies in Dresden.

Francisco de Goya

Portrait of the Duke of Wellington
1812-14

National Gallery

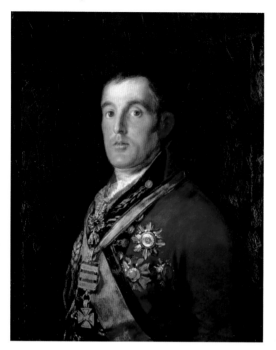

On 22 July 1812, Lieutenant General the Earl of Wellington (as he then was), at the head of an army of perhaps 50,000 men inflicted a severe defeat on a French force of similar size near Salamanca in a battle which military historians consider to be 'Wellington's Masterpiece'. A few days later he liberated Madrid, a city on the verge of starvation, receiving a delirious welcome. Although only a temporary respite for the denizens of the Spanish capital, in the long term the battle turned out to be a turning point in the war against Napoleonic France in the Iberian Peninsula.

It was during this first stay in the Spanish capital that Wellington sat for Goya who, before the war, had been the principal painter to the Spanish court but who had also completed, only two years before, a portrait of the puppet King Joseph, brother of Napoleon. As soon as Wellington left, the French swept back into Madrid later in the same year, so it obviously paid to be outwardly politically flexible. In fact Goya was torn — as a liberal he initially welcomed certain aspects of the French regime (compared to the rigid conservatism and stifling religious orthodoxy of the Bourbon monarchy) but as a patriot he hated the military occupation of his country.

It seems that this painting may have been based on a wonderfully executed drawing of Wellington now in the British Museum — presumably the general could not spare the time even for Goya's notably modest requirements for sitters. The same drawing also appears to have been the basis for an equestrian portrait which Goya also made at the same time and which now hangs in Wellington's London home, Apsley House.

Wellington's dress uniform is encrusted with decorations bestowed by a number of grateful European monarchs. Around his neck hangs the emblem of the Golden Fleece and beneath that the Peninsular Gold Cross; on his breast the star of the Order of the Bath glitters above two equally lustrous Iberian gongs, the Portuguese Order of the Tower and Sword and the Order of San Fernando from Spain. Bolstered by this impressive assortment of honours the general stares imperiously out of the canvas, his eyes penetratingly alert, his mouth very slightly open as if he might be about to bark an order to an attentive member of his staff. As one would expect, he holds himself ramrod straight aware of his lofty status and reputation.

Wellington went on to achieve even greater glory and eventually to become Prime Minister. Sadly, Goya's hopes (with those of a great many of his countrymen) for the emergence of a more liberal government, after the upheavals of the years of war, were dashed when the viciously reactionary Fernando VII was restored to power in 1814. After living for ten years under an increasingly brutal and repressive regime, Goya eventually chose exile in France, dying in Bordeaux in 1828.

Contemporary Works

1814	Théodore Géricault: *Officer of the Imperial Horse Guards Charging*; Paris
	Caspar David Friedrich: *Early Snow*; Hamburg
1815	Joseph Mallord William Turner: *Dido Building Carthage*; London, Tate Britain

Francisco de Goya

1746	Born in Fuendetodos in Aragon.
1771	Goya travels to Rome after studying in Saragossa.
1773	Goya marries Josefa Bayeu, the sister of his colleagues and mentors, Francisco and Ramón Bayeu.
1774	Moves to work under Francisco Bayeu in Madrid.
1780	He is elected to the Real Academia de Belles Artes de S Fernando in Madrid.
1785	Becomes assistant director of painting at the Real Academia.
1786	Goya is appointed Painter to the king.
1792	Travels to Cádiz to stay with a friend and collector, Sebastián Martínez. While there Goya becomes very ill resulting in a total loss of hearing.
1793	Returns to Madrid in a weakened state and profoundly deaf.
1796	Stays in Andalusia as the guest of the Duchess of Alba.
1799	Publishes a series of 80 satirical aquatints known as the *Caprichos*.
1800	Spends the spring at the palace of Aranjuez, working on the group painting of the family of Carlos IV.
1808	French forces take control of several Spanish fortresses. Further French troops cross the Pyrenees. Carlos IV abdicates. Goya visits Saragossa and records the horrors he sees during the siege of the city in a sketchbook.
1809	Joseph Bonaparte is installed on the Spanish throne.
1810	Begins to work on a series of prints based on his Saragossa sketchbooks entitled the *Disasters of War* which remain unpublished until 1863.
1812	Goya's wife dies. He paints portraits of the Earl of Wellington.
1814	The ferociously reactionary Fernando VII is restored to the Spanish throne.
1819	Buys a property in the Madrid suburbs called the Quinta del Sordo.
1820	Starts to decorate the walls of two rooms in his house with the 'Black Paintings'.
1824	Horrified by a wave of terror unleashed by Fernando, Goya leaves Spain. Visits Paris but settles in Bordeaux.
1828	Dies in Bordeaux.

Joseph Mallord William Turner

The Fighting Temeraire tugged to her Last Berth to be broken up 1839

National Gallery

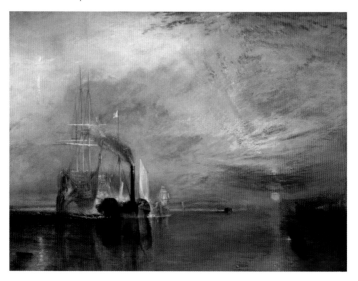

The *Temeraire* was launched in 1798, a 98-gun Second Rate ship of the line. She was the second ship to carry the name — her predecessor had been built in France, launched as *Le Téméraire*, but was captured in 1759, during the Seven Years War, becoming a British ship but keeping her name, minus the accents. In 1805 the (second) *Temeraire* played an exceptionally gallant part in the battle of Trafalgar attacking the Franco-Spanish line directly behind the *Victory* and taking not one but two enemy ships captive. So she was a vessel with an heroic pedigree.

But by the 1830s the age of these leviathans was at an end. Oak and sail were giving way to steam and on 5 and 6 September 1838 it was the *Temeraire's* turn to succumb to inevitable progress. A hulk, stripped to an empty hull, she was towed from her moorings at Sheerness by two steam tugs on her last journey to Rotherhithe where she was broken up. Turner would have read of this in the newspapers — it is highly unlikely that he witnessed the journey himself. However the story elicited a response from him which resulted in a most remarkable picture — perhaps his most-loved painting.

Half of the picture is filled with a glorious sunset. To the left, buoyed on a calm and tranquil sea the *Temeraire* is towed to her doom. Turner has used colour to impart an ethereal quality to the old vessel — she seems to loom over her nemesis like a ghost ship — anticipating her eventual demise. The real *Temeraire*, during her last journey would not have been masted but Turner has given her some stunted masts so that she should retain a semblance of dignity. The tug paddles remorselessly towards the viewer; other sailing vessels retreat towards the setting sun.

At first sight the message is clear — the *Temeraire*, valiant emblem of the age of sail, is being ushered unceremoniously to her demise by a squat tug belching acrid smoke and flame — an era of grace, power and heroism is replaced by ugly, brutalistic utility and the exigencies of money. But Turner may not necessarily have attached such negative associations to the tug. He had included steamers in many works prior to this and he may well have seen the tug as a symbol of necessary and inevitable change. It is the sunset, as much a focus of the composition as the two disparate vessels, which betrays an underlying significance — all things come to an end including our own lives.

And what a sunset it is. Noone does sunsets like Turner. He was always striving to better his hero Claude in his portrayal of light, and particularly the sun. In paintings such as this Turner succeeds triumphantly. This part of the canvas, in contrast to other areas, is covered with thickly impastoed paint — very unlike Claude. Golds, crimsons and reds are built up to produce a quite extraordinary evocation of the different colours which the setting sun imparts to cloud and atmosphere.

When it was exhibited at the Royal Academy in 1839 it received ecstatic reviews. One reviewer thought that the painting was 'the most wonderful of all the works of the greatest master of the age'. But it was William Makepeace Thackeray who put his finger on it when he likened the picture to 'a magnificent national ode'.

Contemporary Works

1838	Christen Købke: *View of Lake Sortedam*; Copenhagen
	William Dyce: *Madonna and Child*; Nottingham
1840	Jean-Baptiste-Camille Corot: *Breton Women at the Well*; Paris
1841	Théodore Chassériau: *The Toilet of Esther*; Paris

Joseph Mallord William Turner

See page 165

Jean-Auguste-Dominique Ingres

National Gallery

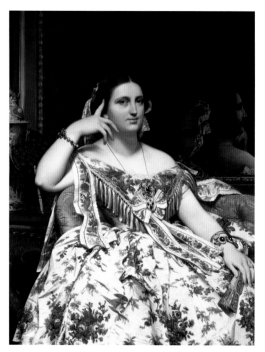

Ingres was a perfectionist given to compulsively reworking canvases, his unfortunate clients often waiting years for the release of their commissions. An extreme example is his *Venus Anadyomene* commenced in 1807 but which remained in his studio for over forty years until it was at last deemed complete in 1848. The gestation of this portrait was not quite so protracted but the young wife of the banker Sigisbert Moitessier, aged twenty-three at the time of the commission, was nevertheless a more mature 35-year-old when she was finally able to hang it on her wall.

When first approached by M. Moitessier in 1844, Ingres initially refused to accept the commission, never really considering portraiture to be a sufficiently elevated art form and was consequently somewhat dismissive of the genre, even though he was an outstanding exponent. But on meeting Marie-Clotilde-Inès he was enthralled by her beauty and changed his mind.

He originally planned to include the young daughter of the sitter but presumably the hours of inactivity required for such a portrait (especially one executed by such a painter) did not prove to be popular with the child who does not appear in the finished painting. In any event Ingres would have found it difficult to complete her likeness as she was no longer a child by the time the picture was delivered. Many other changes were made over the years including the repainting of the sumptuous dress which, considering the complexity of the final pattern would not have been a decision taken lightly.

In 1849 the death of his wife rendered Ingres incapable of work — he seems to have despaired, feeling that his working life was at an end; in 1851 he donated his art collection to the museum at Montauban, his birthplace. However, in the same year he began work again on two portraits, one of them representing a standing Madame Moitessier resplendent in a black gown (now in Washington) which he completed within the year. This uncharacteristic alacrity was possibly the result of complaints from M. Moitessier regarding the slow progress of the original commission. But within months he had also resumed work on this portrait which continued to occupy him for a further four years.

Of course his technique needed time. A pupil of David, Ingres surpassed even his mentor in his superfine finish and exquisite rendition of every detail, be it jewel, fabric, glass or the refined quality of pampered feminine flesh (although coming perilously close here to a quality not unlike a waxworks model). He also emulated David, the arch neo-classicist, in his appreciation of the antique, fostered by his years of domicile in Rome. And indeed the sitter's pose, her head resting on her forefinger, probably derives from a Roman wall painting found at Herculaneum.

Contemporary Works

1855	Gustave Courbet: *The Painter's Studio*; Paris
	Eugène Delacroix: *A Moroccan Saddling a Horse*; St Petersburg
1856	John Everett Millais: *The Blind Girl*; Birmingham

Jean-Auguste-Dominique Ingres

1780	Born in Montauban near Toulouse, the son of a painter and sculptor.
1797	After receiving instruction from his father and attending the academy at Toulouse, he enters the studio of David in Paris.
1801	Wins the Prix de Rome.
1806	Travels to Rome to take up his position at the Académie de France.
1808	Sends two paintings back to Paris (now thought of as masterpieces) but their reception is unenthusiastic.
1810	After receiving a number of commissions he decides to stay in Rome.
1813	Completes commissions for the Napoleonic administration in Rome. Marries Madeleine Chapelle.
1815	The fall of the Napoleonic regime in Italy sharply reduces commissions. He resorts to drawing portraits of tourists.
1819	Further submissions to the Paris Salon are greeted with little interest. Ingres resolves to stay in Italy.
1820	Moves to Florence.
1824	*Entry into Paris of the Future Charles V* and the *Vow of Louis XIII* are exhibited at the Salon and are received favourably.
1825	Ingres is awarded the Cross of the *Légion d'honneur*. Opens a studio in Paris taking in students.
1834	Again disappointed by the reception of a painting at the Salon, Ingres leaves Paris to become director of the Académie de France in Rome.
1840	*Antiochus and Stratonice*, started in 1807 is delivered to the Duc d'Orléans in Paris. When exhibited, the picture is greeted with acclaim.
1841	Returns to Paris.
1849	Ingres becomes vice-president of the École des Beaux-Arts. In July his wife Madeleine dies. Ingres is devastated and ceases to work for some time.
1851	Donates his art collection to Montauban museum.
1852	His spirits are raised by his second marriage to Delphine Ramel.
1867	Dies in Paris.

Pierre-Cécile Puvis de Chavannes

The Beheading of St John the Baptist   c1869

National Gallery

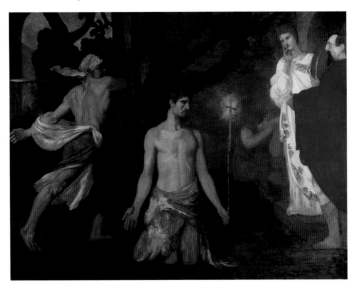

St John the Baptist had denounced Herod for his incestuous marriage and not unnatually Herodias, Herod's wife, had been displeased. When Salome, her daughter by her first marriage later danced in front of Herod, he was so entranced by her that he promised her anything she wanted. Prompted by her mother, Salome famously asked for the Baptist's head on a plate and Herod, true to his word, ordered John's summary decapitation.

We are witness here to the very last second of the life of St John. The executioner's sword is poised at the point from which it will depart for its swift terminal journey; the executioner's body is packed with kinetic power, flexed to impart maximum velocity to the blade — enough energy to make the coming stroke the only one necessary to do the job. Soon, very soon, the Baptist's head will be rolling on the stone-flagged floor. An impassive Salome (whose features are said to resemble the artist's life long partner) looks on with academic interest, her dish ready to receive the saintly head.

Puvis was famous in the late nineteenth century for his huge decorative murals and oversize canvases which combined simplicity of form and colour with monumental scale. His admiration for Piero della Francesca and the art of the early Italian Renaissance led him to use flat expanses of colour in emulation of fresco and a great many of his compositions present us with an Arcadian paradise. This picture shows no idyll but the sparse covering of matt paint, the suppression of perspective, and concentration of the action along the picture plain is pure Puvis. (This painting is probably unfinished — a smaller version now hanging in the Barber Institute in Birmingham was exhibited at the Salon of 1870).

He was, of course, painting at the same time as the Impressionists and it would be difficult to think of a contemporary artist who produced work less in tune with the outdoor immediacy of much Impressionist output. However, it is of course wrong to think of the various groups and individuals who participated in the rich artistic life of late nineteenth-century Paris as being in some way hermetically sealed against what was happening around them. Puvis's art was hugely influential and was greatly admired by most of the Impressionists and especially by the next generation of painters such as Seurat, Signac, Gauguin, Picasso and Matisse, the latter giving expression to his debt to Puvis in such ground-breaking paintings as *Luxe, Calme et Volupté*. His fame spread beyond France, bringing him a commission to produce frescoes for the Public Library in the American city of Boston.

Contemporary Works

1868	Édouard Manet: *The Execution of the Emperor Maximilian*; London, National Gallery
1869	Hilaire-Germain-Edgar Degas: *The Orchestra of the Paris Opera*; Paris
1870	John Everett Millais: *The Boyhood of Raleigh*; London, Tate Britain

Pierre-Cécile Puvis de Chavannes

1824	Born in Paris, the son of the Chief Engineer of Mines.
1846	After serious illness interrupts his studies, he travels to Italy and there discovers an interest in art being particularly impressed with the frescoes of Piero della Francesca.
1848	Visits Italy again. On his return he briefly studies with Delacroix and then Thomas Couture but then studies independently.
1850	He exhibits for the first time at the Salon.
1852	Three submitted works are rejected by the Salon.
1856	Begins a relationship with Princess Marie Cantacuzène which lasts until her death.
1861	Puvis wins a medal at the Salon with two murals, *Peace* and *War*.
1864	He wins his first public commission for the Musée Napoléon after which he rapidly gains recognition as a mural painter.
1872	Puvis resigns as a member of the Salon jury marking his disapproval of their conservatism.
1874-8	Works on murals of St Geneviève for the Panthéon in Paris.
1884-6	He is in Lyon decorating the staircase of the Musée des Beaux-Arts.
1891-4	Undertakes a series of murals at the Hôtel de Ville in Paris.
1896	He is invited to decorate the Boston Public Library and travels to the United States to undertake the commission.
1897	Puvis marries Princess Marie Cantacuzène.
1898	Princess Marie dies in August and Puvis dies in October.

Georges-Pierre Seurat

Bathers at Asnières 1884

National Gallery

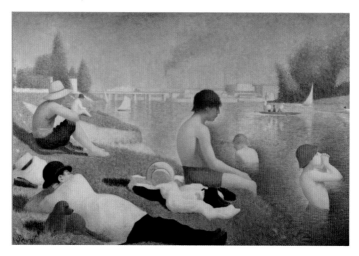

The picture captures those stultifying moments we all experience on a hot summer afternoon. There are occasional cooling flurries of wind — the flag on the ferry hangs limply but there seems to be enough breeze to fill the sails of the larger sailing craft that populate the river, and the smoke from a nearby factory is carried away from the perpendicular. But the heat is palpable; Seurat has perfectly captured the visible by-products of the high temperature — the trees in the middle distance dance and shimmer in the sunlight; the haze unites the sky and river in a blur of light; the white clothing, either worn or discarded on the bank dazzles us with reflected light; the occasional dark shadow points up the slightly faded colour of the grass in the intense sunlight. The bathers in the water and the *flaneurs* on the bank are caught in a mid-summer ennui, each absorbed in their own reverie, contemplating the river but seemingly unable to break a heat-imposed trance.

Unlike most of his Impressionist contemporaries, Seurat did not achieve these effects by setting up his easel out of doors and creating the finished work *en plein air*. Apart from anything else the monumental size of the canvas, at over three metres wide, would preclude any such thought. Instead he worked slowly and painstakingly in the studio putting together the finished composition with the help of a considerable number of drawings and oil studies on panel, many of which were executed *in situ*. Seurat was therefore working more in the tradition of Poussin and, in particular that immensely influential contemporary, Pierre Puvis de Chavannes, a similarity which was noted by contemporary critics. The *Bathers* has that feeling of compositional rigour which you would expect from Poussin and Puvis, but although Seurat is using the same visual grammar, he departs from their Arcadian dreamscapes, transplanting the 'lower orders' in place of the semi-heroic beings which inhabit Puvis's universe. In this he was at one with the Impressionists.

Seurat famously developed a working method later called pointillism (he prefered the rather clumsy label chromo-luminarism) based on his extensive researches into colour theory which led him to study optics, chemistry and other scientific disciplines. Essentially, and without going into great detail, his method involved the application of juxtaposed dabs of pure but complementary colour which when viewed from a distance fused and mixed within the spectator's eye. *Bathers at Asnières* is an early piece in which full-blown pointillism is not used to any great extent. Instead, Seurat uses a number of techniques from bold brush strokes to cross-hatching (especially in depicting the grass) but the actual method matters less than the fact that in the *Bathers* his colour combinations conform to his theories of colour harmony. He added some pointillist detail later, especially in the orange hat worn by the boy blowing into cupped hands, where small dots of yellow, lighter orange and dark blue (reflecting the water) resonate and complement each other.

The painting was predictably rejected by the conservative jury of the Salon of 1884 but in that year the Groupe des Artistes Indépendants was formed, organised by artists who, after years of frustration, decided to follow in the footsteps of the Impressionists and challenge the monopoly of the Salon. The *Bathers* was exhibited at this alternative forum in the spring of that year and although it was rather disappointingly displayed (in the bar) it was noticed by the critics and received some charitable if occasionally somewhat puzzled reviews.

Contemporary Works

1883	Arnold Böcklin: *Ulysses and Calypso*; Basel
1884	Edward Burne-Jones: *King Cophetua and the Beggar Maid*; London, Tate Britain
1885	Vincent van Gogh: *The Potato Eaters*; Amsterdam

Georges-Pierre Seurat

1859	Born in Paris
1878	Seurat enters the École des des Beaux-Arts studying under Henri Lehmann who had been a pupil of Ingres.
1879	Visits the Fourth Impressionist Exhibition which has a profound influence on him. Starts one year's military service and is posted to Brest.
1880	Returns to Paris.
1883	A drawing by Seurat is accepted for exhibition at the Salon.
1884	*Bathers at Asnières* is rejected by the Salon but the painting is shown at the first exhibition of the Sociéte des Artistes Indépandants.
1886	Seurat exhibits various works at the eighth (and last) Impressionist Exhibition, chief among them the huge *A Sunday Afternoon on the island of La Grande Jatte*, which is again exhibited later in the same year at the second Sociéte des Artistes Indépendants. Paints at Honfleur in the summer.
1888	Seurat visits Normandy, where he paints at Port-en-Bessin.
1889	Works at Le Crotoy in Normandy.
1890	Seurat's mistress Madeleine Knobloch gives birth to their son. Few of his associates are aware of their relationship. Works at Gravelines in the summer.
1891	Seurat falls ill and dies at the age of 31.

Vincent van Gogh

Sunflowers 1888

National Gallery

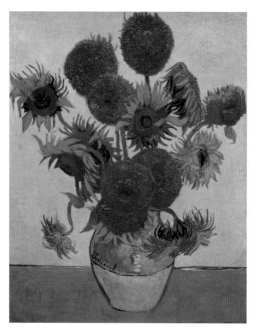

The *Sunflowers* is probably the most popular (and therefore the most famous) painting housed in the National Gallery — one of the most instantly recognisable images in Western art, made by the world's favourite painter. The outline of Vincent's life is well known and the tragic irony of the loneliness and penury endured by him, when contrasted with the fact that his posthumous fame contributed to a record auction price (for another version of this image) of nearly £25 million in 1987, adds an unavoidable piquancy to one's response to the picture.

In February 1888 van Gogh left Paris and travelled to Provence where he rented a diminutive house in Arles. Vincent wanted this modest dwelling to become the embryonic focus for a community of artists and to this end he had written repeatedly to his friends Émile Bernard and Paul Gauguin asking them to leave Brittany and join him in the south. Gauguin eventually agreed and it was following this news that Vincent painted a series of four sunflower canvases (he later made more copies) as decorations for the house. He selected and signed two of them and it was these two which adorned Gauguin's bedroom when he arrived. The National Gallery's version is one of these signed works, the other now hangs in Munich. Gauguin was very taken with them and responded by producing a portrait of van Gogh engaged in painting one of the later copies —Vincent is shown gazing intently at a somewhat withered vase of flowers.

In retrospect, this explosive and short-lived cohabitation was probably one of the worst ideas in the history of art. One can only wonder at the sort of atmosphere which was generated within the tiny 'Yellow House' by two such temperaments — one, manically passionate, already showing signs of mental instability, or at best acute depression, the other equally obsessive, famously egotistical and much more self assured. After two months Gauguin announced that he wished to leave Arles. This news precipitated the celebrated incident of self mutilation triggering van Gogh's descent into terminal mental illness.

But the sunflowers represent a more hopeful period when he was looking forward to the arrival of his friend, and when the prospect of a community of artists based in Arles was still a possibility. Yellow was a colour he equated with happiness and it is also the colour of the south — of the dazzling sun. Indeed, in the only favourable article to appear during his lifetime, in the year of his death, the critic and poet Albert Aurier asks: 'And how could we explain that obsessive passion for the solar disk that he loves to make shine forth from his emblazoned skies, and, at the same time, for that other sun, that vegetable-star, the sumptuous sunflower, which he repeats tirelessly, monomaniacally, if we refuse to accept his persistent preoccupation with some vague and glorious heliomythic allegory?'

Contemporary Works

1888	Paul Gauguin: *Old Women of Arles*; Chicago
	Camille Pissarro: *Apple Picking at Eragny-sur-Epte*; Dallas
1889	Philip Wilson Steer: *Knucklebones*; Ipswich

Vincent van Gogh

1853	Born at Grooot-Zundert in the southern Netherlands, the son of a pastor.
1869	Becomes an apprentice at the French art dealers Goupil & Co. in The Hague.
1873	Van Gogh is transferred to the firm's London branch. He falls in love with the daughter of his landlady but is rejected — a bitter personal blow.
1875	He is transferred to the head office of Goupil & Co. in Paris.
1876	Increasingly obsessed with religion, van Gogh is sacked. Travels to England and works in church schools in Ramsgate and West London.
1877	Returns to the Netherlands and decides to become a minister but fails to gain a place in the Theological Faculty at Amsterdam.
1878	Becomes a lay preacher in a mining area of Belgium.
1879	His contract is not renewed. Decides to become an artist.
1880	Studies drawing in Brussels. Becomes dependent on the financial support of his brother Theo who works for Goupil & Co. in Paris.
1881	Returns to live with his parents. In December moves to The Hague where he lives with a prostitute Clasina (Sien) Hoornik.
1883	Leaves Sien and after a spell in the province of Drenthe returns to live with his parents in Nuenen where he paints peasant life.
1885	His father dies. In November he moves to Antwerp.
1886	Joins his brother Theo in Paris who introduces him to the Impressionist circle.
1888	In February he leaves Paris for Arles where he wants to found a community of artists. Gauguin is persuaded to join him in October but in December announces that he wants to leave. A disheartened van Gogh famously cuts off a small part of his ear. He is committed to the Hôtel Dieu in Arles.
1889	In January van Gogh discharges himself from hospital. After suffering further hallucinations and attacks of paranoia he is admitted to the asylum near Saint-Rémy-de-Provence where he continues to paint.
1890	A favourable article appears in *Mercure de France*. Makes the only sale of a picture during his life. In May he leaves the asylum and travels to Auvers-sur-Oise where Dr Gachet keeps an eye on him. Vincent shoots himself on 27 July. Two days later he dies.

Henri Rousseau

National Gallery

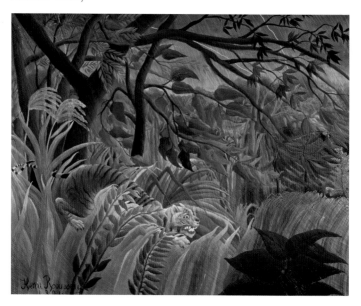

In 1908 Pablo Picasso hosted a banquet at his rooms in the Bateau Lavoir, a run-down apartment block in Montmartre. A host of 'big names' from the Parisian avant garde were there including Gertrude Stein, Guillaume Apollinaire and Georges Braque. But the guest of honour at the banquet was an elderly man who had spent a good deal of his working life as an attendant at the toll gates which then surrounded Paris. The Bateau Lavoir group had mockingly christened him 'Le Douanier' as, during his working life, he had failed to attain even the relatively modest status of customs officer.

Henri Rousseau had started to paint in early middle age; completely self taught, he was unwittingly the first exponent of what was later labelled Naïve Art. Not that Rousseau would have accepted this appellation for a moment. He took himself very seriously and as far as he was concerned his output was firmly in the academic tradition of such officially respectable painters as Gérôme and Bouguereau whose work was feted at the Salon. He had a great sense of his own importance and once told Picasso 'we are the two great painters of our time, you in the Egyptian style and I in the modern style'. It was for this reason that the atmosphere at the banquet was laced with gentle mockery most of which would undoubtedly have gone right over Rousseau's head. However, Picasso had genuine regard for his work and owned several of his pictures.

In this painting, a tiger, normally an object of awe and fear, is shown as itself fearful of the violence of a tropical storm; its awkward stance has also conspired to rob it of the grace inherent in real tigers. The forest vegetation is depicted with considerable gusto. No matter that some of the undergrowth can be identified as scaled up house plants, the effect is sensational as the trees strain under the weight of the wind. And it is difficult to think of many other pictures in which rain has been better portrayed. Rousseau's solution to this problem was to streak the canvas with slightly opaque glazes of paint or varnish.

Rousseau claimed that his twenty jungle scenes (of which this was the first) were the product of direct observation. He had been a bandsman in the army and he claimed to have served in Mexico, but this tour of duty seems only to have taken place in his own imagination as it appears that he spent his time in the army in the delightful but rather less exotic climes of Angers in the Loire valley. It is much more likely that the plants in this painting have their origin in his visits to the Jardin des Plantes in Paris.

Rousseau's influence on various twentieth century movements was considerable but it was the Surrealists who really took him to their hearts. They loved the dreamlike quality which he achieved in much of his work — presumably his somewhat eccentric grasp of scale and perspective only served to heighten his appeal. His legacy can be seen clearly in the output of Max Ernst and Paul Delvaux.

Eventually Picasso gave his collection of Rousseau's works to the Louvre. How Rousseau would have liked to know that he now is admired far more than the academicians whom he had esteemed so highly.

Contemporary Works

1891	Fernand Khnopff: *I Lock My Door upon Myself*; Munich
	Lawrence Alma-Tadema: *Love's Votaries*; Newcastle-upon-Tyne
1892	Henri de Toulouse-Lautrec: *Jane Avril Dancing*; Paris

Henri Rousseau

1844	Born at Laval (May). Later attends the lycée in Laval but receives no artistic training.
1871	He is working by this date for the Paris municipal toll service, collecting dues at the entry gates to the city. This gave rise to his later nickname of 'Le Douanier' but he never rose to the rank of customs officer.
1884	He is known to have had a permit to copy works in the Louvre by this date.
1885	Showed two works at the Salon, both derided by the critics.
1886	Paul Signac encourages Rousseau to exhibit at the Salon des Indépendants. Thereafter, he exhibits regularly at this annual show.
1893	He retires in order to spend more time painting.
1905	Exhibits his work at the Salon d'Automne (the year of Les Fauves). Meets Picasso, Robert Delaunay and the poet and critic Guillaume Apollinaire.
1908	Picasso holds a banquet in Rousseau's honour.
1910	Dies in Paris (September).
1911	The Salon des Indépandants holds a retrospective of his work.

The architect Sir John Soane's house, museum and library at No. 13 Lincoln's Inn Fields has been a public museum since the early nineteenth century. Between 1794 and 1824 Soane rebuilt three houses on the north side of Lincoln's Inn Fields, beginning with No. 12, and concluding with No. 14.

He first opened his house when he was appointed Professor of Architecture at the Royal Academy in 1806, giving Royal Academy students access to his books, casts and models.

In 1833 Soane negotiated an Act of Parliament to settle and preserve the house and collection for the benefit of 'amateurs and students' in architecture, painting and sculpture. On his death in 1837 the Act came into force, a crucial part of the brief for the Board of Trustees being to maintain the fabric of the museum, keeping it 'as nearly as circumstances will admit in the state' in which it was left at the time of Soane's death and to allow free access for students and the public to 'consult, inspect and benefit' from the collections.

Sir John Soane's Museum

13 Lincoln's Inn Fields London WC2A 3BP
Tel. +44 (0)20 7405 2107

Opening Hours

Tuesday to Saturday 10am – 5pm. Closed Sunday and Monday, Bank Holidays and Christmas Eve. Extended opening on the first Tuesday of every month 6pm – 9pm.

Admission

Free. Every Saturday there is a tour of the museum (at 2.30pm) costing £3.00. The number of visitors allowed entry to the museum at any one time is limited due to the unique nature of the collection and the house. This can lead to queues forming at busy periods, especially on Saturdays.

How To Get There

The nearest underground station is Holborn (Piccadilly and Central Lines).

William Hogarth

Sir John Soane's Museum

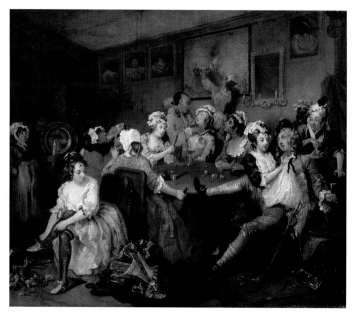

In 1732 William Hogarth published a set of engravings based on a series of paintings he had recently completed entitled *The Harlot's Progress*. He had originally painted a single picture showing a prostitute in her room, counting her takings. He then hit on the idea of expanding the story by adding paintings, each one illustrating a particular stage in the narrative. His original picture became the third in a series of six paintings which together constituted a new concept, being the first of his 'modern moral narratives', which used the downfall of a particular social type (in this case of a prostitute) to ram home a moral lesson but, as importantly, to highlight hypocrisy and to satirise contemporary society. The engravings were an immediate success bringing Hogarth fame throughout Europe.

Keen to capitalise on this triumph, he immediately started work on *The Rake's Progress* charting the fortunes of Tom Rakewell as he squanders an inheritance, descending, inevitably it would seem, into dissipation, penury and eventual madness. This time Hogarth encapsulated the descent in eight scenes and here we join Tom on his third step down the ladder to Bedlam. He is in the Rose Tavern, a well-known haunt of prostitutes, two of whom have been ministering to his needs but are now taking advantage of his obvious drunkenness to fleece him of his watch and anything else they can get their hands on. One of their compatriots is taking off her stockings in readiness for her part in the continuing entertainment. A man has just entered the room carrying a pewter plate and a candle — accessories which she will use when she dances naked on the table.

After the debauchery of the Rose Tavern we follow Tom into the gambling house, see him as he is arrested for debt and is forced to marry an elderly crone for her money, eventually following him into the prison cell and the madhouse. The locations for these scenes are recognisable (he is arrested in St James's) and indeed a number of the faces in the cacophonous backdrops to Tom's exploits were identifiable as contemporary minor celebrities.

Hogarth was not interested in happy endings. He painted a number of striking portraits, some very moving, like the multiple portrait of his servants, but aside from these, his best work is his coruscating satires of human failings and social pretensions. And he had personal experience of life at the bottom of the pile. His father, a Latin teacher, was consigned to debtor's prison after his attempts to publish a dictionary ended in failure. In Hogarth's day this resulted in the family accompanying the offender into his place of incarceration.

Somewhat ironically, the success he enjoyed with his moral narratives unfortunately resulted in the dashing of his own pretensions as a portraitist; he became pigeonholed, known as the originator of the progresses and was not taken seriously when trying to move on to other things.

Contemporary Works

1733	Jean Siméon Chardin: *La Fontaine*; Stockholm
1734	Giambattista Tiepolo: *Immaculate Conception*; Vicenza
1735	Canaletto: *Bacino di S Marco*; Boston

William Hogarth

1697	Born in London.
1708	Hogarth's father is consigned to the Fleet Prison as a debtor.
1712	His father is released from the Fleet.
1713	Hogarth becomes apprenticed to an engraver.
1720	Has his own engraving business. Enrols in the academy in St Martin's Lane.
1724	One of his early engravings is pirated. The St Martin's Lane academy having closed, Hogarth joins James Thornhill's free academy.
1729	Marries James Thornhill's daughter.
1732	Hogarth publishes engravings of his first 'moral progress' series, the *Harlot's Progress*, based on six oil paintings. It is a great success but pirate copies appear almost immediately.
1735	Sets up a new academy in St Martin's Lane. This became the centre of a circle of likeminded artists. Lobbies Parliament (successfully) urging the passage of a bill establishing copyright for print makers. Publication of the engravings of *Rake's Progress*.
1740	Paints the portrait of his friend Thomas Coram to mark the inauguration of his Foundling Hospital.
1748	Hogarth travels to France with other artists but is arrested as a spy while sketching in Calais. His xenophobic response is to paint *O the Roast Beef of Old England*.
1751	Publishes engravings of Beer Street and Gin Lane.
1753	Publishes his theories on art in *The Analysis of Beauty*.
1757	Becomes Sergeant Painter to the King.
1761	Elected to the committee of the Society of Artists of Great Britain.
1764	Dies at his house in Leicester Fields, London.

Tate Britain is the national gallery of British art from the sixteenth century to the present day.

In 1889 Henry Tate, who had made a fortune from refining sugar, offered his collection of British art to the nation. Furthermore, if the government was willing to donate a site, he also promised to provide a building to house the collection. The offer was accepted and in 1897 the Tate Gallery opened, containing Henry Tate's collection of sixty-seven paintings together with other British works transferred from the National Gallery. The original building forms only a small part of today's gallery which was extended twice in the first decade of the twentieth century.

In 1917 the Tate Gallery was given responsibility for forming a national collection of modern art. More extensions were built in order to house this collection. In 1987 the Clore Gallery extension to the Millbank building was opened to house the Turner bequest. In 1988 Tate Gallery Liverpool was opened, followed in 1993 by Tate Gallery St Ives.

In 1992 the trustees decided to create a new museum for the national collection of modern art, which opened in 2000 leaving Tate Britain to fulfill its original function as a repository for British art.

Note: British twentieth-century artists, some of whom have been exhibited in both galleries, have been listed in this chapter.

Tate Britain

Millbank, London SW1P 4RG
Tel. +44 (0)20 7887 8000
www.tate.org.uk

Opening Hours

Every day 10am – 5.30pm

Admission

Free

How To Get There

The nearest underground station is Pimlico (Victoria Line).
The following bus routes take you to the area: 2, 3, C10, 36, 77A, 88, 159, 185 and 507.
The Tate Boat plies between Tate Modern and Tate Britain also stopping at the London Eye.

Access for the Disabled

Parking spaces and wheelchairs are available on request — telephone 020 7887 8888. The entrance on Atterbury Street has level access with two ramps and handrails. Access to the galleries is by lift and stairs. The Clore Gallery entrance, to the right of the main gallery on Millbank, has level access and a lift to the main gallery floor. The North Entrance on John Islip Street at the back of the gallery has ramp access and parking for disabled visitors.

Gallery Shop

Open Monday to Saturday 10am – 5.30pm. Sunday 10.30am – 5.30pm
The Tate Britain shop stocks an impressive range of art books, posters and prints, stationery, greetings cards, slides and postcards There is also a range of gifts, from silk scarves, watches and jewellery to bags, T shirts and toys.

Gallery Café

Open every day 10am – 5.40pm
For coffee, sandwiches, light meals etc.

Tate Britain Restaurant

For special occasions — reservations recommended: tel. +44 (0)20 7887 8825.

John Constable

Sketch for Hadleigh Castle c1828

Tate Britain

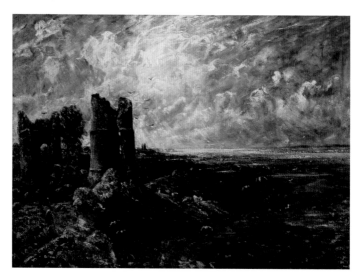

In November 1828 Constable's beloved wife Maria died. Theirs had been a difficult courtship — for many years the disapproval of her parents had precluded any meaningful relationship; they were reduced to clandestine meetings, filling in the gaps as best they could with correspondence. The death of Constable's father in 1816 resulted in a financial settlement which enabled him, in the face of continued displeasure from her family, to marry Maria. However, their long delayed happiness was soon marred by the onset of tuberculosis, the scourge familiar to so many nineteenth-century families. They moved from London to the nearby airy village of Hampstead in an effort to stave off the inevitable decline in her health but just twelve years after their marriage she succumbed leaving John with seven children.

Constable was devastated and never really recovered from his grief. His belated election as a Royal Academician a few months later, after many rebuffs, only seems to have served to heighten his loss. However at about this time he wrote to his great friend John Fisher that despite his depression 'could I get afloat on a canvas of six feet, I might have a chance of being carried away from myself'. And it seems that something like this happened because a few months later he submitted *Hadleigh Castle* to the Academy.

Constable was unique (for his generation and earlier) in often producing full-size oil paintings executed on the spot, some of which were sketches, some more 'finished' ready for the Academy. He painted two versions of *Hadleigh Castle*; the picture shown at the Academy is now at the Yale Center for British Art in the United States. The Tate version is stunningly expressionistic — thick, unmixed paint is applied to the canvas in a frenzy of daubs and dashes which animate the surface with a restless energy. These patches of colour coalesce to give a palpable sense of shifting light as clouds race over the windswept estuary and heath. Constable's mood imbues the exposed estuarine landscape with a dark bleakness — the shepherd and his dog seem to be subsumed in the enveloping loneliness of the scene, a loneliness which of course mirrors the painter's despair at the loss of his wife.

Constable's deeply held conservative beliefs in the virtues of the twin pillars of Parliament and the Church as the immutable bastions of British society found expression in such paintings as the *Hay Wain* through their depiction of the order and peace of the English countryside. But there is very little peace to be found in this picture — the bluish palette increases the cold and desolate feel and the ruined castle echoes the destruction of his own happiness.

Contemporary Works

1826	Thomas Cole: *Daniel Boone and his Cabin at Great Ossage Lake*; Amhurst, MA
	Jean-Baptiste-Camille Corot: *The Forum seen from the Farnese Gardens*; Paris
1830	Eugène Delacroix: *Liberty Leading the People*; Paris

John Constable

1776	Born at East Bergholt in Suffolk, the son of a gentleman farmer who also had a milling business.
1796	Meets Sir George Beaumont who owns Claude Lorrain's *Landscape with Hagar and the Angel*, a painting which inspires the young Constable to pursue his artistic ambitions.
1799	Begins his studies at the Royal Academy Schools.
1802	Exhibited at the Royal Academy for the first time.
1806	Visits the Lake District.
1809	Falls in love with Maria Bicknell, granddaughter of the rector of East Bergholt but her family disapproves.
1811	Visits Salisbury, staying with the Bishop, Dr John Fisher.
1816	The death of his father brings some financial security and despite her family's opposition Constable marries Maria. In December they settle in London.
1819	Constable rents a house in the London suburb of Hampstead, prompted by Maria's illness with tuberculosis. Becomes an ARA.
1820	Visits Salisbury and sketches in the surrounding countryside.
1824	Wins a Gold Medal at the Paris Salon.
1828	Maria dies of tuberculosis leaving seven children.
1829	Belatedly becomes a full member of the Royal Academy.
1837	Dies at Hampstead.

Joseph Mallord William Turner

Norham Castle, Sunrise   c1845-50

Tate Britain

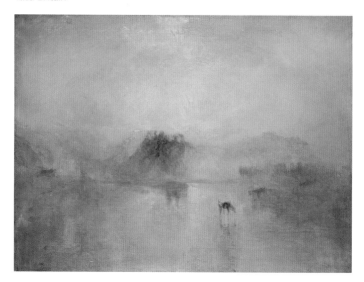

If it were possible to effect a pictorial manifestation of the sublime then surely this is the work which would come nearest to qualifying. If I were ever given the opportunity to choose one painting to accompany me to a desert island this would be it.

A product of his later years, *Norham Castle* epitomises Turner's fascination with the representation of light and colour. Turner's yellows seem to be spiked with some sort of supernatural energy providing a light source which appears to emanate from the canvas itself. How does he do it? When looking at some of his pictures, the illusion is so powerful that one often instinctively shields one's eyes from the glare. Here the effect is more muted, perfectly conveying the more diffused light experienced when the sun is burning off the mist at the dawn of a fine summer day. Indeed, at this moment, the sun is engaged in dispersing the wreaths of mist from the castle, which is represented by a thin glaze of purplish blue. On the left side of the river a skein of mist clings to the surface of the water. In the shallows on the right a cow is drinking, its presence captured by a few dabs of paint but its form dissolved, like everything, by the light of the rising sun.

It was in 1797 that Turner first saw this view of the castle perched on a cliff above the river Tweed, during one of his tours, and it was a view to which he returned on many occasions producing drawings, watercolours and eventually this oil painting dating between 1845 and 1850. This picture was never exhibited at the Royal Academy — it would have been met with a bemused puzzlement and would have provoked a recurrence of the attacks to which some of his exhibited work had been subjected. It may have been a sketch, a precursor to a more 'finished' picture, or it may have been painted for Turner's own personal satisfaction; there is no evidence either way but it is tempting to favour the latter.

Norham Castle represents the culmination of Turner's life-journey from a topographical watercolourist to a visionary genius producing works of profound beauty, works which led the way to a new art, to a new way of representing the effects of light and of perceiving the world. As is well known, his paintings influenced the Impressionists but the radical nature of a work like *Norham Castle* surpasses, in terms of its approach to light and colour, anything produced for many decades after his death, perhaps until the twentieth century.

Contemporary Works

1847	George Caleb Bingham: *Raftsmen Playing Cards*; St Louis
1848	Eugène Delacroix: *The Entombment of Christ*; Boston
1850	Dante Gabriel Rossetti: *Ecce Ancilla Domini (The Annunciation)*; London, Tate Britain
	John Everett Millais: *Christ in the House of His Parents*; London, Tate Britain

Joseph Mallord William Turner

1775	Born in Covent Garden, London, the son of a barber and wig-maker.
1789	He is admitted to the Royal Academy Schools.
1790	At the age of fifteen he exhibits a watercolour at the RA.
1796	He is elected as an Associate Member of the Royal Academy.
1799	Rents a house in Harley St which he later buys. He installs his mistress, probably Hannah Danby, nearby.
1800	Turner's mother is committed to the Royal Bethlehem Hospital as a result of her insanity.
1802	Becomes a full Royal Academician at the age of 26. After the Treaty of Amiens, Turner makes his first visit to continental Europe, visiting Paris then Switzerland.
1804	Turner opens his own gallery in Harley St. His mother dies.
1807	Elected Professor of Perspective at the Royal Academy.
1808	Tours the north of England, which he visits many times over next two decades.
1811	Tours the west of England.
1813	Moves to Solus Lodge, Twickenham, probably built to his own design.
1817	Travels to the battlefield of Waterloo and then to Germany where he sketches in the Rhine gorge before returning to the Low Countries.
1819	Tours Italy, visiting Venice, Rome and Naples.
1821	Tours northern France.
1825	Revisits the Rhineland.
1827-37	Spends much time at Petworth, the home of Lord Egremont, who provides him with a studio.
1828	Returns to Italy and sets up a studio in Rome. His work was not well received.
1829	Turner's father, who had been his constant companion, dies
1835	Visits Copenhagen, Berlin, Dresden and Vienna.
1843	The first volume of *Modern Painters* by John Ruskin appears, much of it devoted to an impassioned defence of Turner who had been the subject of attacks from a conservative faction at the Royal Academy.
1841-4	Visits Switzerland each year basing himself in Lucerne.
1845	Turner's health is deteriorating.
1846	Turner acquires a small house in Chelsea for Mrs Sophia Booth with whom he had frequently stayed on visits to Margate.
1851	Dies in December at Chelsea in west London.

John Everett Millais

Ophelia   1852

Tate Britain

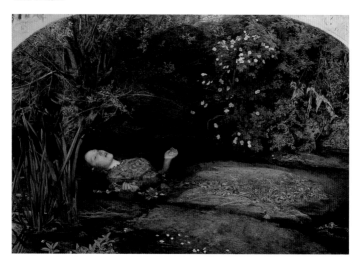

The demented Ophelia, driven to despair after the murder of her
father by her lover Hamlet, is shown here floating in the stream
which will soon close over her, unable to comprehend her fate and still
singing to herself — 'Her clothes spread wide, And mermaid-like, awhile
they bore her up'. She is clutching some of the flowers she picked before
her fall into the brook; others, carried by the current have lodged
themselves in the still buoyant parts of her sumptuous dress, 'but long it
could not be Till that her garments, heavy with their drink, Pull'd the poor
wretch from her melodious lay To muddy death'.

Millais spent many months of intensive work on this composition. At the
beginning of July 1851 he set up his easel by the side of the river Hogsmill
near Ewell in Surrey. There, occasionally plagued by flies, heat and a bull, he
worked with astonishing obsessiveness on the background detail of the
painting, often spending eleven hours a day in front of his canvas. His
obsessive meticulousness was shared by his Pre-Raphaelite colleagues (in
particular William Holman Hunt) in their determined espousal of 'truth to
nature'.

The luminosity of early Pre-Raphaelite work was attained by painting
directly onto a pure white ground. Sometimes, to gain extra intensity the
'wet white' technique was used whereby colour was applied on top of a
white ground which had been laid the same day and it was this technique
that was used by Millais for most of the flowers in this picture, giving them
extra brilliance.

The picture contains a huge variety of flowers and plants all painted with
botanical exactitude, although not all of them would have been flowering
at the same time as they appear in the picture. Many plants are there for
symbolic reasons. The willow gets a big part not only because Shakespeare
mentions it ('There is a willow grows aslant a brook') but because it is

associated with forsaken love. The nettle growing within it, rather obviously, denotes pain, the daisies are associated with innocence, the pansies caught in Ophelia's dress signify love in vain, the poppy is a symbol of death, and so on.

Eventually, in mid-October Millais had finished his labours by the river bank and after his return to London from Surrey it only remained for him to insert the figure of Ophelia. In early December he started work, using as his model Elizabeth Siddal (who met Dante Gabriel Rossetti in 1850 and eventually married him in 1860). Her task was to lie submerged in a bath filled with warm water which was kept at a reasonable temperature by placing lamps beneath the bath. This being Millais, the poor woman was no doubt subjected to this peculiar form of water torture for many hours a day and for many weeks (he did not finish her head until March 1852). A forced break in this bizarre routine was occasioned by the lamps failing one day resulting in Elizabeth catching a severe cold. Millais, threatened with legal action by her father was forced to pay her doctor's bills. Such were the perils inherent in the role of Pre-Raphaelite muse.

Contemporary Works

1851	Gustave Corbet: *Burial at Ornans*; Paris
1852	Arthur Hughes: *Ophelia*; Manchester
1854	Théodore Rousseau: *The Edge of the Woods*; New York

John Everett Millais

1829	Born in Southampton.
1840	Becomes the youngest ever student to attend the Royal Academy Schools.
1846	Has a painting accepted for exhibition at the Royal Academy.
1848	Millais, together with William Holman Hunt, Dante Gabriel Rossetti and others form the Pre-Raphaelite Brotherhood at a meeting at Millais' parental home in Gower St in London.
1849	*Isabella*, his first painting in the Pre-Raphaelite manner is exhibited at the Royal Academy.
1850	The extreme realism of *Christ in the Carpenter's Shop* provokes attacks on grounds of blasphemy.
1852	Exhibits *Ophelia* and *A Huguenot* at the RA to critical acclaim.
1853	Elected ARA. Spends the summer on holiday in Scotland with the critic John Ruskin and his wife Effie. Millais and Effie fall in love.
1854	Ruskin's six-year (unconsummated) marriage to Effie is annulled.
1855	The marriage of Millais and Effie causes a scandal. The couple move to Perth near Effie's parents.
1860's	Increasingly moves away from the tenets of Pre-Raphaelitism.
1870's	Cultivates a highly successful commercial portrait practice.
1885	Created a baronet.
1886	Elected President of the Royal Academy. Dies in London.

John Martin

The Great Day of His Wrath   1853

Tate Britain

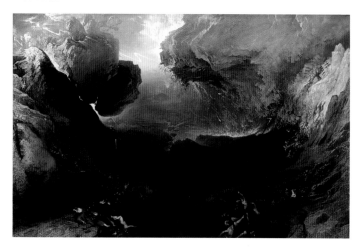

John Martin never lets you down, you always get your money's worth — huge canvases stuffed full of all manner of pyrotechnic effects, supernatural intervention, storms and huge architectural inventions (usually in the process of being destroyed). Romanticism by the yard. Martin really hams it up, but that is his appeal. His vision of nature casts man as a grain of sand in a huge, and sometimes terrifying, universe, reminding us, even in our complacent age, that latent natural forces are capable of unleashing a personal or collective Armageddon at any time.

The Great Day of his Wrath forms one element of the Judgement Pictures, a triptych comprising the Plains of Heaven to the left, The Last Judgement in the centre and this picture concluding the narrative on the right. They are the last major works painted by the artist before his death, the final flourish in an extraordinary catalogue of destruction, cataclysm, awe-inspiring landscapes and natural disasters.

They are based upon the visions of the Last Judgement experienced by St John the Divine and written down as the Revelation, the last book of the New Testament. In this bizarre prophecy, the seven seals of the Book of Judgement are broken by the Lamb. The opening of each seal heralds various apparitions but the breaking of the sixth seal precipitates a truly apocalyptic earthquake:

> and the sun became black ... and the whole moon became as blood ... And every mountain and island were moved out of their places ... And the kings of the earth and the princes ... say to the mountains and to the rocks, Fall on us and hide us from the face of him that sitteth on the throne and from the wrath of the Lamb: For the great day of their wrath is come.

Martin has endeavoured to visualise this passage in concrete terms — a pretty tall order. But he has succeeded triumphantly. The rocks and mountains do indeed tumble in to crush the wretched souls beneath and it is with horror that one notices that the huge mountain being hurled upwards from the right is encrusted with a large city which is about to disappear into the bottomless chasm in the centre of the composition. All is lit by volcanic fire and bolts of white lightning; surely this is as close as one would like to get to the end of the world.

The contemporary response to Martin's pictures was sensational. He often hired halls to exhibit his works and the public flocked to see them. Perhaps it is not too fanciful to see a parallel between his paintings and today's action packed popular American films; Martin was the 'special effects' master of his day.

Contemporary Works

1852	William Holman Hunt: *The Hireling Shepherd*, Manchester
1853	Franz Xavier Winterhalter: *Portrait of the Empress Eugénie Surrounded by Her Maids of Honour*, Compiégne

John Martin

1789	Born in Haydon Bridge, Northumberland.
1803	Apprenticed to a coachmaker in Newcastle upon Tyne.
1804	Martin receives tuition from a Piedmontese painter by the name of Boniface Musso.
1805	Settles in London.
1809	Employed in the glass painting studio of William Collins but works on oil paintings in his spare time.
1810	His first submission to the Royal Academy is rejected.
1812	*Sadak in Search of the Waters of Oblivion* is a success when exhibited at the Royal Academy. The picture is sold and this marks the start of his career.
1821	50,000 people pay to see his painting *Belshazzar's Feast* which is exhibited at the British Institution.
1830's	Martin devotes himself to printmaking but his copyright is constantly infringed by imitators, bringing him to financial disaster.
1851-3	Paints the three huge *Last Judgement* paintings.
1854	Feb: Dies in Douglas, Isle of Man.

William Holman Hunt

The Awakening Conscience   1854

Tate Britain

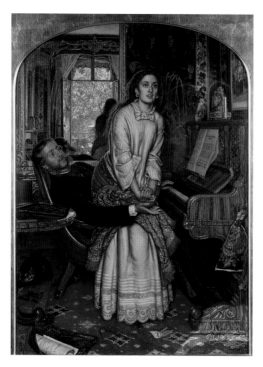

One of the founder members of the Pre-Raphaelite Brotherhood, Hunt always considered himself to be the artistic and intellectual powerhouse of the movement and he was the only one of the core triumvirate (Rossetti and Millais being the other two) to remain faithful to Pre-Raphaelite technique and principles. Always deeply concerned with religious and moral questions, in this painting he confronts the issue of the 'Fallen Woman', the subject of much debate among the Victorian chattering classes and a concern which inspired a number of contemporary novels, including Mrs Gaskell's *Ruth*. Hunt and his circle held liberal views on the subject, his friend Edward Lear writing to him that 'I think with you that it is an artificial lie that a woman should so suffer and lose all, while he who led her … encounters no share of evil from his acts'.

We are transported to the very heartland of the *maison de convenance*, to St John's Wood, a district of north London which was notorious as the location chosen by wealthy gentlemen for the installation of their mistresses — within easy reach of the respectable central areas of the metropolis but just far enough away to avoid embarrassment. Hunt hired Woodbine Villa in St John's Wood and with typical meticulousness and Pre-Raphaelite rigour has captured every aspect of the modern, somewhat vulgar, studiedly bourgeois, interior down to the last exhaustive detail.

A gentleman is slouched on a chair and a young woman has just risen from his lap, a wide-eyed revelatory expression on her face. (Hunt used the beautiful Annie Miller as his model — a working class lass who he had found working in a pub, had infatuated him and whom he was trying to educate). She is wearing a loose-fitting shift which contemporaries would have seen as tantamount to being in a state of 'undress'. But the detail which confirms her status becomes evident when one looks at her left hand — she wears no wedding ring. Hunt underlines the nature of their relationship with a number of further visual hints and symbols. The song which has presumably just been played on the piano and the sheaf of sheet music on the floor (a recently published piece by Lear) both refer to the loss of innocence; the clock on the mantelpiece shows the triumph of Chastity over Cupid. Beneath the table a cat has been toying with a captured bird — its vicious game of ensnarement mirroring the equally cruel motives of the seducer. But the bird looks as if it is about to escape and it is this moment of release, of revelation and recognition which is echoed in the woman's face. She has 'seen the light' which literally and symbolically floods in through the window reflected in the mirror.

Hunt considered this piece to be the earthly counterpart of his painting the *Light of the World*, the famous work which depicts Christ the Saviour holding a lantern. In *The Awakening Conscience* the 'still small voice' is seen at work, entering the soul of the young woman and unleashing a new understanding and the light of redemption.

Contemporary Works

1854	Ford Madox Brown: *An English Autumn Afternoon, Hampstead*; Birmingham
	Gustave Courbet: *Bonjour Monsieur Courbet*; Montpellier

William Holman Hunt

1827	Born in London, the son of a warehouse manager.
1839	Becomes an office clerk but attends drawing classes in the evening.
1844	Finally accepted into the RA Schools after three attempts.
1847	Reads *Modern Painters* by John Ruskin which radically alters his approach to his own painting.
1848	Meets Dante Gabriel Rossetti, and together with John Everett Millais, the three are instrumental in the formation of the Pre-Raphaelite Brotherhood.
1852	His financial circumstances improve with the sale of *The Hireling Shepherd*.
1853	Paints *Light of the World*. His replicas, and the spread of engravings, ensure that this image becomes the most popular religious icon of the 19th century.
1854	Leaves for Egypt. Travels on to Jerusalem.
1855	Visits Nazareth, Damascus and Beirut, making his way home via the Crimea.
1865	Marries Fanny Waugh.
1866	They leave for a journey to Palestine but are detained in Italy by quarantine regulations. Their son is born in Florence. Fanny dies of fever.
1867	Hunt returns to England with his new-born son.
1868	Returns to Florence to work on a memorial to Fanny.
1869	Travels on to Jerusalem which he reaches in August.
1875	Marries Edith Waugh, his deceased wife's sister, in Neuchâtel in Switzerland. Such a union was then illegal in England. They travel on to Jerusalem.
1876	Their daughter is born in Jerusalem.
1878	The family return to England.
1892	Again visits the Middle East.
1905	Awarded the Order of Merit.
1910	Dies in London, his ashes interred in St Paul's Cathedral.

Richard Dadd

Tate Britain

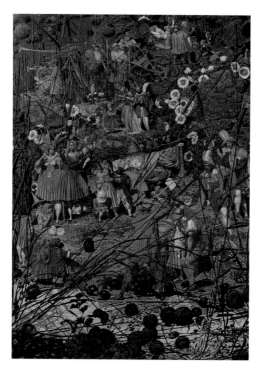

In 1842 Richard Dadd left England with his patron Sir Thomas Phillips on a journey through Europe to the Middle East. It was probably during their visit to Egypt that Dadd's mental health began to deteriorate, becoming convinced that he was receiving messages from the Egyptian god Osiris. Later, in Rome, on the return leg of their trip, Dadd was seized by an irrepressible desire to attack the Pope during a public appearance. He became increasingly violent towards Phillips and on his return to England his family sought the advice of a specialist doctor who counselled that he was indeed insane. Unfortunately, no further measures were taken and in order to give Richard some rest, he and his father travelled to Cobham in Surrey. There, Dadd murdered his father, believing him to be the devil in disguise, and dismembered his body. He fled to France where he attempted to carry out another murder. Apprehended and later extradited to Britain, he was committed to Bethlem Hospital in Lambeth — the infamous Bedlam, now the Imperial War Museum.

The staff at the hospital were supportive and seem to have recognised the importance of his art as a therapy and it was in Bethlem that he painted *The Fairy Feller's Master Stroke*, the second of his two fairy paintings for which he is now famous. Although nominally inspired by *A Midsummer Night's Dream* the picture is really a product of Dadd's fertile imagination. Oberon and Titania can be seen above the central patriarchal figure with the voluminous white beard but the rest of the extraordinary cast is pure invention.

We are down at ground level, strands of grass cutting across our field of vision. We have the feeling that we are secret witness to this strange gathering of miniature folk, hidden as we are behind the vegetation. This multitude of diminutive personages are gathered before us in order to observe the (perhaps) ceremonial cracking of a hazelnut. The fairy woodman stands with his back to us, axe raised above his head, about to make the 'master' stroke, awaiting the signal from the patriarch whose raised hand will soon fall. The patriarch seems to be wearing something akin to a papal tiara on his head — possibly a reference to Dadd's murderous obsession with that office.

The onlookers, 'Fays, gnomes and elves' as Dadd calls them in an explanatory poem, are arrayed in various forms of dress, some contemporary and some historical, each one depicted with obsessionally minute detail, the influence of Blake and Fuseli detectable in some passages. To the left two women are portrayed with exaggerated breasts and tightly corseted-waists — Dadd devoted a number of lines in his poem to these two ladies and they may well be the product of the sexual frustration he must have experienced during his incarceration. Above the Shakespearian fairy king and queen, a line of figures represent the characters in the children's rhyme 'soldier, sailor, tinker, tailor', which in Dadd's day continued 'ploughboy, apothecary, thief'. On the evidence of a portrait drawn by Dadd before his illness, the penultimate member of this group bears a strong resemblance to his dead father who was an apothecary. It is difficult to imagine what emotions Dadd would have experienced while working on this part of his extraordinary work.

Contemporary Works

1857	Jean-François Millet; The Gleaners; Paris
1859	Arthur Hughes: The Long Engagement; Birmingham
1863	Édouard Manet: Déjeuner sur l'Herbe; Paris

Richard Dadd

1817	Born in Chatham, Kent, the fourth child of Robert Dadd, an apothecary.
1834	Dadd's family move to London.
1837	Enters the Royal Academy Schools where he becomes friends with Augustus Egg and William Powell Frith.
1841	His painting Titania Sleeping is a critical success. Dadd is commissioned to produce over a hundred panels for the home of Lord Foley.
1842	Journeys through Europe to the Middle East making many drawings. His mental health begins to show sign of deterioration whilst in Egypt.
1843	Returns from the Middle East. Becomes increasingly violent. In August he stabs his father to death, fleeing to France where he attempts another murder.
1844	After spending some time in a French asylum he is extradited to Britain. He is certified insane and committed to the criminal lunatic wing of Bethlem Hospital in London. Continues to paint throughout his many years of incarceration, mostly in watercolour.
1855	Starts work on the Fairy Feller's Master-Stroke.
1857	Six of Dadd's paintings are exhibited at the Manchester Art Treasures Exhibition.
1864	He is transferred to the newly opened secure hospital at Broadmoor.
1886	Still incarcerated in Broadmoor, Dadd dies of consumption.

James Abbott McNeill Whistler

Nocturne in Blue and Gold: Old Battersea Bridge 1875

Tate Britain

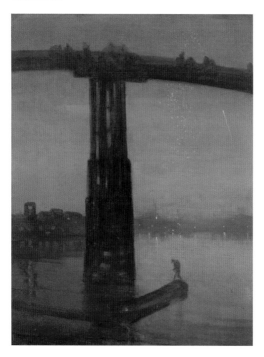

Whistler left the United States — never to return — some twenty years before the completion of this painting, settling in Paris where he mixed with the likes of Manet, Courbet and Monet. A few years later he moved to London which became his home for much of the rest of his life, first taking rooms in the dockland area of Wapping and later moving up the river to the more salubrious location of Chelsea. The Thames, the link between these two homes, became his principal muse.

This picture is one of a series of views of the Thames by night which he entitled 'Nocturnes'. The term was inspired by the Chopin piano pieces of the same name possibly at the suggestion of Whistler's patron, F. R. Leyland, for whom he produced the stunning *Peacock Room* at about this time. He later used other musical expressions in his titles including Arrangement, Symphony and Variation and retrospectively changed existing titles.

The picture shows one of the massive piers of the old wooden bridge extending to a much exaggerated height. A section of the bridge arcs across the top of the composition: our viewpoint is from below. A somewhat formless blob of darker paint denotes a boatman steering his craft like Charon across the Styx. Some fireworks are represented with flecks of gold, otherwise colour is constrained to a very narrow range. In a letter to his friend Henri Fantin-Latour, Whistler explained that 'the same colour ought to appear in the picture continually here and there … in this way the whole will form a harmony. Look how well the Japanese understood this'.

Whistler's admiration for the stylised simplicity of Japanese art can be plainly seen in this piece, based as it is directly on similar Japanese motifs.

Whistler is not concerned with making an exact naturalistic representation of Old Battersea Bridge. He believed — in line with the ideals of the Aesthetic Movement, of which he was a key propagandist, thinker and exponent — that art should not be slavishly descriptive or aspire to representational accuracy, nor should it be concerned with matters such as morality or instruction. Rather a painting should be appreciated as a beautiful object in its own right, its composition and colour harmonies being of more aesthetic value than mere subject matter: in other words 'art for art's sake'. In the Nocturnes — and especially in the famous *Nocturne in Black and Gold: The Falling Rocket* — Whistler pushed these ideas to their logical conclusion; he was flirting on the fringes of abstraction.

In this he found himself on a collision course with Ruskin whose battle cry of 'Truth to Nature' had had a deep impact on many artists, not least the youthful Pre-Raphaelites. Ruskin's reaction on seeing The Falling Rocket was to write his infamous letter to The Times, castigating Whistler for 'flinging a pot of paint in the public's face'. The celebrated court case ensued but that is another story…

Contemporary Works

1873	Pierre Puvis de Chavannes: *Summer*, Paris
1875	Hilaire-Germain-Edgar Degas: *The Dancing Examination*, Paris

James Abbott McNeill Whistler

1834	Born in Lowell, Massachusetts, the son of a railway engineer.
1843	His family moves to St Petersburg.
1848	Lives with his step-sister in England. Attends lectures at the Royal Academy.
1849	Returns to the USA after his father's death.
1851	Enters West Point Military Academy.
1854	Dismissed from West Point after failing his chemistry examination.
1855	Determined to become an artist he leaves America for France.
1856	Attends Charles Gleyre's studio in Paris.
1859	The Salon rejects *At the Piano*. Moves to London taking rooms at Wapping.
1861	*Symphony in White No. 1: The White Girl* is rejected by the Royal Academy and by the Salon.
1863	*The White Girl* hangs with *Déjeuner sur l'herbe* at the Salon des Refusés. Moves from Wapping to Chelsea, near Rossetti. His mother moves to live with him.
1865	Paints at Trouville with Courbet and Monet.
1866	Travels to Chile.
1872	*Arrangement in Grey and Black; Portrait of the Artist's Mother* is exhibited at the Royal Academy.
1877	*Nocturne in Black and Gold: the Falling Rocket* is exhibited at the Grosvenor Gallery. Ruskin writes to *The Times*. Whistler sues for libel.
1878	Whistler wins his libel case against Ruskin but is awarded a farthing in damages.
1879	Facing huge legal costs, Whistler is declared bankrupt losing his newly constructed house. He destroys work rather than see it go to creditors.
1880	Leaves for Venice to undertake a commission for etchings.
1885	Delivers his Ten o'clock Lecture advocating his aesthetic ideas.
1888	Marries Beatrice Godwin.
1894	Beatrice becomes ill with cancer.
1896	Beatrice dies.
1903	Dies in London.

Edward Burne-Jones

King Cophetua and the Beggar Maid 1884

Tate Britain

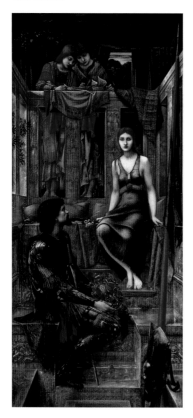

The story of King Cophetua is told in an early seventeenth-century ballad which later formed the basis for a short poem by Tennyson. One day, the king whilst idly looking out of his window saw among the beggars at the palace gate a girl of such exquisite beauty that he had her brought to him and immediately vowed to make her his queen.

Burne-Jones depicts this meeting: the young maid sits wide eyed in the sumptuous surroundings of Cophetua's palace seemingly struck dumb by this decidedly unexpected turn of events. The king sits at her feet equally stunned by her beauty. Two singers self-consciously study their music perhaps awaiting a sign from Cophetua or maybe just waiting for him to come to his senses. But they are all lost in a timeless moment — beauty has prevailed over privilege and power.

They sit in a highly implausible setting. Of course we are in the midst of a fairy tale, but it is difficult to envisage the precise use to which this room could be put. And yet one feels that it would be possible to feel at home in it; drapes and cushions give it a comfortable ambience. Through the open door or window the sun is setting, enhancing that sense of a golden yet evanescent experience.

The maid is clad in a very curious outfit — not exactly rags, a touch threadbare perhaps, but certainly not the usual Burne-Jonesian loose-fitting robe either. Apparently he agonised over her attire — she must be suitably down at heel but on the other hand not too beggarly lest the king should be put off. According to the ballad, Cophetua was African and so Burne-Jones has given him a Moorish complexion with tightly curled black hair. The king is kitted out in a mythic suit of armour which looks as though it has been partly modelled on the scales of a large (possibly prehistoric) fish. His crown, which he has taken off as if in the presence of a higher being, was based on a metalwork model specially made to the artist's specifications.

Burne-Jones visited Italy on four occasions. He greatly admired Botticelli as well as Michelangelo. But here the highly decorated architectural setting in which the king and the maid sit betrays Burne-Jones' admiration for Mantegna and especially Carlo Crivelli (see page 84)

Yet Burne-Jones mixes these Italian Renaissance influences with his highly personal medievalism. And this personal vision became immensely popular during the last quarter of the nineteenth century. When this picture was exhibited at the Grosvenor Gallery in 1884 it was received with rapturous reviews. *The Times* thought that it was 'not only the finest work that Mr Burne-Jones has ever painted, but one of the finest ever painted by an Englishman'. This sort of opinion was not confined to Britain. In France it attracted such admiration that the artist was awarded the *Légion d'honneur*.

The best explanation for the secret behind Burne-Jones' appeal comes from the man himself. His pictures, he said, are 'a beautiful romantic dream of something that never was, never will be … in a land no-one can define, or remember, only desire'.

Contemporary Works

1883	Arnold Böcklin: *Odysseus and Calypso*; Basel
1884	Georges Seurat: *Bathers at Asnières*; London, National Gallery
1886	Mary Cassatt: *Young Woman Sewing*; Paris

Edward Burne-Jones

1833	Born in Birmingham. His mother dies shortly after his birth.
1853	Begins his studies at Exeter College, Oxford, destined for the church. Meets William Morris.
1855	After a tour of French cathedrals and inspired by Ruskin's writings, Burne-Jones and Morris decide to follow artistic vocations.
1856	Meets Dante Gabriel Rossetti. Settles in London.
1857	Collaborates with Rossetti and others in decorating the Oxford Union.
1859	Visits Italy.
1860	Marries Georgiana Macdonald.
1861	Burne-Jones is involved in the founding of Morris, Marshall, Faulkner & Co. being particularly involved in the design of stained glass windows.
1862	Visits Italy again with Ruskin.
1871	Visits Florence, Pisa, Orvieto, Rome etc.
1873	Again in Italy.
1877	Exhibits eight pictures at the opening exhibition of the Grosvenor Gallery. They are a great critical success.
1878	Gives evidence in support of Ruskin in the case brought by Whistler against Ruskin. Enjoys success exhibiting his work in Paris.
1894	Created a baronet.
1898	Dies at Fulham.

John Singer Sargent

Carnation, Lily, Lily, Rose   1886

Tate Britain

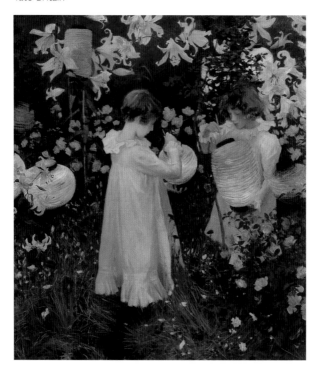

Sargent is chiefly known as a society portrait painter although a glance at this composition will reveal that this description of him does not do justice to the range of his art. Trained in the Parisian studio of the fashionable portraitist Charles Carolus-Duran, he was soon competing with his mentor for the custom of the most glamorous clients in Paris. However, it was one such society portrait of 1884 which precipitated a decision to move from Paris to London. His mildly louche portrait of 'Madame X' draped in a revealing evening gown was considered to be too provocative by some of the more conservative elements in the French art world. Sargent was offended and, after some prevarication, decided to move across the channel.

He spent the summers of 1885 and 1886 as the guest of an American amateur painter in the beautiful Cotswold village of Broadway which was at the time frequented during the summer and early autumn by a number of British and American artists. It was here that he decided to recreate on canvas a scene which he had witnessed some time before of two girls in a garden, amidst beds of lilies, engaged in lighting Chinese lanterns at twilight. He dressed the two daughters of a local Broadway friend in white dresses and set to work on a number of preparatory sketches.

But he found that the special light which accompanies the waning of a summer evening, and which he wanted to capture, could only be glimpsed for a few minutes. His work on this composition was consequently restricted to a very short interlude each day. Sargent usually worked with some speed but the exigencies of painting this picture led him to become frustrated — he wrote to his sister about this 'Fearful difficult subject. Impossible brilliant colours… Paints not bright enough, and then the effect only lasts ten minutes.' Unable to finish the painting during his first sojourn at Broadway he was obliged to pack it away and resume the following summer.

The title he gave to the piece comes from a popular nonsense song of the time — in answer to the question 'Have you seen my Flora pass this way' the answer is 'Carnation, Lily, Lily, Rose'. The exasperated Sargent privately dubbed the work 'Darnation, Silly, Silly, Pose'. However, when it was eventually exhibited at the Royal Academy in 1887, the painting was a huge success, it was immediately bought for the nation and its popularity has continued to this day.

Sargent's technique — having just decamped from the city of Impressionism — is a synthesis of Impressionist exuberance, especially in the treatment of the lilies and background foliage, and a more controlled and measured style for such areas as the children's faces.

The picture is a superb evocation of that sublime, transient moment in a summer evening when the fading light seems to play tricks with one's senses and actually intensifies the colour of garden flowers. The use of children as his protagonists enhances the inherent nostalgia of the piece — we all have powerful memories of childhood episodes which are recalled with a heightened sense of perfection. This picture fixes one such instance.

Contemporary Works

1886	Pierre Auguste Renoir: *The Umbrellas*; London, National Gallery
	Georges Seurat: *A Sunday on La Grande Jatte*; Chicago
1887	Atkinson Grimshaw: *Liverpool Quay by Moonlight*; London, Tate Britain

John Singer Sargent

1856	Born in Florence to wealthy expatriate American parents.
1874	Enters the studio of Charles Carolus-Duran in Paris.
1877	His portrait of Miss Fanny Watts is accepted by the Salon.
1884	His portrait of 'Madame X' is attacked on grounds of being decadent. This minor scandal persuades Sargent he should move to London.
1885-6	Spends the late summer of both years at Broadway in the Cotswolds, the guest of an American doctor.
1886	Settles in London permanently following encouragement by his friend Henry James.
1887	Visits the USA (his second trip) where he is fêted, receiving numerous commissions.
1894	Accepts a commission to paint a series of murals at the Boston Public Library.
1907	At the height of his fame as the pre-eminent portrait painter in both Britain and the USA, Sargent announces that he will accept no further portrait commissions. Exceptions are in fact made for friends.
1916	Begins work on murals for the Boston Museum of Fine Arts. Visits the Rocky Mountains.
1918	Visits the front in France and produces watercolours and other works such as *Gassed*.
1925	Dies in London.

Stanley Spencer

Tate Britain

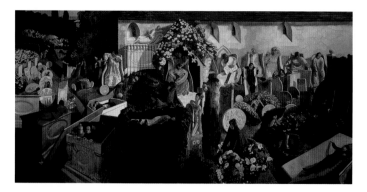

Stanley Spencer's childhood in Cookham, a pleasant Thames-side village in Berkshire, was so blissful that he came to see these environs as a specially hallowed corner of creation. When he attended the Slade School of Art in London he did so as a day student, travelling back to Berkshire each evening (his contemporaries nicknaming him 'Cookham'). Spencer wrote 'When I left the Slade and went back to Cookham, I entered a kind of earthly paradise'. His experiences during the Great War, serving first with the Medical Corps in Macedonia and then as an infantryman, shattered his pre-war idyll, but only reinforced his mystical belief in Cookham as a personal Arcadia. He returned to his native village after the war and continued where he had left off, using it as a backdrop for a series of biblical compositions such as the *Last Supper* and *Christ's Entry into Jerusalem*.

The Resurrection, Cookham is the most ambitious single work of this period and it was the centrepiece of a one-man exhibition at the Goupil Gallery in London in 1927. It was immediately purchased for the nation at the handsome price of £1,000. *The Times* hailed it as '…the most important picture painted by any English artist in the present century…'.

Almost hidden in the gloom of the porch, God the Father presides over the resurrection of the dead who stir from their graves in Cookham churchyard and miraculously assume the corporeal form of their former lives. Lined against the wall of the church we can see a number of white-robed prophets including Moses holding his tablets and pointing to the first Commandment.

In front the Almighty, sitting beneath the profusely flowering white climbing rose which obscures the structure of the porch, is a Madonna figure nursing not one but three children. This figure may be modelled on Spencer's first wife, Hilda Carline, whom he married in 1925 and who also appears as if deep in sleep enfolded in an ivy nest atop a tomb surrounded by railings. Spencer himself stands naked in a central position, arms resting rather jauntily on a pair of tombstones: the fully clothed man lying on top of two unstable brick tombs, looking rather like a giant book that might snap shut at any minute, is also him. The couple appear again near the left edge of the painting where Hilda smells a yellow flower and Stanley watches her from the top of a tomb.

To the left of the porch, a section of the churchyard (the earth cracked by heat and drought, contrasting with the lush grass which surrounds it) is host to a small community of black bodies struggling from their places of burial. Spencer's intentions here seem to have been that their presence was symbolic of the inclusive nature of his vision — to emphasise that all humanity will experience this moment, not just the inhabitants of a comfortable part of the Thames Valley. Soon, every emergent soul will walk from the churchyard, through the gate and onto a Thames pleasure cruiser (two of which can be seen in the top left corner of the composition). Presumably these have been pressed, Dunkirk-like, into unlikely action by some heavenly bureaucracy for the journey along the Thames to Heaven — a paradise which, in Spencer's eyes will no doubt look very much like the village they have just left.

Contemporary Works

1923	Max Ernst: *Ubu Imperator*, Paris
1924	Pierre Bonnard: *Signac and his Friends Sailing*, Zurich
1926	René Magritte: *The Menaced Assassin*, New York

Stanley Spencer

1891	Born in Cookham, Berkshire, on the Thames to the west of London.
1907	Attends Maidenhead Technical Institute, Berkshire.
1908	Enrols at the Slade School in London.
1915	Joins the Army Medical Corps, serving in Macedonia.
1918	After volunteering as an infantryman with the Royal Berkshire Regiment, Spencer was eventually appointed as a War Artist. After the war he returns to Cookham.
1923	He is commissioned to decorate the Sandham Memorial Chapel in Burghclere, Hampshire, in memory of Lieutenant Henry Sandham who had been killed in Macedonia.
1925	Marries the painter Hilda Carline.
1927	One-man exhibition at the Goupil Gallery London.
1932	Completes the decoration of the Sandham Memorial Chapel. Elected as an Associate Member of the Royal Academy.
1935	Resigns from the RA after the committee refuses to hang two of his submissions.
1940	Spencer is appointed as a War Artist and is commissioned to paint the ship-building yards of Port Glasgow.
1950	His quarrel with the Royal Academy ends and he is made a full Academician.
1954	Visits China as a member of a cultural delegation.
1955	A retrospective of his work is held at the Tate Gallery.
1958	He accepts a knighthood.
1959	Dies in Cliveden, Berkshire.

Francis Bacon

Three Studies for Figures at the Base of a Crucifixion   1944

Tate Britain

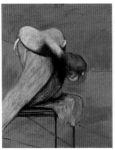 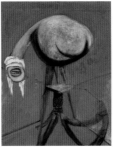 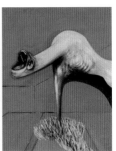

This was Bacon's first mature work. It was completed in 1944 shortly after the artist devoted himself to painting full time. Although an early work it is quintessential Bacon encapsulating the horror, pain and revulsion which are essential elements of his output. Of course the timing of its execution during the climax of the most destructive war in history must have been influential. The work was exhibited in London in 1945 and according to one critic it 'caused total consternation'. One can imagine that this would not have been an exaggeration.

Each part of the triptych contains a bestial mass of amorphous flesh imprisoned in a nightmare space of livid orange. Each of these indeterminate creatures has a phallus-like neck; the central beast, its body reminiscent of something from the darker passages of a Bosch triptych, turns its neck towards the viewer, a grotesque mouth to the fore; some sort of cloth forms a blindfold but perhaps these creatures are without eyes. The being in the right wing of the triptych certainly seems to be blind but we cannot know for sure as its mouth is so extended in a silent howl that any eyes may be obscured. The creature in the left hand panel seems to be cowed into a state of enforced introspection, perched on a table, swathed in, or perhaps bound by, a clashing violet and orange cloth, head lowered in mute subjection.

According to the artist these images represent the Eumenides — the Furies of Greek drama; Bacon may have been influenced here by T. S. Eliot whose play *The Family Reunion*, in which the Eumenides play a part, was first performed in 1939. The use of the triptych is interesting — of course it has obvious connections with centuries of Christian imagery but the artist was not a believer and his use of this format, strongly linked as it is with the Crucifixion, is more to do with its place in the portrayal of human suffering.

Bacon's long fascination with the depiction of the cry or the scream takes flight in this picture and continued in such iconic works as the *Screaming Pope* (to use the popular title). The roots of this fascination can be traced to an interest in photography and film, specifically to a still from the Eisentein film *Battleship Potemkin* showing the scream of a woman who has just been shot on the Odessa Steps, and to later Surrealist photographs and writings and even to clinical books on oral disease.

The list of sources is wide ranging but Bacon draws from them a very personal and intensely shocking vision of human frailty and suffering.

Contemporary Works

1943	Piet Mondrian: *Broadway Boogie-Woogie*; New York
1945	René Magritte: *The Rape*; Paris
1946	Pablo Picasso: *La Joie de Vivre*; Antibes

Francis Bacon

1909	Born in Dublin to English parents. He is brought up in Ireland. Because of ill health he receives very little formal education.
1927	Leaves home – lives in Berlin (then the capital of European decadence) and in Paris.
1929	Returns to London. Tries his hand at interior decoration and painting but the next ten years are characterised by drift.
1943	Commits himself to becoming a full-time artist having been excused military service as a result of his asthma.
1945	*Three Studies for Figures at the Base of a Crucifixion* causes a sensation when first exhibited at the Lefevre Gallery in London.
1950's	Develops an international reputation.
1960's	His partner George Dyer becomes the subject of many paintings.
1971	Dyer dies the day before the opening of a major retrospective of Bacon's work in Paris.
1992	Bacon dies during a visit to Madrid.

David Hockney

Tate Britain

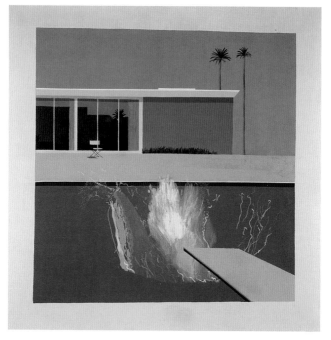

Born in Bradford in 1937, David Hockney had already become a success in Britain when, late in 1963, he arrived in Los Angeles, a city which had fascinated him for a long time. 'Within a week of arriving there in this strange big city, not knowing a soul, I'd passed the driving test, bought a car, driven to Las Vegas and won some money, got myself a studio, started painting, all within a week. And I thought, it's just how I imagined it would be.'

Perhaps only those who experienced the grey drabness of 1950s Britain can understand the full intensity of this culture shock. Another work in the Tate collection acts as a reminder; Carel Weight's *The Dogs* shows a crowd leaving a south London greyhound stadium. Although a beautiful sunset illuminates the scene, the mood remains relentlessly downbeat, the crowd dressed almost uniformly in grey, trudge home, unaware of the spectacular sky, shoulders hunched, heads down. Hockney left all that behind him and embraced the light and colour of California (as well as a number of beautiful young men). This picture is a celebration of that dazzling light and the lifestyle he now enjoyed.

In 1966 he had painted a small piece called *The Little Splash* which he completed in about two days. Later that year he produced a larger version, *The Splash* but, he tells us in his book *David Hockney by David Hockney*, 'I thought the background was perhaps slightly fussy, the buildings were a little too complicated, not quite right. So I decided I'd do a third version, a big one using a very simple building and strong light.' So in 1967 *A Bigger Splash* took shape.

Hockney had switched to acrylic paint which chimed in well with the intense light producing flat, bold colours — he tells us that he used a roller to apply the broad areas of paint in *A Bigger Splash*. There are almost no shadows, just an overwhelming sense of heat and penetrating light. A single chair swelters at the poolside, two slender palm trees rise into the featureless sky, the blind glass of the low-rise house reflects another palm behind us. A diver has just departed from the diving board a split second before; he has broken the unnaturally becalmed surface of the pool and has disappeared beneath the water causing the eponymous splash to erupt. In contrast to the rapid application of the flat background planes of acrylic Hockney worked intensively on the splash using fine brushes in his effort to capture a frozen instant.

In a minute fraction of a second gravity will recall the plumes of water which now hang at their apogee, and the placid surface of the pool will be disrupted. In another second the re-emergence of the diver will cause more ripples. But for now we can stand for as long as we want, as though we are in a realm in which the laws of time have ceased to work, enabling us to contemplate the light, the heat and the silence, the diver permanently consigned to the blue-tiled depths.

Contemporary Works

1967	Andy Warhol: *Electric Chair*, Paris
1969	Patrick Heron: *Cadmium with Violet, Scarlet, Emerald, Lemon and Venetian*; London, Tate Britain

David Hockney

1937	Born in Bradford.
1953	Enrols at Bradford College of Art.
1957	As a conscientious objector Hockney spends two years working in hospitals as a substitute for national service.
1959	Begins a postgraduate course at the Royal College of Art.
1961	Visits New York.
1962	Awarded the Royal College of Art Gold Medal. Visits Berlin.
1963	Completes a series of prints which are a modern version of Hogarth's *Rake's Progress*. Visits Egypt. Travels to Los Angeles.
1964	Settles in Los Angeles. Teaches at the University of Iowa.
1965	Teaches at the University of Colorado.
1967	Spends ten weeks teaching at Berkeley.
1968	Returns to Britain with his lover Peter Schlesinger.
1970	Hockney's relationship with Schlesinger breaks up. A major retrospective exhibition of his work is put on at the Whitechapel Art Gallery in London.
1973	Lives for a time in Paris.
1975	Designs sets for the Glyndebourne Opera production of Stravinsky's *The Rake's Progress*.
1978	Design's sets for Mozart's *Magic Flute* at the Metropolitan Opera in New York. Returns to live permanently in Los Angeles.
1982	Develops a photo-collage technique, taking hundreds of photographs of a subject and then piecing them together to form an image.
1986	Starts to produce work using a colour photocopier and fax machine.
1996	A retrospective of his drawings is mounted at the Royal Academy Continues to live in Los Angeles.

David Inshaw

Tate Britain

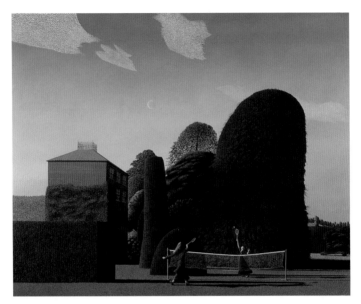

David Inshaw has given us a most enchanting image — a beautifully conceived conceit. His technique enables him to craft a wonderful intensity. Each leaf and each blade of grass seems to have been individually painted. It is almost Pre-Raphaelite in its precision. However, the painting transcends mere verisimilitude for it is this very meticulousness that seems in some way to be the catalyst for the sense of mystery which emanates from it.

The artist conjures a scene which awakens in us a flash of recognition, not that we know the place but that we ought to know it, that we should like to know it, that maybe we will stumble across it in our dreams. The scene is a proxy for those fragments of life which are filed away only to be recalled in flashes of delicious nostalgia. It stands for all those moments which fix themselves in our memory. To quote T. S. Eliot:

'… the moment in the rose-garden,
The moment in the arbour when the rain beat
The moment in the draughty church at smokefall.'

And yet the idyll is by no means perfect. One remembers that dreams have a habit of turning nasty. The towering evergreen trees dwarf the two badminton players — a vague just-discerned feeling of unease inhabits the topiary. Perhaps this is because, as the artist has told us, he remembers being in love with both of the badminton players. The long shadows tell us that the light will soon fade, ending the game. The two women will presently move towards the house. And we suddenly comprehend that this is no ordinary dwelling, it exudes a slightly nightmarish quality. The red brick wall which faces us appears to have no openings and is fast succumbing to the choking ivy which before long will be at the roof. The other visible wall is topped by blank windows. How do the rooms on lower floors receive any sunlight? How does one get in? Presumably there is an entrance around the other side but, were it possible for us to walk on that lush grass, past the cool high hedges and the blue hydrangea, it wouldn't be a complete surprise to find that like Alice, we had entered a world where the usual rules do not apply.

Contemporary Works

1971	David Hockney: *Mr and Mrs Clark and Percy*; London, Tate Britain
1973	Gerhard Richter: *1024 Colours*; Paris
	Anselm Kiefer: *Resurrexit*; Amsterdam

David Inshaw

1943	Born in Wednesfield, Staffordshire.
1950	The family moves to Biggin Hill in Kent.
1963-66	Studies at the Royal Academy Schools.
1964	Awarded a French Government scholarship and lives in Paris.
1967	Moves to Bristol where he teaches painting.
1969	First one-man exhibition at the Arnolfini Gallery, Bristol.
1971	Moves to live in Devizes, Wiltshire.
1975	The Brotherhood of Ruralists is formed comprising David Inshaw, Peter Blake, Graham and Ann Arnold, Jann Howarth and Graham and Annie Ovendon. Resigns from teaching post at Bristol. Appointed Fellow Commoner in Creative Art at Trinity College, Cambridge.
1983	Resigns from the Brotherhood of Ruralists.
1989	Moves to Clyro on the Welsh border.
1995	Moves back to Devizes..
2004	Solo Exhibition at Agnews, London.

The original Bankside Power Station, now home to Tate Modern, was designed by Sir Giles Gilbert Scott who was also the architect of the Liverpool Anglican cathedral and the famous red telephone boxes which used to be such a feature of the British urban landscape. It was built in two phases between 1947 and 1963.

In the late 1980s it became clear that the collection at the Tate Gallery had outgrown its home on Millbank. It was decided to create a new gallery to house the Tate's international modern art. The decision to convert the redundant Bankside Power Station was an inspired choice. An international architectural competition was held, with over seventy architectural practices entering. The final choice was the Swiss architects Jacques Herzog and Pierre de Meuron.

Decomissioning work began in 1995 with contruction of the new gallery starting in 1996. Tate Modern was opened to the public on 12 May 2000.

Please note that because of the size and nature of the Tate collection, and because the collection is spread over four sites, it is unlikely that all of the chosen paintings will be on display at Tate Modern at the same time.

You will also note that the hanging policy of Tate Modern is to arrange works thematically but I have decided to maintain the convention employed in previous chapters by ordering the chosen works chronologically.

Tate Modern

Bankside, London SE1 9TG
Tel. +44 (0)20 7887 8000

Opening Hours

Sunday to Thursday 10am – 6pm
Friday and Saturday 10am – 8pm
Closed 24, 25, 26 December (Open 1 January)

Admission

Free

How To Get There

The nearest underground stations are Southwark (Jubilee Line) and Blackfriars (District and Circle Lines). Both are about ten minutes walk from the gallery.

The Tate Boat runs every forty minutes along the Thames between Tate Britain and Tate Modern, stopping at the London Eye.

The RV1 bus runs direct to Tate Modern from Covent Garden and the following buses stop either at Blackfriars Bridge Road or in Southwark: 45, 63, 100, 381, 344.

Access for the Disabled

All levels are accessible by lifts from either the North or West entrance. Ten wheelchairs are available on request for visitors; to book a wheelchair telephone +44 (0)20 7887 8888.

Gallery Shop

Open Sunday to Thursday 10am – 6pm; Friday and Saturday 10am – 8pm

The shops at Tate Modern stock a range of books which extends to 10,000 titles as well as postcards, posters, prints and gift items.

Tate Modern Restaurant and Café

The restaurant is situated on Level 7 with spectacular views over London. Open Sunday to Thursday 10am – 6pm; Friday and Saturday 10am – 9pm (Last orders 7.30pm). To book telephone +44 (0)207 401 5020.

The café on Level 2 provides a more informal menu as well as coffee and light refreshments. It is open Sunday to Thursday 10am – 6pm; Friday and Saturday 10am – 8pm.

Gustav Klimt

Portrait of Hermine Gallia 1904

Tate Modern

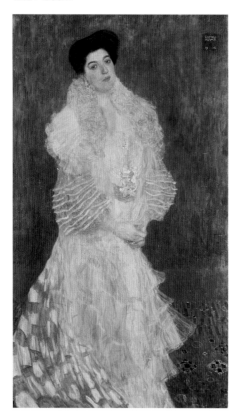

K limt is sometimes dismissed as merely a decorative artist — implying membership of some sort of sub-category operating below the exalted levels of 'great' art. But his landscapes and his erotic drawings speak otherwise, as do his portraits.

It is true that the women (for they are nearly all women) in his portraits are invariably depicted against decorative backgrounds which are not explicitly three-dimensional. Indeed, in a famous example, the first of his two portraits of Adele Bloch-Bauer, the sitter's body and dress are dissolved in a swirl of stunning golden decoration. But this does not detract from the skill with which Klimt teased out the essentials of the personality and character of his sitters even though they have to compete for attention with his sumptuous backgrounds or with the elaborate dresses which Klimt delighted in further elaborating. And so it is with his *Portrait of Hermine Gallia*.

Hermine's head is held slightly to one side, she looks out at the viewer through limpid eyes, a certain melancholy pervading her features. Compared to the profusion of gold leaf used in his later portrait of Adele Bloch-Bauer or the richly coloured backgrounds of his last portraits, he is relatively subdued is his choice of colouring for this picture. There is a hint of space behind the figure, the carpet pattern seems to be shown in perspective but even so we are not at all sure how Hermine fits into the space. She is dressed in a truly fabulous confection; unfortunately we may not be seeing the true colours chosen by Klimt — the pigments in this picture have degraded over the years. Nevertheless, we can see what a tour de force this exotic creation must have been.

Klimt's portraits have a dual function — they are profoundly satisfying records of elegant women from the first two decades of twentieth-century Vienna but they also often function as semi-abstract exercises exploring the use of colour and pattern. Above all they are ravishingly beautiful.

Contemporary Works

1904	Pierre Auguste Renoir: *Portrait of Misia Sert*; London, National Gallery
	Henri Matisse: *Luxe, Calme et Volupté*; Paris
1905	Pablo Picasso: *Saltimbanques*; Washington

Gustav Klimt

1862	Born at Baumgarten near Vienna (July).
1876	Enters the School of Applied Art (Kunstgewerbeschule) in Vienna.
1879	Starts working with his brother Ernst and a fellow student Franz Matsch on a number of projects.
1883	Completes his studies and forms the Artists' Company (Kunstlercompagnie), opening a studio with his brother and Matsch.
1888	The Artists' Company complete decorative work on the staircases of the new Burgtheater in Vienna.
1891	The Company works on the decoration of the staircase at the Kunsthistorisches Museum in Vienna.
1892	Klimt's brother Ernst dies.
1894	Klimt and Matsch are commissioned to paint the ceiling of the grand auditorium at Vienna University (known as the 'Faculty Paintings').
1897	The Vienna Secession is founded with Klimt as first president.
1898	The First Secession exhibition takes place.
1900	Exhibits one of the unfinished paintings for the university, representing Philosophy, to a storm of protest centred on its suitability for its intended home.
1901	Klimt exhibits *Medicine*, the second of the pictures destined for the university. A similar furore erupts, leading to the matter being debated in the Austrian Parliament.
1905	Klimt renounces the contracts for the 'Faculty Paintings' and buys them himself. He resigns from the Secession.
1908	Exhibits 16 paintings at the Kunstschau in Vienna. His iconic work, *The Kiss* is bought by the Austrian State Gallery.
1911	The Villa Stoclet is completed in Brussels with a frieze designed by Klimt for the dining room combining mosaic and painted panels.
1913	Spends the summer at Lake Garda.
1918	Suffers a stroke in January and, weakened by this, succumbs to influenza in February, one of the many killed in the pandemic.

Henri Matisse

Portrait of André Derain

Tate Modern

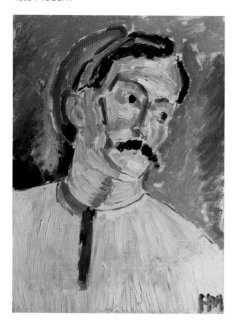

There must have been something in the air. During 1905 Debussy wrote *La Mer*, Elgar published *Introduction and Allegro for Strings*, Picasso was producing some of his most memorable 'rose period' work and in Switzerland, Albert Einstein published his *Special Theory of Relativity*, which completely revolutionised our understanding of the universe.

During that summer two French artists made their own contribution to this *annus mirabilis*. Henri Matisse and André Derain were spending the summer in the Mediterranean fishing village of Collioure. They developed a feverish rapport, an empathy based on the use of pure colour. 'We were at that time like children in the face of nature' wrote Matisse, 'we rejected imitative colours… with pure colours we obtained stronger reactions.'

The Tate owns the two portraits they painted of each other during this fertile summer — one of Matisse by Derain and this painting of Derain by Matisse. They illustrate how stylistically close the pair had become during their time in Collioure (somewhat like the relationship between Picasso and Braque a few years later during the development of Cubism — see page 194). Both artists were admirers of Gauguin and took the opportunity to see some of his late Tahitian paintings which were at the home of his executor not far from Collioure. Gauguin's use of flat areas of anti-naturalistic and purely decorative colour were influential but Matisse and Derain now took things much further.

In this picture Matisse has used paint in broad undiluted swathes, in particular the lighter yellows of Derain's shirt towards the bottom of the painting seem to have been applied with a near-frenzy which would not look out of place in a painting by van Gogh. The shadow on one side of Derain's face has been suggested by using various hues of green; the same greens are used for a section of the background, resonating with the red of Derain's beret. Against the flesh and sunburnt orange tone of the face Matisse has used a complementary blue for the background. Matisse, fresh from his dalliance with Neo-Impressionism, has retained his interest in Seurat's ideas relating to colour relationships, and the colour juxtapositions in the paintings executed at Collioure are a direct homage to his system.

All this cut little ice with the Parisian public and critics who, confronted at the Salon d'Automne of that year with recent work by Matisse and Derain together with other like-minded artists such as Maurice de Vlaminck, Henri Manguin and Albert Marquet, reacted with outrage and indignation. One critic, Louis Vauxcelles, commenting on the room in which the work of this group was concentrated, and in which an Italianate sculpture by Marquet occupied a central position, thought that the sculpture was like a '*Donatello parmi les fauves*' (a Donatello among the wild beasts). Just like the insult hurled by Louis Leroy in 1874, which came to define the Impressionists, Matisse, Derain, Vlaminck and their circle came to be known as the Fauves.

Contemporary Works

| 1905 | Gustav Klimt: *The Three Ages of Woman*; Rome |
| | Edvard Munch: *Four Girls on a Bridge*; Cologne |

Henri Matisse

1869	Born at Le Cateau-Cambrésis, near Cambrai, Picardy.
1887	After working in a solicitor's office he begins to study law in Paris.
1889	On returning to Picardy, he attends drawing classes.
1891	Studies painting at the Académie Julian in Paris.
1892	Studies at the studio of Gustave Moreau.
1894	A daughter is born to Matisse's mistress Caroline Joblaud.
1895	Passes the entrance examination for the École des Beaux-Arts.
1898	Marries Amélie Parayre. The couple honeymoon in London.
1902	Unable to sell his work the family returns from Paris to Picardy.
1904	A one-man exhibition is mounted by Vollard. It is not a success. Stays with Paul Signac at St Tropez in the summer.
1905	Spends the summer at Collioure near the Spanish border with André Derain.
1906	Good sales at a second one-man exhibition enable Matisse to visit Algeria. Also paints again at Collioure. Meets Picasso.
1908	Publishes *Notes d'un peintre*.
1909	The Russian businessman Sergey Shchukin commissions two of Matisse's masterpieces, *Dance* and *Music*.
1910	Travels to Munich for an exhibition of Islamic art. Travels to Spain to see more Moorish architecture.
1911	Visits St Petersburg and Moscow.
1917	Stays in Nice which will become his home base for much of the rest of his life.
1920	Serge Diaghilev invites him to London to work on the set designs for a Stravinsky ballet.
1930	Travels to Tahiti via New York and San Francisco.
1933	Completes murals for the Barnes Foundation in Pennsylvania.
1941	Matisse undergoes an operation for a tumour which leaves him in poor health.
1948	Begins work on designs for stained glass, and decoration for the Chapelle du Rosaire at Vence. This commission occupied him until his death.
1954	Dies in Nice.

Georges Braque

Tate Modern

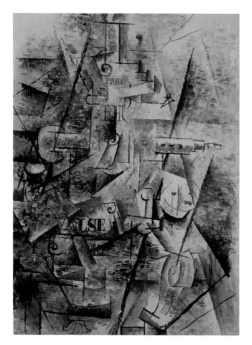

After a flirtation with the work of Matisse and *les Fauves*, in 1907 Braque became fascinated by Cézanne and for the next few summers he chose to visit sites favoured by the great man in order to paint the same motifs. In 1908 he was in L'Estaque near Marseille where, inspired by Cézanne's late style, he explored ways of taking the tight structure of Cézanne's work and pushing it a little further towards another possible logical conclusion. The result was a series of paintings which were rejected by the Salon d'Automne, but when exhibited at the Galerie Kahnweiler elicited a review from the critic Louis Vauxcelles which talked of 'cubes'. And indeed this is what Braque had created — he had taken Cézanne's broken planes and facets as his starting point and fashioned a series of more monumental blocks of various shapes, some of them unquestionably cuboid. All extraneous detail had been removed and colour restricted to greens, ochres and browns.

In 1907 Braque had been introduced to Picasso by Guillaume Apollinaire and had seen Picasso's ground-breaking, iconoclastic painting *Demoiselles d'Avignon*. Braque and Picasso gradually became friends and collaborators and by 1911 when this picture was painted the close chemistry between them was such that it has been claimed they could not tell their work apart. The three intervening years between Braque's visit to L'Estaque and 1911 had been intensely creative and in forging this new conceptual art Braque likened their collaboration to being 'roped together like two mountaineers'.

This was the high tide of Cubism — appealing to a very small group of cognoscenti, their work was not shown at the various Salons but channelled through one dealer, Daniel-Henry Kahnweiler, who showed it to a select band of clients.

The triangular composition is broken into a multitude of facets many of them creating multiple parallel faces which resonate on different planes throughout the composition. Colour is extremely muted — ochres and browns predominate. Dappled, almost pointillist brushstrokes create a textured effect, in some passages looking like woven cane or raffia. At the top of the pyramid stands the bottle of rum; the first two capital letters RH (French — Rhum) can be seen on its label followed by half of the U as it disappears around the curve of the bottle. Just below we can see the shaft of the clarinet, part of which disappears behind the bottle as well as another indecipherable plane. In a quintessentially Cubist passage, the bell of the clarinet is seen from a different angle. At the bottom of the composition we can see the moulding which supports the mantelpiece, tipped at a jaunty angle and again seen concurrently from different angles. Continuing the musical theme running through this and many other Cubist compositions, this moulding doubles as a treble clef. A smaller bass clef appears to the left beneath the word 'valse'.

The only object in the composition not to be fragmented or otherwise deformed is the nail, represented along with its shadow, perhaps waiting to receive this canvas in a parallel universe, or maybe a shifted plane.

Contemporary Works

1911	Henri Matisse: *The Red Studio*; New York
	Umberto Boccioni: *The City Rises*; New York
	Vasily Kandinsky: *Cossacks*; London, Tate Modern

Georges Braque

1882	Born at Argenteuil, just outside Paris.
1890	Braque's family move to Le Havre where his father has a decorating business.
1897	He attends the municipal art school where he meets Raoul Dufy.
1902	Moves to Montmartre.
1903	Studies at Léon Bonnat's studio.
1905	Influenced by the work of Matisse which he sees at the Salon d'Automne.
1907	Sells five Fauvist paintings at the Salon des Indépendants. Visits Picasso's studio and sees *Demoiselles d'Avignon*.
1908	Work produced at L'Estaque near Marseille in the summer gives rise to a review in which Braque is described by the critic Louis Vauxcelles as a painter of cubes.
1909	Paints views of the castle at La Roche-Guyon in an early Cubist style. Braque and Picasso, both living in Montmartre, are constantly in each other's company.
1911	Spends part of the year working in Céret in the Pyrenees.
1912	Marries Marcelle Lapre. Works with Picasso at Sorgues near Avignon. Introduces the papier collé technique.
1914	Braque is called up for military service.
1915	He is wounded while serving on the Western Front.
1924	Designs sets for the Ballet Russes production of *Les Fâcheux*.
1929	After visiting the Normandy coast he decides to build a studio at Varengeville for use during future summers.
1940	Braque leaves Paris after the German occupation but soon returns.
1953	Commissioned to decorate the Etruscan room in the Louvre.
1954	Designs stained glass windows for the church at Varengeville.
1963	Dies in Paris.

Giorgio de Chirico

Tate Modern

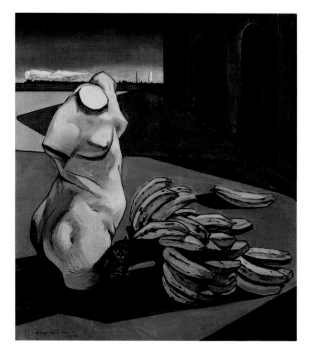

De Chirico was a true innovator — a 'one off' — he invented a new artistic vocabulary which he used for a decade or so to create dream-like images full of foreboding and anxiety. They are characterised by a vision of a world where everyday objects take on a new and often malign significance merely by their unexpected juxtaposition with articles which, in another context, would remain unremarkable. De Chirico called this state 'the solitude of signs' and in an article published in 1919 he wrote that his art 'is essentially serene; yet it gives the impression that something new is about to happen within that serenity, and that other signs, apart from the obvious ones, will enter and operate within the bounds of the canvas.'

De Chirico's favourite motif in his 'metaphysical' period is the deserted piazza, full of menace, filled with unmoving, soundless air, bordered by equally deserted, dark loggia casting deep, enigmatic shadows cutting across the open square. In this painting we have just such a piazza. No sentient being inhabits this place — instead it is populated by a large bunch of bananas and a headless sculpted torso. They are 'exhibited' on some sort of plinth which has an unresolved relationship with the wider space of the square. In the distance de Chirico has used another favourite device: a steam train, half hidden behind a wall, hurtles across the horizon beneath the ominous sky (for him, the train is a symbol of nostalgia redolent of emotional partings at railway stations, but at the same time perhaps an icon of modernity). The deep shadow cast by the loggia contrasts with the unremitting glare beyond in the open piazza, represented with a startling yellow. And yet the lowering indigo sky is surely incapable of emitting such strong light, seeming more likely to be the harbinger of a violent and ugly storm. If an unfortunate individual were to find themselves in such a place it would be difficult to decide which part of the square would be least inhospitable — the unforgiving heat out in the open or the nightmare darkness within the blind arcade.

In the same year that this picture was created, de Chirico met the poet, writer and critic Guillaume Apollinaire who became an inspirational friend. It was Apollinaire who first used the term 'metaphysical' to describe de Chirico's work (and who also coined the expression 'surrealist'). And indeed it was via their admiration of Apollinaire that the Surrealist group came to discover de Chirico's painting. It is now difficult not to think of de Chirico's work as quintessentially Surrealist but his metaphysical paintings were executed a decade before the publication of the *Manifesto of Surrealism*. He was in fact a precursor of that movement whose profound influence on Surrealist painting is obvious. This even extends to his enigmatic titles which were adopted some years later by Max Ernst, René Magritte and other Surrealist artists.

Contemporary Works

1913	Pierre Bonnard: *Dining Room in the Country*; Minneapolis
	Ernst Ludwig Kirchner: *Five Women in the Street*; Cologne
	Marc Chagall: *Self Portrait with Seven Fingers*; Amsterdam

Giorgio de Chirico

1888	Born in Vólos in northern Greece, the son of an Italian railway engineer.
1903	Begins three years of studies at the Higher School of Fine Arts in Athens.
1906	After the death of his father in 1905, the family move to live in Munich.
1911	After studying in Munich he joins his family who are in Milan, but de Chirico and his mother then move to live in Paris.
1912	Exhibits three paintings at the Salon d'Automne in Paris.
1913	Sells his first paintings at the Salon d'Automne. Meets the critic Guillaume Apollinaire and through him Picasso, Derain, Brancusi and others.
1915	De Chirico is conscripted into the Italian army as Italy enters the war. He is based in Ferrara, a city which inspired him to continue painting despite the demands of military life.
1917	Meets Carlo Carrà in a military hospital. Together they found Pittura Metafisica.
1918	First one-man show at the Galleria Bragaglia in Rome.
1924	Returns to Paris where he meets the Surrealists who have, during his absence, enthusiastically received his early work. However they are less keen on his more recent output.
1931	His marriage to his first wife Raissa ends and he later marries Isabella Pakszwer Far.
1935	De Chirico travels to New York where he stays for two years. He is now producing work in a new 'classical' style which provokes hostility from former supporters.
1942	Paints a portrait of Mussolini's daughter.
1946	Declares the contents of an exhibition of his metaphysical paintings to be fakes.
1950s	It becomes clear that de Chirico has been making copies of his own early work, selling them as originals. He defends this by saying that the concept is his and the time of execution is of no consequence. He campaigns against Modernism.
1978	Dies in Rome, active to the end.

Pierre Bonnard

Coffee 1915

Tate Modern

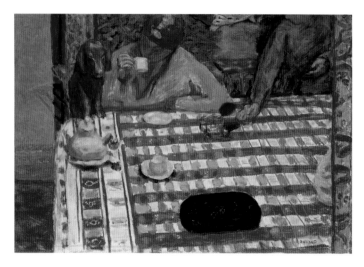

To stand in front of a painting by Bonnard is to be assailed by colour, to be enraptured by the profusion of rainbow colours which find a home in his canvases. He is one of the great colourists, not just of the twentieth century but of any century.

This canvas is quintessential Bonnard. More than half of the picture is taken up with a red gingham tablecloth which slants towards the viewer. The centre of our attention, two figures and a dog are jammed up in the top third of the composition; one of the figures has lost its head beyond the picture space. On the table we see a coffee pot and cups together with one or two other objects. A woman — Bonnard's partner Marthe who later became his wife — sips from her cup; beside her a dog stands on a chair, its two front paws on the table. It is an everyday scene but Bonnard delights in the unremarkable rhythm of daily life much as the Impressionists did a generation before him. From this mundane starting point he creates memorable images using gorgeous colour. Here the red of the tablecloth interacts with the blazing gold of Marthe's dress which is picked up again in the colour of the wall, the picture frame behind the dog and the curious strip down the right hand edge of the picture. Marthe's face is modelled in red and gold and her fingers are picked out in gold as is the dog's head.

Much of Bonnard's output, particularly in the last half of his life, is a catalogue of intimate domesticity. Marthe appears in most of these pictures either as the principal subject or making an appearance as a 'bit player' — almost part of the furniture. This is no accident — Bonnard's art, and indeed his life, came to be dominated by her. She was plagued by concerns about her health, some of these concerns requiring various dietary regimens, others leading to her spending considerable amounts of time ensconced in the bath. This, of course, accounts for the great number of paintings in existence showing Marthe either in the bath or in the process of getting out of it. She also became increasingly reclusive and may have suffered from some sort of persecution complex which led her to disapprove of visits from fellow artists to their home. Not unnaturally their friends referred to her as a demon or a 'tormenting sprite'. Bonnard, however seems to have borne all this with a resigned fatalism and none of his difficult home life comes through in his paintings — they are full of light and, of course, colour and it is interesting that Marthe always appears in the later paintings as a young woman. Bonnard refused to allow her to age on canvas and so, rather like Dorian Gray, our image of her, via the brush of her husband, remains forever youthful, except that thankfully the paintings did not remain in the attic.

Contemporary Works

1915	Kasemir Malevich: *Black Cross*; Paris
	Juan Gris: *Still Life (Fantomas)*; Washington
	Pablo Picasso: *The Harlequin*; New York

Pierre Bonnard

1867	Born at Fontenay-aux-Roses near Paris.
1887	Attends law school at the behest of his father but also enrols at the Académie Julian where he meets Paul Sérusier who has already painted with Gauguin in Brittany.
1889	Sworn in as a barrister. Becomes a member of the Nabi, a group founded by Sérusier and dedicated to furthering the aims of Gauguin's art.
1891	First Nabi group exhibition is held in the château of Saint-Germain-en-Laye. Bonnard produces a poster, *France-Champaigne* which is well received; the income from this persuades him to give up the law and become an artist.
1893	Meets Maria Boursin (Marthe), who becomes his constant companion, model and muse.
1896	Bonnard, other Nabi members and Toulouse-Lautrec design sets for the Théâtre d'Art. First one-man exhibition at Durand-Ruel.
1901	Travels to Portugal and Spain with his friend Vuillard.
1903	He is a founding member of the Salon d'Automne.
1906	Exhibits at both Vollard's gallery and Bernhein-Jeune. Visits the Midi for the first time.
1911	Buys his first automobile. Motoring becomes an important part of his life.
1912	Purchases a house at Vernon in Normandy.
1913	Visits Hamburg with Vuillard.
1916	Visits the Somme battlefields.
1925	Marries Marthe who suffers from ill health and becomes increasingly paranoid, discouraging visits from friends and fellow artists.
1926	Purchases a small villa 'Le Bosquet' at Le Cannet in the south of France. Travels to the USA to serve on the jury of the Carnegie International Exhibition.
1927	Le Bosquet becomes his main home but he keeps properties in Normandy and Paris.
1942	Madame Bonnard dies.
1947	Bonnard dies at Le Cannet.

George Grosz

Tate Modern

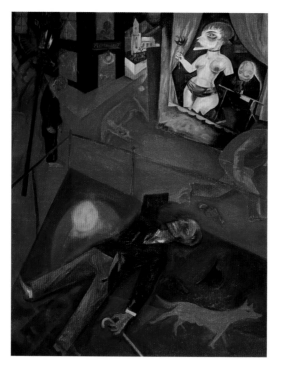

In November 1914, three months after the beginning of the Great War, George Grosz volunteered for the army. He was discharged on medical grounds in May 1915 but for the rest of the war he lived in fear of being recalled for military service. His military experiences, which included a short spell on the Western Front, confirmed and exacerbated an already strong tendency towards misanthropy.

His apoplectic rage directed at those he held responsible for taking Germany into the war as well as those who supported it, such as journalists who spewed craven patriotic propaganda, knew no bounds. Particular venom was reserved for industrialists (who are always portrayed as fat), the officer class, prostitutes and the Church. Capitalism was identified as an unequivocal evil; everyone and everything had become a commodity.

In *Suicide* Grosz deploys his personal lexicon of shocking images in pursuit of some of his obsessions, producing a horrifying panorama of corruption and degradation. It is an apocalyptic vision of a modern dystopia. The painting is bathed in a hellish red light; on the red streets red scavenging dogs prowl. In the foreground a man has just shot himself — his red revolver lies nearby — his head has already taken on the characteristics of a fleshless skull. Another corpse hangs from a lamp post at the corner of the street. In an indeterminate space in the top right corner of the composition (perhaps a shop window?) a near naked, hard-faced prostitute displays herself to the world; her bald and corpulent suited client leering expectantly behind her. In the distance a church, positioned centrally at the top edge of the picture stands witness to the carnage and squalor around it, symbolising its own impotence and complacency.

'My views of the war years can be summarised: men are swine ... Life has no meaning except the satisfaction of one's appetites for food and women. There is no soul.' The end of the war and the atmosphere of febrile decadence which characterised Berlin during the Weimar years did nothing to assuage the artist's intense pessimism and anger. He continued to produce similarly coruscating commentaries on contemporary dissipation until his emigration to the United States in 1933 just before the Nazis gained power.

Contemporary Works

1916	Gustav Klimt: *Houses at Unterach on the Attersee*; Vienna
	Giorgio de Chirico: *The Amusements of a Young Girl*; New York
1917	Fernand Léger: *The Cardplayers*; Otterlo, Netherlands

George Grosz

1893	Born Georg Grosz in Berlin but grew up in Stolp, Pomerania, now Slupsk, Poland.
1909	Entered the Akademie der Künste in Dresden.
1913	Influenced by an exhibition of Italian Futurists in Berlin.
1914	In November he joins the army.
1915	Honourably discharged from the army on medical grounds.
1916	Grosz changes his first name to George.
1918	Joins the German Communist Party and the Berlin Dada group.
1928	A drawing showing Christ on the cross wearing boots and a gas mask leads to Grosz being tried for blasphemy.
1932	Grosz is invited to teach for two terms at the Arts Student League in New York.
1933	He emigrates to the United States.
1937	His works are displayed by the Nazis with those of Cézanne, Matisse, Picasso, Chagall and others in an exhibition of 'degenerate' art.
1959	Returns to West Berlin where he dies soon after his arrival.

Max Beckmann

Tate Modern

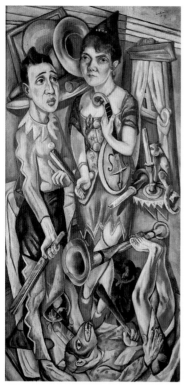

Max Beckmann was one of the many German artists in a particularly talented generation whose mental health was shattered by the outbreak of the First World War. He joined the medical corps as a hospital orderly and served for some time at a field dressing station. Like George Grosz (see page 200) his experiences precipitated a severe mental breakdown and he was invalided out of the army in 1915.

Before the war he had been fêted as a great talent. He had been influenced by Impressionism, Symbolism and by Cézanne, rejecting the move towards abstraction spearheaded by his German contemporaries in the Blau Reiter group. After his encounter with the horrors of war his style changed dramatically. He was still concerned to depict objects and people in a way which conformed recognisably with reality but now he began to cram his subjects into claustrophobic spaces where normal perspectival laws break down, heightening the inherent tension and alienation of his subject matter.

In *Carnival*, three figures find themselves in a chaotic and perplexing space rather like the 'crooked house' fairground attractions where everything is designed to challenge your sense of balance. Various objects litter the scene, presumably part of Beckmann's complex web of symbolism; in particular, the gramophone horn seems to have been of particular significance as it appears in many of his pictures during this period.

The three figures are dressed in the costume of the *Commedia dell'arte*. The woman dressed as Columbine is a portrait of Fridel Battenburg, the wife of a close friend and fellow artist who had looked after Beckmann during and after his breakdown. Harlequin is the art dealer I. B. Neumann who had supported his post-war shift to a new style and the clown, lying on the floor with a trumpet held by his feet, is thought to be a self portrait hidden behind the monkey mask. It has been suggested that the clown symbolises a world gone mad. Certainly Fastnacht (the German title of the picture), facilitated a sort of madness; it was the climax of the carnival season, traditionally celebrated with unrestrained revelry featuring fancy dress and street processions.

Beckmann's was an essentially pessimistic vision. He said that 'the sole justification for our existence as artists ... is to confront people with the image of their destiny'. Weighed down by his experience of war and his disappointment at the political chaos that ensued in Germany after 1918, Beckmann foresaw that Europe's destiny would again descend into turmoil and disorder.

Contemporary Works

1919	Pierre Bonnard: *The Bowl of Milk*; London, Tate Modern
1920	George Grosz: *Republican Automata*; New York
	Stanley Spencer: *Christ Carrying the Cross*; London, Tate Britain

Max Beckmann

1884	Born in Leipzig.
1900	Enrols at the Kunstschule in Weimar.
1906	Beckmann marries Minna Tube. Exhibits for the first time at the Berlin Secession.
1910	Becomes the youngest member of the committee of the Berlin Secession.
1914	At the outbreak of war Beckmann joins the medical corps and works as a hospital orderly.
1915	He is discharged from the army because of the deterioration of his mental health.
1917	Settles in Frankfurt am Main.
1925	Exhibits with the Neue Sachlichkeit movement in Mannheim. Divorces his first wife and marries Mathilde von Kaulbach. Appointed professor at the Städelsches Kunstinstitut in Frankfurt.
1932	Begins work on the first of his triptychs.
1933	Declared a 'degenerate' artist by the Nazis; he is dismissed from his academic post and all works by him in museums are confiscated.
1937	Leaves Germany to live in Amsterdam.
1947	Moves to the USA.
1950	Dies in New York.

Max Ernst

Tate Modern

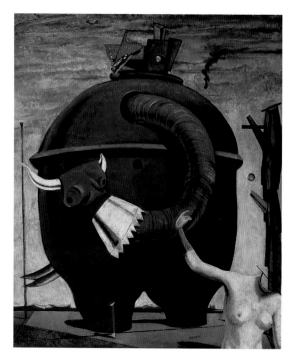

Painted in Cologne before Ernst abandoned his wife and child for the cultural mecca of Paris, *Celebes* is a seminal work heralding the birth of Surrealism. It would be another three years before André Breton published his manifesto of Surrealism but Ernst is already employing here (and in other contemporary works) a personal lexicon of childhood and dream images partly inspired by the writings of Sigmund Freud which he read whilst at university before the Great War (where he read psychology as well as philosophy and art history).

The ideas associated with the Surrealist movement had been in the air for some time. Guillaume Apollinaire (who appears in another work by Ernst housed in Tate Modern, *Pietà or Revolution by Night*) had coined the term in 1917 in relation to his own play *Les Mamelles de Tirésias* and *Parade*, the ballet for which Picasso had designed the sets. There were other precursors, notably the poet Comte de Lautréamont who as early as 1869 had written of the beauty of 'the chance encounter of a sewing machine and an umbrella on an operating table'.

But in this painting Ernst leaned heavily on the most obvious prophet of Surrealist painting, Giorgio de Chirico. The picture is dominated by a monstrously bulbous metallic object which, according to the artist, derives from a photograph of an African container for storing corn. Some industrial hosing emanates from a dark hole in the top of this object, the other end culminating in a bull's skull. Perched on top of this half-mechanical — half-animate being an indeterminate apparatus (very reminiscent of de Chirico's later metaphysical paintings) performs an undefined role — perhaps one of directional control, for a partly obscured eye stares disconcertingly back at the viewer from behind its blue eyrie.

This semi-sentient automaton looms threateningly over an agoraphobic landscape — exactly the sort of place which features in nightmares where one is being pursued, because there is no possible cover from the inherent menace in such a setting. And, of course, these landscapes, instituted by de Chirico, were later to appear again and again in the Surrealist canon. The sky is also pregnant with dreamlike surprise. Two fish swim through the ether and a strange trail of smoke seems to suggest a downed aeroplane (possibly a reference to Ernst's wartime experiences on the Western Front) although there is no discernable craft from which the smoke could issue.

To the right a curious entity teeters unsteadily, echoing the ambiguous nature of the central 'elephant' — is it made up of metallic coffee pots? Or is it supposed to be organic — some kind of tree? Obscuring the lower portions of this object stands a headless female torso, perhaps a mannequin, devoid of life but possessed of an animated claw-like hand which seems to be pointing to the red phallic spout to its right.

Contemporary Works

1921	Paul Signac: *Port of La Rochelle*; Paris
	Pablo Picasso: *Three Women at the Fountain*; New York
	Piet Mondrian: *Painting 1*; Cologne

Max Ernst

1891	Born in the town of Brühl near Cologne, the son of a keen amateur painter.
1909-12	Studies philosophy, psychology and art history at the University of Bonn.
1914-18	Serves in the German Army but continues to paint.
1918	After demobilisation he joins the Dada movement. Marries the art historian Louise Strauss.
1921	The Parisian Dada group mount an exhibition of Ernst's collages. Paul Eluard and his wife Gala visit him in Cologne.
1922	Leaves his wife and moves to Paris where he lives with the Eluards.
1924	Eluard travels to the Far East. Ernst and Gala meet him in Saigon. Ernst stays as the Eluards return.
1925	Back in Paris he moves into his own studio.
1926	Ernst develops the frottage technique. Designs sets for Diaghilev's production of Prokofiev's *Romeo and Juliet*.
1927	Marries Marie-Berthe Aurenche.
1928	Exhibition of his work at the Galerie Georges Bernheim.
1938	Moves to St Martin d'Ardeche with the English painter Leonora Carrington.
1939	Ernst is interned as an enemy alien on the outbreak of war.
1941	After suffering a mental breakdown he escapes to New York.
1942	Marries Peggy Guggenheim but the relationship does not last.
1946	Ernst marries the surrealist painter Dorothea Tanning and settles in Arizona.
1948	Becomes an American citizen.
1953	Returns to live in Paris.
1954	Wins the Grand Prix at the Venice Biennale.
1955	Ernst and his wife move to live near Chinon in France.
1958	Becomes a French citizen.
1975	Major retrospectives of his work are held in New York and Paris.
1976	Dies in Paris.

Pablo Picasso

Tate Modern

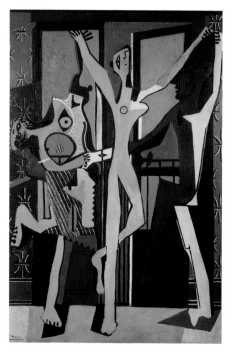

This painting was a product of one of the frequent periods of reassessment which punctuate Picasso's art. Since the end of the Great War, whilst continuing to produce Cubist works, he had also become involved in a general revival of interest in classical forms (dubbed by Jean Cocteau as 'the return to order'). *The Three Dancers*, a large painting with life size figures, represents a clear break with the predominantly classicist output of the recent past and in many respects marks a return to the jarring 'primitive' imagery of *Demoiselles d'Avignon*, painted in 1907, and inspired by African art. It was immediately hailed by André Breton, leader of the recently emerged Surrealist movement and as a result of their overtures Picasso made another break with the past and agreed for the first time to participate in a collective exhibition, showing some Cubist pieces in the first Surrealist group show.

Since 1916 Picasso had also been closely associated with the Ballets Russes, collaborating with Diaghilev, Eric Satie and Jean Cocteau. Through these connections he met the dancer Olga Koklova whom he married in 1918. So the theme of dancers was a natural choice during this period. But the work is hardly a celebration of poise and graceful movement. In fact the character of the painting changed as Picasso was working on it, for during its gestation he heard of the death of his friend Ramón Pichot who was then introduced into the composition, silhouetted in profile behind the right-hand dancer. Pichot's death triggered painful personal memories for

Picasso dating back to an earlier tragedy when in 1901 a close friend and fellow painter Carlos Casagemas had committed suicide. The cause of Casagemas's despair was rejection by his lover Germaine who may have left him because he was impotent. Soon after this traumatic event Germaine married Pichot who had accompanied Picasso and Casagemas from Barcelona when all three had made their first extended visit to Paris.

Therefore *The Three Dancers* might be seen as a dance of death. The female figure on the left of the picture may be Germaine, her grotesque teeth and exposed breasts symbolising her role as a man-eater. The ghostly Casagemas had already made an appearance in a number of paintings including the Blue Period work *La Vie*. It is probable that he now makes another posthumous appearance as the central figure in this painting. Is he dancing or is he crucified — trapped between Germaine and Pichot?

Evidence of the importance of this work to the artist (because of this personal and biographical content) is provided by the fact that it remained in his possession for forty years until he sold it directly to the Tate.

Contemporary Works

1924	Gwen John; *Interior (Rue Terre Neuve)*; Manchester
1925	Paul Signac: *The Lighthouse, Groix*; New York

Pablo Picasso

1881	Born Pablo Ruiz in Málaga, 25 October.
1895	After a period in La Coruña, the family move to Barcelona. Picasso, aged 14, passes the examination to enter the Escuela de Bellas Artes.
1900	Picasso and his friend Casagemas leave for Paris.
1901	While in Madrid, Picasso hears of the suicide of Casagemas in Paris. In May he returns to Paris. He starts to sign his works using his mother's surname, Picasso.
1902	His work at this time uses a predominantly blue palette.
1904	After returning to Spain, Picasso is back in Paris in April 1904, he rents a studio at Le Bateau-Lavoir. Meets Guillaume Apollinaire. Rose Period begins.
1906	Spends the summer at Gosol, in the Pyrenees with his lover Fernande Olivier.
1907	Inspired by African and Oceanic art he paints *Les Demoiselles d'Avignon*.
1909	Picasso and Braque develop Cubism.
1912	Picasso produces the first collage, *Still Life with Chair-caning*.
1915	His current companion Eva Gouel dies.
1916	Meets Jean Cocteau who introduces him to Diaghilev.
1917	Designs the sets for the Ballets Russes production of *Parade*.
1918	Marries the dancer Olga Koklova.
1925	Picasso shows some works at the first Surrealist group exhibition.
1927	Meets Marie-Thérèse Walter who later becomes his mistress.
1931	Picasso's marriage to Olga breaks down.
1933	Designs the cover for the first edition of the Surrealist periodical *Minotaure*.
1935	Marie-Thérèse Walter gives birth to Picasso's daughter.
1937	In a reaction to the Fascist bombing of the Basque town during the Spanish Civil War, Picasso produces the huge iconic painting *Guernica*.
1940	Picasso continues to live in Paris during the Nazi occupation.
1944	Joins the Communist Party after the liberation of Paris.
1946	Living with Françoise Gilot. They have two children; she leaves him in 1953.
1950	The *Vollard Suite*, 100 etchings produced in the 1930s goes on sale.
1958	Buys the Château de Vauvenargues near Aix-en-Provence.
1961	Marries Jacqueline Roque who has been his companion since 1955.
1967	Refuses the *Légion d'honneur*.
1973	Dies at Mougins, France.

Salvador Dalí

Metamorphosis of Narcissus 1937

Tate Modern

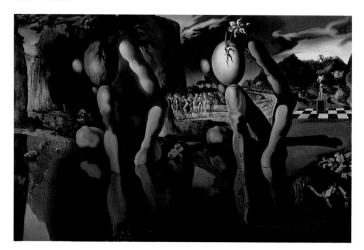

According to Greek myth Narcissus was a youth of flawless beauty. Many nymphs fell in love with him but none more passionately than Echo who had attracted the displeasure of Hera (the consort of Zeus), and who had consequently been condemned to repeat only the last syllable of any words she uttered. Echo, unable to declare her love for Narcissus, was duly spurned by him, as indeed were all his other suitors. She then died of a broken heart, only the echo of her voice surviving. Her fate, and the clamour of other rejected lovers alerted the gods, and Nemesis, the goddess of vengeance, punished Narcissus by arranging for him to fall in love with his own reflection in a pool of water. Unable to possess the object of his desires, he eventually expired in the same manner as Echo — the eponymous flower springing up where he died.

This subject greatly appealed to Dalí who was deeply interested in the psychology of the subconscious and the new science of psychoanalysis. Indeed in 1938 he visited Sigmund Freud in London taking this picture with him. Apparently Freud was impressed by his visitor, somewhat against his own expectations. Dalí's interest in such matters led to the development of a working method for his paintings which he called 'paranoiac-critical'. Essentially this involved the simulation of a state of delirium during which visual reality and the relationship between objects became skewed. Dalí described his method, typically somewhat opaquely, as 'the critical and systematic objectification of delirious associations and interpretations'.

In *Metamorphosis of Narcissus* we can marvel at the inventiveness of Dalí's imagery and at his inimitable technique. These two aspects of his art conspire to produce extraordinarily memorable paintings with a super-fine photo-realist finish of which this is a virtuoso example.

Narcissus appears twice — statuesque on a pedestal in the background to the right — reminding us of his self centred 'narcissism', and again in the foreground, kneeling in the clear waters of a desert pool, his body reflected as in a mirror, but caught in the process of transformation. The transformative image is a breathtaking piece of invention; on the shore of the pool a giant hand, fashioned from stone, holds an egg from which emerges a single narcissus flower. The nail of the giant thumb mirrors the knee of Narcissus whose head becomes the egg, and so on. An army of ants gathers by the side of the pool — they have started to climb up the stone thumb — soon, no doubt, they will be at the cracked thumbnail and onto the egg. Ants were a favourite item in Dalí's arsenal of symbols, turning up in a number of his most dazzling creations such as the *Great Masturbator*. In the background, cavorting around another shallow pool one can see a group of naked men and women waiting, according to Dalí in 'preliminary expectation'. Always fearful of sexual inadequacy, always anxious that, like Narcissus and Echo, he will not be able to fulfill his desires, Dalí perhaps sees this group, with their overt potency, to be in some way as threatening as the black cloud which billows behind them.

Contemporary Works

1937	Pablo Picasso: *Guernica*; Madrid
	Henri Matisse: *Woman in Blue*; Philadelphia
	Paul Delvaux: *The Break of Day (L'Aurore)*; Venice

Salvador Dalí

1904	Born in Figueres in Catalonia, the son of a notary.
1921	Enters the Real Acadamia de Bellas Artes de San Fernando in Madrid where he meets the poet Federico Garcia Lorca and the film maker Luis Buñuel.
1925	Dalí has his first one-man exhibition at the Galeria Dalmau in Barcelona.
1926	Expelled from the Acadamia. Visits Paris for the first time.
1929	Dalí collaborates with Luis Buñuel in making the famous surrealist film *Un Chien andalou*, shot in Paris and le Havre. André Breton, René Magritte and Paul and Gala Eluard visit Dalí at Cadaqués in Catalonia. The Galerie Camille Goemans mounts his first show in Paris. Accepted as a member of the Surrealist group. Travels to Paris where he and Gala begin a lifelong relationship.
1933	Shows eight pieces at the Exhibition of Surrealist Objects in Paris.
1934	Exhibits at the Zwemmer Gallery in London. Visits the USA.
1936	Takes part in the International Surrealist Exhibition in London giving a lecture dressed in a diving suit complete with helmet.
1938	Visits Sigmund Freud in London.
1940	After the fall of France, where he has been living, he flees to the USA.
1941	A rift with the Surrealists is formalised when he is attacked in print by André Breton. Retrospective at MOMA New York.
1948	Returns to Europe but continues to spend some time each year in the USA.
1958	Marries Gala in Spain.
1964	Dalí is awarded the Grand Cross of Isabella, Spain's highest decoration.
1979	A major retrospective takes place at the Centre Georges Pompidou in Paris.
1982	Gala dies.
1984	He suffers severe burns as a result of a fire in his current home, the castle of Púbol.
1989	Dies in Figueres where his body is buried in the Teatre-Museu Dalí.

Paul Delvaux

Tate Modern

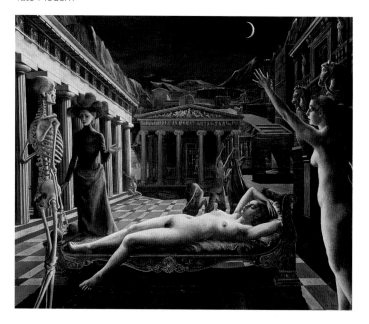

Anaked woman lies sleeping on an ornate couch in the middle of a classical piazza set amongst dark and lifeless mountains. A crescent moon is suspended in the black sky, its light surely insufficient to provide the silvery radiance which illuminates the eerie townscape. The sleeping Venus is oblivious to the other inhabitants of the square. A further naked female enters from the right, one arm held aloft, a look of blank concern on her face as though she may be sleepwalking. A skeleton approaches Venus from the left; a woman dressed in the costume of the Belle Époque silently glides like an automaton towards the viewer, her eyes fixed in a glassy stare which might suggest that she is also sleepwalking. Alternatively she may just be a dressmaker's dummy. Otherwise the square is uninhabited save only for another group of nude women who seem to be submerged in anguish, two of whom are looking up to the sky.

Delvaux explained that the picture was painted at a time when Brussels was under attack, before its liberation. The women are looking to the sky in fear of aerial bombardment. However the genesis of the Venus figure, which Delvaux used in a great many compositions, can be found in an experience at a fairground nearly fifteen years before. One of the stalls was the grandly entitled Spitzner Museum inside which could be viewed (in the words of the museum brochure) a 'Reclining Venus modelled from life'. This seems to have been some sort of waxworks figure complete with an internal mechanism which simulated breathing. It was certainly arresting enough to captivate Delvaux, who visited the museum many times.

Shortly after his encounter with the waxworks Venus, Delvaux discovered the art of Giorgio de Chirico. The fusion of these two influences gave birth to Delvaux's distinctive form of Surrealism. His dreamscapes are almost invariably constructed using a relatively restricted inventory of pictorial elements — naked, heavy-breasted women, classical architecture, skeletons, airless landscapes redolent of ennui or menace; later, railway trains either trapped on dead end sidings or on lines which look as if they might invade a domestic interior.

It is the juxtaposition of these disparate elements, which in isolation might appear relatively benign, but which when placed incongruously in a context heavy with foreboding, reminds us of the panic of childhood dreams. The *Sleeping Venus* is the stuff of nightmares but in common with other Surrealist work we are also able to walk away from it with a smile of recognition.

Contemporary Works

1943	Piet Mondrian: *Broadway Boogie-Woogie*; New York
	Jackson Pollock: *Guardians of the Secret*; San Francisco
1944	Frida Kahlo: *Broken Column*; Mexico City

Paul Delvaux

1897	Paul Delvaux is born at Antheit near Huy in Belgium.
1916	Enrols at the Royal Academy of Fine Arts in Brussels.
1923	He exhibits for the first time at the gallery of Georges Giroux in Brussels. Pictures by René Magritte were exhibited in the same show.
1930	Delvaux comes across the 'Spitzner Museum' at the Midi Fair in Brussels.
1932	He paints his first *Sleeping Venus*.
1934	The Minotaure exhibition is held in Brussels including works by de Chirico, Dalí and Magritte. This show had a profound effect on Delvaux and influenced the development of his mature style.
1938	Delvaux takes part in the International Surrealist Exhibition organised by André Breton in Paris.
1939	Visits Florence, Pompeii and Herculaneum; classical architecture becomes more important in his work after this trip.
1950	Appointed Professor of Painting at the École Supérieure d'Art et d'Architecture in Brussels.
1956	Visits Greece.
1975	A retrospective of his work takes place in Tokyo.
1981	Andy Warhol visits him in Brussels.
1991	A retrospective of Delvaux's work is held at the Grand Palais in Paris.
1994	Paul Delvaux dies.

Yves Klein

Tate Modern

If you are not keen on the colour blue then this is not for you. Klein has covered the entire canvas with the same colour — but what a colour. It is the modern equivalent of those ultramarine blues used for the robes of late medieval and Renaissance Madonnas; they are so rich and intense that they stay with you long after the memory of the rest of the painting has faded. And so it is with this work. It exerts a strong magnetic pull drawing you to it as you enter the room. Klein's blue is of such an intensity that it seems to enter your soul.

Klein was not the first person to exhibit works consisting of one single colour. My particular favourite dates back to 1883 when the French journalist and wit Alphonse Allais exhibited a sheet of white paper which he entitled *First Communion of Anaemic Young Girls in the Snow*. He followed it up with *Apoplectic Cardinals Harvesting Tomatoes on the Shore of the Red Sea*. In a less facetious vein, around 1918 Kazimir Malevich produced his Suprematist piece *White Square on White*. But this was not good enough for Klein who wanted no lines in his paintings. Monochrome for him was an 'open window to freedom… the possibility of being immersed in the immeasurable existence of colour'. In 1956 he displayed 20 monochrome works in different shades of red, purple, yellow, orange and blue in an exhibition in Paris.

But it was the colour blue that embodied the spiritual values for which he strove; it was the colour of the sky and it symbolised infinity. He experimented with a chemist to find a new binding material which would better retain the intensity of pigments, in particular blue. The result was IKB, standing for International Klein Blue, which he then patented. He also developed a red which he called Monopink and a yellow (Monogold). In 1960, in a series of extraordinary 'performance' works naked models smeared with IKB pressed their bodies against the walls and floors of the gallery to the accompaniment of an orchestra playing *Symphonie Monoton*, a piece composed by the artist in which the orchestra played a single note.

Will we ever look at 'blue' in quite the same way!

Contemporary Works

1957	Victor Pasmore: *Abstract in White, Black and Lilac*; London, Tate Britain
1958	Kenneth Noland: *First*; Paris
1960	Frank Stella: *Six Mile Bottom*; London, Tate Modern

Yves Klein

1928	Born in Nice, the son of a Dutch painter, Fred Klein and Marie Raymond, who is an abstract artist.
1946	Studies with the Rosicrucian Fellowship. Influenced by esoteric mystical writings and East Asian religions.
1947	Begins making monochrome paintings.
1948	Moves to live in London.
1950	First exhibition of Klein's paintings takes place in London.
1952-3	Spends a year in Japan studying judo. His monochrome paintings are exhibited in Tokyo.
1954	Teaches judo in Madrid.
1955	Returns to Paris.
1956	An exhibition in Paris of twenty monochrome paintings is well received by some critics. Conducts experiments with the help of a chemist to find a binding material which would retain and enhance the intensity of pigments, in particular blue. Patents the resulting colour which he calls International Klein Blue (IKB).
1957	Exhibitions of his paintings and sculpture take place in Milan and Paris.
1958	An exhibition called *La Vide* comprises an empty space painted white by Klein.
1959	Klein anticipates conceptual art when he exchanges 'Zones of Immaterial Pictorial Sensibility' for gold leaf.
1960	The Nouveau Réalisme movement is founded at a meeting at Klein's flat.
1962	Klein dies in Paris of a heart attack.

Mark Rothko

Red on Maroon (The Seagram Murals) 1959

Tate Modern

These murals were part of a commission to provide 600 square feet of paintings for the Four Seasons restaurant at the recently finished Seagram Building in New York — the work of the celebrated architects Mies van der Rohe and Philip Johnson. It was a prestigious and lucrative contract but in 1959, after having completed most of the elements in his proposed scheme, Rothko withdrew from the agreement and returned his fee. A decade later he gave nine of the murals intended for the Four Seasons restaurant to the Tate Gallery with the proviso that they be permanently exhibited in a room exclusively set aside for them. He was influenced by the fact that they would be in the same collection as the works of J. M. W. Turner. They arrived in London on the day that he was found dead in his studio in New York having committed suicide by cutting the blood vessels in his arms.

As Rothko worked on the Four Seasons series his habitual motif of juxtaposed areas of colour developed into window-like compositions. He also began to use a very restricted palette of black and sombre reds. Rothko commented that as he worked he realised that both these developments were in part attributable to the influence of the architecture of Michelangelo, in particular the vestibule in the Laurentian Library in Florence which is renowned for its blind windows and startlingly brooding decorative scheme. He had recently returned from a trip to Italy and had been much impressed by Michelangelo's disturbing creation.

But there was another reason for this change of heart. Looking at these pictures now in the space set aside for them is an undeniably spiritual experience – the sombre colours resonate to induce a reflective quietude. But apparently this is not what Rothko intended. He was a political radical and he determined that he would paint murals that were designed to produce a state of agitation in the wealthy clientele who were the only people who could afford to eat at the Four Seasons. He is quoted as saying that he wanted to 'ruin the appetite of every son of a bitch who ever eats in that room' and that he wanted to make them 'feel that they are trapped in a room where all the doors and windows are bricked up'. This must be a reference to the Laurentian Library which does indeed exude an aura of claustrophobia.

Eventually however, Rothko withdrew from the commission; after a visit to the newly opened Four Seasons he reportedly told his assistant 'Anybody who will eat that kind of food for those kind of prices will never look at a painting of mine'.

There is no doubt that whatever effect Rothko strove to produce through these paintings, they have transcended his intentions and have become icons to the power inherent in purely abstract arrangements of colour and form. So strong an effect can they exert that they are often the only exceptions cited by museum-goers who say they are unable to empathise with any other abstract compositions.

Contemporary Works

1958	Ad Reinhardt: *Painting 1954-1958*; Canberra
1959	Jasper Johns: *Numbers in Colour*; Buffalo, NY
1960	Renato Guttuso: *The Discussion*; London, Tate Modern

Mark Rothko

1903	Born Marcus Rothkowitz at Dvinsk in Russia (now Daugavpils in Latvia).
1913	He emigrates to the USA with his mother and sister arriving in Portland, Oregon where his father and the rest of the family had settled.
1921	Begins his studies at Yale University.
1923	Leaves Yale in his third year without taking a degree and moves to New York where he begins to paint.
1933	First one-man exhibition at the Portland Art Museum.
1935	Co-founder of The Ten, a group of Expressionist artists.
1940	First starts to use the shortened version of his name.
1942-7	His work is influenced by Surrealism, in particular Ernst and Miró. Also works extensively in watercolour.
1947	Teaches at the California School of Fine Art in San Francisco. Turns to abstraction, painting compositions with large soft-edged areas.
1959	Legally changes his name to Mark Rothko.
1964-67	He works on a commission for John and Dominique de Menil to produce murals for a chapel at the University of St Thomas in Houston, Texas.
1968	Ill health means that for a time he is unable to work on large compositions. Becomes depressed.
1970	Commits suicide in New York in 1970 the very day that the murals originally destined for the Four Seasons Restaurant are delivered to the Tate.

Anselm Kiefer

Parsifal III   1973

Tate Modern

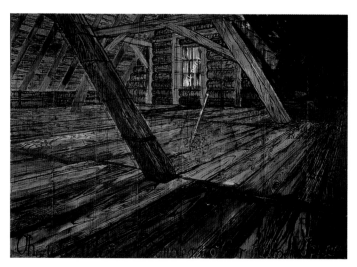

nselm Kiefer was born in the brutal year of 1945. His art explores the twin themes of German history and myth seen through the eyes of a generation having to come to terms with the truth of the recent Nazi past. In a reaction against the attitude of many Germans in the immediate aftermath of the war, who seemed to be content to ignore the horrific revelations which had been uncovered by Allied troops in the year of his birth, Kiefer, Gerhard Richter and other left-wing artists, chose to confront the issue through their art. In a particularly provocative project in 1969, Kiefer photographed himself making the Nazi salute in front of a number of famous European landmarks.

In 1973 Kiefer made a series of four paintings — three of which are in Tate Modern — inspired by the legendary exploits of Parsifal (Percival) in pursuit of the Holy Grail, and by Richard Wagner's opera of the same name which had been based on the Grail romances, in particular Wolfram von Eschenbach's *Parzival*. According to these romances Parsifal's father had died heroically in battle during his infancy and as a result, his mother had sought to shield him from the world of chivalry. However after a chance encounter with some knights, Parsifal decides to travel to Arthur's court where he is initiated and knighted and eventually achieves, after many trials and adventures, what others have failed to do in finding the Holy Grail. He is able to save the Grail from destruction by recovering the Holy Spear (used to pierce Christ's side) and using it to heal the Guardian of the Grail.

All three of the Tate paintings are set in an attic room, reminiscent of the artist's beamed studio — each painting views the room from a different angle. The space is empty and nothing relieves the claustrophobic monotony of the wooden interior (perhaps a reference to the unbroken forests which formed the backdrop to the Germanic myths) save for the symbolic articles which are placed within it. In the first part of the triptych

(*Parsifal I*) a lonely cot refers to the hero's pacific childhood. In the second panel, Parsifal's sword is shown with its point rammed into the wooden floor. Nearby, another sword lies broken and smeared with blood (Kiefer has used real blood in the painting) — a reference to Parsifal's defeat of the wicked Ither. The central part of the triptych, *Parsifal III*, shows the holy spear, again with its tip stuck in the wooden floor. In each case the names of the protagonists are scrawled nearby but in this picture another list of names appears — those of the left wing Baader-Meinhof terrorist group whose members had been responsible for a number of killings in Germany during the early seventies and who were representative of the most extreme elements of discontent within Kiefer's generation.

The parallels between the sanctified violence of Parsifal and the revolutionary violence of the Baader-Meinhof group are interesting especially as they sandwich (in the mind of Kiefer and his contemporaries) the state-sponsored and industrialised slaughter of the Holocaust.

Contemporary Works

| 1972 | Richard Diebenkorn: *Ocean Park No. 49*; Los Angeles |
| 1973 | Gerhard Richter: *Annunciation after Titian*; Washington |

Anselm Kiefer

1945	Born in Donaueschingen, Germany.
1965	Studies law in Freiburg.
1966	Switches to art.
1969	Continues his studies in Karlsruhe. During travels through Switzerland, Italy and France he produces a series of photographic works called *Occupations* which show Kiefer imitating a Nazi salute.
1970	Moves to Düsseldorf where he meets Joseph Beuys.
1971	Moves to live in Hornbach where he works on large landscape paintings.
1980	Represents Germany at the Venice Biennale.
1984	Visits Israel.
1992	Moves to live in Barjac, France.

The V&A (as it is universally known) bills itself as the world's greatest museum of art and design, with collections unrivalled in their scope and diversity. The collections, running to perhaps four million exhibits, include ceramics, furniture, fashion, glass, jewellery, metalwork, photographs, sculpture, textiles and paintings.

Founded in 1852, drawing inspiration from the success of the Great Exhibition, the museum has been housed in the present grand building since 1909. As the museum grew new buildings were erected, some of which were intended to be semi-permanent exhibition halls, but all have survived and together represent one of the finest groups of Victorian buildings in the country.

Victoria and Albert Museum

Cromwell Road, London SW7 2RL
Tel. +44 (0)20 7942 2000

Opening Hours

Every day 10am – 5.45pm
Wednesdays (and the last Friday of the month) 10am – 8pm
Closed 24 – 26 December

Admission

Free

How To Get There

The nearest underground station is South Kensington (District, Circle and Piccadilly Lines).
Bus routes 14, 414, 74 and C1.

Access for the Disabled

The museum provides access for the disabled to all floors. For further information telephone +44 (0)20 7942 2211.

Museum Shops

Open as above. Three shops cater for all tastes and offer a wide range of books, stationery, gifts and jewellery.

Museum Café

Open as above. The museum has a number of places to eat offering hot dishes, salads, sandwiches and cakes.

Nicholas Hilliard

Young Man leaning against a Tree among Roses

c1585-95

Victoria and Albert Museum

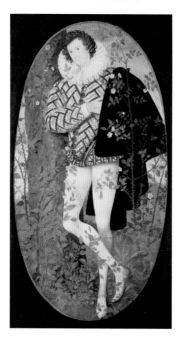

This image is an example of that characteristically Elizabethan preoccupation with staging courtly protestations of devotion to the queen's majesty.

A young man gazes dolefully at nothing in particular, engrossed in a private misery and with his hand on his heart. We are therefore left in no doubt as to the cause of his suffering. However, the object of his desires may be less easy to divine and this gem of a picture may fulfil a dual role. The sitter is dressed in black and white, the queen's colours, and he is surrounded by the barbed beauty of the eglantine rose, also associated with Elizabeth, but at the same time, a reference to the pains of love.

It is possible that the young man might be identified as Robert Devereux, 2nd Earl of Essex, a particular favourite of the queen, who had incurred Elizabeth's wrath when he married in secret. It has been postulated that this picture could have been a small part of Essex's strategy to restore his position at court but it has to be said that there is no evidence for this and there is equally no evidence that the subject is Essex. The cryptic legend at the top of the picture which may be translated as 'a praised faith is its own scourge' is of little help. It is a quote from Lucan in a piece which goes on to recommend a political assassination (which sits rather uneasily above a lovesick youth) so it may be urging the viewer to think along lines of political loyalty; or it may merely be a quote which holds a special private significance for two or more people. Perhaps it is best to think of it straightforwardly as the image of a man who wishes to appraise his lady of the depth of his feelings, and at the same time needs to reaffirm his fidelity to the queen — Hilliard was after all painting almost exclusively for court circles and we must not forget the heightened political and patriotic atmosphere of the period in which it was probably produced — in or around 1588 — the year of the Armada.

This piece was probably the first of a series of larger scale miniatures for which Hilliard usually chose a rectangular format — in this case he has used an elongated oval. The style of the picture betrays the influence of his stay in France during the mid-1570s when he would have seen the palace of Fontainebleau. The sinuous and attenuated outline of the young man is reminiscent of the mannerist proclivities of the Fontainebleau school and it fits perfectly into his chosen oval format. This most charming miniature has become deservedly famous not only as a near perfect and original example of the limner's art but as embodying the quintessence of a heady period of English history.

Contemporary Works

1586	El Greco: *The Burial of Count Orgaz*; Toledo
1587	Jacopo Tintoretto: *Flight into Egypt*; Venice
1595	Caravaggio: *The Lute Player*; St Petersburg

Nicholas Hilliard

?1547	Born in Exeter, the son of a goldsmith.
1559	Hilliard is in Geneva having been sent by his staunchly Protestant father during the latter part of Mary's reign.
1560	At the age of thirteen he completes his first miniatures.
1562	Apprenticed to Robert Brandon, a London goldsmith.
1569	Becomes a freeman of the Goldsmiths Company.
1572	Paints his first miniature of Elizabeth I – helped by the patronage of Robert Dudley, Earl of Leicester.
1576	Marries Alice Brandon, the daughter of his former master, and travels to France in the hope of better remuneration. Becomes Valet de Chambre to the Duc d'Alençon.
1578	Returns to England.
1584	Commissioned to re-design Elizabeth's Great Seal.
1585	Elizabeth issues a patent granting Hilliard a monopoly of the production of limned (miniature) portraits of her.
1603	James I maintains Hilliard's position as Royal Limner.
1617	James grants Hilliard a monopoly of engraved royal images.
1619	Dies in London.

In 1797 the 2nd Marquess of Hertford acquired the lease of Manchester House (now Hertford House). His grandson, the 4th Marquess was brought up in Paris by his mother and lived a reclusive life in a large apartment on the rue Laffitte. He never married. The last thirty years of the 4th Marquess's life were devoted to collecting works of art and it is his collection which forms the core of the works on show at the Wallace Collection. He died at his château in the Bois de Boulogne in 1870.

Richard Jackson, the illegitimate son of the 4th Marquess of Hertford and Mrs Agnes Jackson, was never acknowleged by the marquess as his son, and in 1842 Jackson changed his name to Wallace, his mother's maiden name. He inherited his father's collection in 1870 and two years later he took up residence in London. He was known for his philanthropy and was made a baronet in 1871. He purchased further works to add to the collection and on his death in 1890 he left all his property to Lady Wallace. On her death seven years later she left the collection to the nation.

Wallace Collection

Hertford House, Manchester Square, London W1U 3BN
Tel. +44 (0)20 7563 9500

Opening Hours

Every day 10am – 5pm
Closed 24 – 26 December

Admission

Free

How To Get There

The nearest underground stations are Bond St (Central and Jubilee Lines) and Baker St (Hammersmith and City, Metropolitan, Circle, Jubilee and Bakerloo Lines).
Bus routes 2, 10, 12, 13, 30, 74, 82, 94, 113, 137, 274.

Access for the Disabled

The gallery provides access for the disabled to all floors. For further information telephone +44 (0)20 7563 9515.

Shop

Open as above. The Wallace Collection shop sells a wide range of gifts and books, many exclusive to the Wallace Collection, including stationery, mugs, mousemats, scarves, ties, cushions, china and a range of traditional and modern jewellery.

Café Bagatelle

Open every day 10am – 4.30pm. Situated in the elegant Sculpture Garden, in the heart of the collection, the dramatic glass roof provides a light and airy 'outdoor' setting. A French restaurant company, Eliance, manages the Café Bagatelle; their portfolio also includes the Musée du Louvre and the Michelin-starred Jules Verne restaurant on the second floor of the Eiffel Tower.

Frans Hals

Wallace Collection

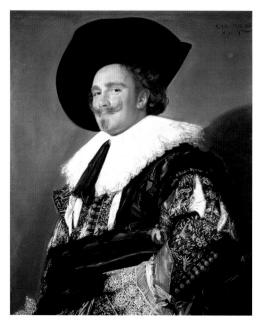

Not really laughing — more like an arrogant swagger. Not really a cavalier — rather a portrait of someone who is probably dressed up for a special occasion. But Hals was not responsible for the title — that was attached in the nineteenth century. It was bought in 1865 by the 4th Marquess of Hertford who bid against Baron de Rothschild for it at auction. The marquess ended up paying an enormous sum for the picture, by an artist who, at that time, was unknown. Indeed, this purchase was the spur to renewed interest in Hals and since then his reputation as one of the great Dutch painters has never been in doubt.

His loose painterly style is the key to his rediscovery but also the reason for the prolonged posthumous obscurity. During the eighteenth century his work had been thought of as unfinished or not up to the mark. This view had persisted into the nineteenth century until the advent of Realism and early Impressionism opened the eyes of connoisseurs and critics to his manifest qualities.

Although his reputation as a painter was resurrected in the nineteenth century, scholars researching his life seemed to uncover a tale of dissolute drunkenness and profligacy. However recent research suggests that there might have been some (not unreasonable) scholarly confusion between the painter and a cousin with the same name who is recorded in Haarlem as having been a drunken wife-beater. Nevertheless, there seems no doubt that Hals was plagued with constant money problems throughout his life. It is diverting to wonder if a putative devil-may-care attitude to life on the part of the artist may have played its part in the production of many paintings from his brush which seem to be suffused with a certain insouciant gaiety.

The Laughing Cavalier is one such portrait. It may have been painted at the time of the sitter's betrothal, or it may be that he wished no more than to show off his finery. But it seems likely that some amorous intent lay behind the painting as a number of motifs used in the Netherlands as symbols of love appear in the embroidery on the jacket — arrows, bees and lovers' knots among others. This could also account for the self-satisfied look on his face! The embroidery, together with the man's expression, and the portrayal of his ruff and lace cuffs provide a challenge for the most accomplished of artists, a challenge which was triumphantly taken up by Hals.

Contemporary Works

1624	Hendrick ter Brugghen: *The Bagpipe Player*, Cologne
1625	Peter Paul Rubens: *'Le Chapeau de Paille'*, London, National Gallery
1627	Guido Reni: *The Immaculate Conception*, New York

Frans Hals

1581-5	Born in Antwerp.
c1591	The Hals family moves to Haarlem where Frans spends most of his life.
1610	Hals enters the Guild of St Luke in Haarlem and also marries his first wife Annetgen.
1615	Hals' wife dies.
1617	He marries Liesbeth Reyniers.
1631	Hals asks the painter Judith Leyster to be godmother to his daughter.
1633	Receives a commission to paint an Amsterdam militia company which leads to a dispute, Hals refusing to go to Amsterdam to finish the work and the company refusing to travel to Haarlem.
1635	Hals becomes involved in a quarrel with Judith Leyster over the poaching of a pupil. He is also noted as being in arrears with his contributions to the guild.
1644	The Haarlem Guild elect him as a warden.
1652	Furniture and paintings are distrained in order to settle an unpaid baker's bill.
1661	The Guild waive his contributions because of his age.
1662	He applies for financial help from the city.
1666	Dies in Haarlem.

Nicolas Poussin

A Dance to the Music of Time   c1635-6

Wallace Collection

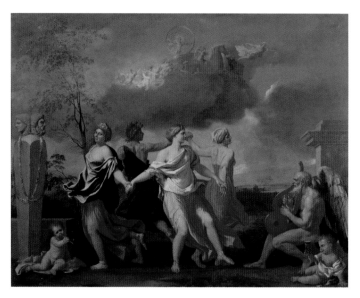

Born in Normandy and having studied in Paris, in 1624, by the age of thirty, Poussin had become resident in Rome. During his early years in Rome, as well as seeking patronage from the Roman ecclesiastical elite, he also mixed with other French expatriate artists, making sketching sorties into the countryside around Rome with Claude Lorrain and his brother in law Gaspard Dughet.

This picture has a strong claim to be thought of as the artist's masterpiece. It was painted at some time between 1634 and 1636 for Cardinal Giulio Rospigliosi who later became Pope Clement XI. Rospigliosi was also a poet and a librettist for the newly emerging art form of opera and it is therefore probable that the subject of the painting was devised by him.

The dancing quartet represent the seasons. Spring wears a white tunic; Summer, clad in blue, has her hair decorated with roses; Bacchus personifying Autumn has his back to us; to his right Winter is wearing a head scarf. They are dancing to music played by Saturn on his lyre. The Roman god Saturn is associated with the Greek god of time, Kronos and to emphasise the point a small child plays with an hour glass at Saturn's feet and another infant, in the opposite corner of the picture, blows bubbles, alluding to the ephemeral nature of human life. This child sits near a term, a pedestal which supports two heads, one youthful the other older. Above, Apollo, the god of light, makes his daily journey across the sky in his chariot, another reference to the passing of time.

There is a parallel interpretation for the identity of the dancers which encapsulates the human condition. Poverty (Autumn) triggers the need for

Labour (Winter) which generates Wealth (Spring) leading to Pleasure (Summer). But too much pleasure may lead to excess which in turn leads back to poverty and the cycle starts again.

Rather than a flowing dance to music, the dancers look more as though they are somewhat frozen in time but Poussin is not striving to create a naturalistic simulacrum; rather he invents a self-contained universe ordered with mathematical precision — a pastoral idyll inhabited by gods set against the landscape of the Roman Campagna.

Contemporary Works

1635	Georges de la Tour: *The Card Cheat*; Paris
	Peter Paul Rubens: *Portrait of Charles I Hunting*; Paris
1636	Francisco de Zurbarán: *St Lawrence*; St Petersburg

Nicolas Poussin

1594	Born at Les Andelys (Normandy).
1612	Arrives in Paris where he studies antique sculpture and Italian painting.
1624	Takes up residence in Rome after first visiting Venice.
1627	Receives his first major commission, *The Death of Germanicus*, from Cardinal Francesco Barberini, a nephew of the Pope. Joines the circle of intellectuals centred on Cardinal Barberini's secretary, Cassiano dal Pozzo who is a friend of Galileo.
1629	Poussin is living with the family of Jacques Dughet.
1630	Marries Jacques Dughet's daughter, Anne-Marie. Explores the Roman Campagna with Anne-Marie's brother Gaspard and with Claude Lorrain, making sketches out of doors.
1632	Poussin is recorded as a member of the Accademia di S Luca in Rome.
1640	Returns to France at the behest of King Louis XIII where he undertakes work in the Grande Galerie of the Louvre.
1642	Poussin returns to Rome.
1665	Dies in Rome.

Jean-Antoine Watteau

The Music Party   c1718

Wallace Collection

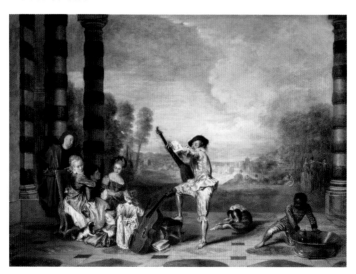

Watteau's relatively small paintings were, in part, a response to a new vogue in Paris at the beginning of the eighteenth century for more intimate, less formal works. He effectively invented a new pictorial genre, the *fêtes galantes* — portrayals of elegant outdoor gatherings engaged in nothing more taxing than the pursuit of fashionable pleasures, often accompanied by music. These paintings create a delightful mood of nostalgic wistfulness and ambiguity. Watteau was not interested in depicting reality let alone specific events. His cast of *commedia dell'arte* characters accompanied by members of the leisured classes inhabit a world of eternal summer in which everyone is at ease and usually in pursuit of an amorous liaison. However the euphoria is tinged with the realisation that life can also be cruel and that youth is not everlasting. Rather like that idyllic summer two centuries later, in 1914, the participants in the *fêtes galantes* appear to be oblivious to the fact that their nemesis may not be far away. Watteau's personal nemesis was indeed very close, taking the form of the tuberculosis which ended his life at a tragically early age.

However, in The Music Party the idyll continues. The gathering is taking place in an indeterminate architectural setting — hardly a ruin but perhaps some sort of external loggia although the pillars do seem a little tall for this. In the parkland other groups are enjoying the day. In the foreground, dominating the centre of the composition, a lute player strikingly dressed in pink silk strives to tune his instrument. To the right a black servant is selecting some chilled wine. To the left of the lute player a group has congregated; a lady sits on a chair playing a guitar; a man in a red cloak leans on the back of her chair. Perhaps he has just made some sort of amorous advance for the young guitarist is studiedly averting her gaze; or perhaps she has been distracted by the two young girls, one in pink, the other playing with a spaniel. We will never know. They will continue to inhabit Watteau's dream world. In the real world we do know with melancholy certainty that life's pleasures are all too transitory.

Contemporary Works

| 1717 | Godfrey Kneller: *Portrait of Joseph Tonson*; London, National Portrait Gallery |

Jean-Antoine Watteau

1684	Born at Valenciennes in northern France.
1702	Probable date of Watteau's move to Paris where he is employed in a picture workshop producing devotional and wholesale paintings.
1705	Assists the painter Claude Gillot in the production of paintings illustrating scenes from the theatre including the *commedia dell'arte*.
1708	Works with an interior decorator, probably providing paintings which were incorporated into the decorative scheme.
1709	Wins second prize in the Prix de Rome competition. Returns for a short time to Valenciennes.
1717	Admitted to the Académie Royale. His reception piece is *Departure for the Isle of Cythera*.
1719	Visits London possibly in order to consult Richard Mead, a renowned doctor, about his failing health.
1720	Returns to Paris. In poor health, he goes to live with his friend the art dealer Edmé-François Gersaint.
1721	Paints *L'Enseigne de Garsaint* – a shop sign for Gersaint's business. Dies at Nogent sur Marne near Paris.

Jean-Honoré Fragonard

The Swing   1767

Wallace Collection

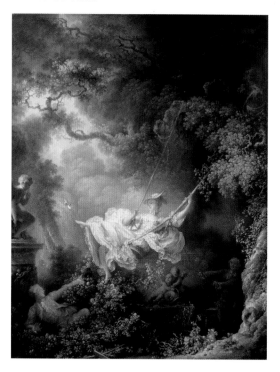

Fragonard was a pupil of both Chardin and Boucher. With such exalted, but in many ways very different mentors, one would expect that his gifts might blossom in various directions, which is indeed what happened — Fragonard became a virtuoso painter, draughtsman and engraver. He won the Prix de Rome and was elected to the Académie, his presentation piece (*morceau d'agrément*) causing a sensation and subsequently being purchased for the Crown. But he turned his back on the Académie, preferring to paint smaller scale works for private collectors.

This picture was one such commission, from Baron de St Julien who originally went to a well respected history painter and pronounced, so the story goes, 'I desire that you should paint Madame (indicating his mistress) on a swing which is being set in motion by a Bishop. You must place me where I can have a good view of the legs of this pretty little thing.' The baron's original choice of painter refused the commission and recommended M. Fragonard. Along the way, the bishop was converted into an elderly husband.

A chocolate box confection, *The Swing* is nevertheless a beautifully crafted piece. The jungle-like foliage is particularly interesting, painted in the strange unnatural, grey-green which was favoured by Boucher and the Rococo painters of the period. The two male members of the cast are clothed in colours which seem to blend in with the surrounding verdure, so much so that the more elderly gentleman, immersed in shadow is easy to miss at a cursory glance. All this provides the backdrop for the swirling 'party' pink dress of the young lady on the swing who has just kicked off her matching pink slipper which is captured at the apogee of its flight before its fall to earth, perhaps quite close to her lover. Artfully hidden behind a rose bower, he is placed in a most appealing position, the better to appreciate the shapely legs — and perhaps more — of his beloved. The cuckolded elderly husband is meanwhile doing all the work in the shadows, oblivious to the treachery of his young wife.

Contemporary Works

1766	Hubert Robert: *Landscape with Stone Bridge*; St Petersburg
1767	Gaimbattista Tiepolo: *Allegory of the Immaculate Conception*; Dublin
1769	George Stubbs: *The Milbanke and Melbourne Families*; London, National Gallery

Jean-Honoré Fragonard

1732	Born in Grasse, Provence, the son of a haberdasher.
1738	The family moves to Paris.
c1749	After spending some time as the pupil of Jean-Siméon Chardin he enters the studio of François Boucher.
1752	Wins the Prix de Rome.
1753	Enters the École Royale des Elèves Protégés.
1756	Arrives in Rome.
1758	Meets the French painter Hubert Robert.
1760	Spends the summer at the Villa d'Este as the guest of the Abbé de Saint-Non, Robert's patron.
1761	Fragonard travels with the Abbé de Saint-Non and Robert on a tour of Italy. Returns to Paris.
1765	Fragonard becomes a member of the Académie Royale. His presentation piece for the Académie, *Coresus Sacrifices Himself to Save Callirhoe* is a great success when exhibited at the Salon and is subsequently purchased for the Crown.
1769	Marries Marie-Anne Gérard.
1770	His fashionable status is confirmed when he is commissioned by Mme du Barry to produce decorations entitled the *Progress of Love* for her pavilion at Louveciennes.
1773	Tours Italy visiting Rome again.
1774	Visits Naples, continuing to Vienna, Prague and Germany.
1789	Moves back to live in Grasse.
1792	Returns to Paris. He manages to negotiate the French Revolution without imprisonment but his style is deeply out of step with the Neo-Classical vogue which accompanies it.
1794	Jacques-Louis David uses his influence to recommend that Fragonard be appointed a member of the Conservatoire des Arts.
1795	Becomes president of the Conservatoire des Arts with responsibility for the new national museum in the Louvre.
1806	Dies in Paris in obscurity.

Joshua Reynolds

Wallace Collection

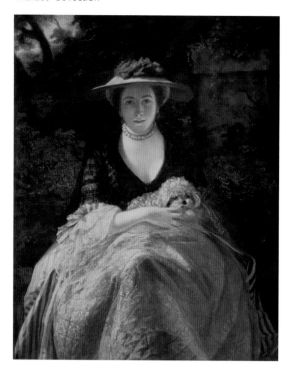

This piece has a curiously 'modern' feel — it would not look out of place in an exhibition of works from the last years of the nineteenth century. The direct and challenging stare, the fact that her hat is casting a shadow over the most important part of any portrait, the head — somehow it seems to belong to a later era. If one contrasts this picture with two admirable portraits, *Mrs Carnac* by Reynolds himself, and *Mrs Robinson* by Thomas Gainsborough hung only a few feet away in the Wallace Collection, or for that matter, with most of the rest of Reynolds' output, the difference in approach is marked. This is interesting as Reynolds is famous as the arch classicist, exhorting his followers and students to follow the precepts of the Grand Style, drawing inspiration from the Italian masters and from the classical world, a path set out so influentially in his *Discourses*, delivered over a number of years to the Royal Academy which was founded just a few years after this painting was created.

Nelly was a friend of Reynolds and a much admired beauty. He used her as a model in a number of his paintings. She was also a courtesan and it is tempting to propose that this might be why she has adopted a very direct stare — as though she is saying 'any problems?' Her elegant hands enclose her lapdog which (true to its role) sits contentedly amidst the folds of her dress. The dress is painted with great skill as is the lace which falls onto it from her sleeves. The dark colour of her bodice encloses an alluring expanse of creamy skin from the choker encompassing her throat to the first swellings of her breasts. She seems so much more interesting and full of life than the equally beautiful but somehow more distant belles who now grace the same wall.

There are fascinating parallels between this picture and another marvellous (and exactly contemporary) portrait by Gainsborough — that of Countess Howe at Kenwood (see page 52). Although the pose is different, that same unswerving stare engages the viewer from beneath similar hats and one feels that one is in the presence of similarly remarkable women, albeit from different social positions.

If, like me, you are a touch bored by much of Reynolds' output then this picture is like a breath of fresh air showing us a different artist from the man who was head of a thriving studio, assistants at hand, to help churn out an endless supply of portraits for fashionable London.

Contemporary Works

1760	Francesco Guardi: *Venice: The Arsenal*; London, National Gallery
c1763	Jean-Baptiste Greuze: *The Broken Mirror*; London, Wallace Collection

Joshua Reynolds

1723	Born at Plympton St Maurice in Devon, the son of the headmaster of Plympton Grammar School.
1740	Following his decision to become a painter he is apprenticed to Thomas Hudson in London.
1743	Reynolds cuts short his apprenticeship, working independently in London and Devon.
1749	Sails to Italy with his friend Commodore Augustus Keppel.
1750	Reynolds lives in Rome for two years.
1752	Visits Florence, Bologna, Naples and Venice before returning via Paris arriving in London in October.
1753	Sets up his own studio in London, quickly becoming successful and establishing himself in society circles.
1756	Meets and becomes friendly with Dr Johnson.
1759	Three of Reynolds' letters are published in Johnson's periodical the *Idler*. Reynolds is elected a governor of the Foundling Hospital.
1760	Moves to larger premises in Leicester Fields.
1762	Meets Oliver Goldsmith.
1764	Founds the Literary Club. Becomes seriously ill but recovers.
1766	He is elected as a member of the Society of Dilettanti.
1768	Visits Paris. The Royal Academy is founded and Reynolds is elected as first President.
1769	Delivers the first of his *Discourses*. Knighted by George III.
1771	Joins Horace Walpole in Paris.
1772	Becomes Alderman of Plympton.
1773	Elected Mayor of Plympton.
1778	The first seven *Discourses* are published.
1779	Suffers a stroke but recovers well.
1781	Visits the Netherlands.
1782	Suffers another stroke which affects his eyesight.
1784	Appointed Principal Painter to the King.
1785	Visits Brussels, Antwerp and Ghent.
1789	His eyesight begins to fail.
1792	Dies in London.

Acknowledgements

Antonello da Messina *St Jerome in his Study* © The National Gallery, London / Bridgeman Art Library; 76

Bacon, Francis *Three Studies for Figures at the Base of a Crucifixion* © Tate, London 2005; 182

Balla, Giacomo *The Hand of the Violinist* © DACS 2005 / Estorick Collection / Bridgeman Art Library; 44

Beckmann, Max *Carnival* © DACS 2005 / © Tate, London 2005; 202

Bellini, Giovanni *Agony in the Garden* © The National Gallery, London / Bridgeman Art Library; 74

Bonnard, Pierre *Coffee* © ADAGP, Paris and DACS, London 2005 / © Tate, London 2005; 198

Bosch, Hieronymus *Christ Mocked* © The National Gallery, London/ Bridgeman Art Library; 86

Botticelli, Sandro *Venus and Mars* © The National Gallery, London / Bridgeman Art Library; 82

Braque, Georges *Clarinet and Bottle of Rum on a Mantelpiece* © ADAGP, Paris and DACS, London 2005 / © Tate, London 2005; 194

Bronzino, *Allegory with Venus and Cupid* © The National Gallery, London / Bridgeman Art Library; 108

Bruegel, Pieter, The Elder *Landscape with the Flight into Egypt* Samuel Courtauld Trust, Courtauld Institute of Art Gallery / Bridgeman Art Library; 18

Burne-Jones, Edward *King Cophetua and the Beggar Maid* © Tate, London 2005; 176

Canaletto *Old Walton Bridge* Dulwich Picture Gallery, London / Bridgeman Art Library; 40

Caravaggio *Supper at Emmaus* © The National Gallery, London© / Bridgeman Art Library; 114

Cézanne, Paul *Lac d'Annecy* Samuel Courtauld Trust, Courtauld Institute of Art Gallery / Bridgeman Art Library; 30

Chardin, Jean Siméon *Young Schoolmistress* © The National Gallery, London / Bridgeman Art Library; 130

Chirico, Giorgio de *Uncertainty of the Poet* © DACS 2005 / © Tate, London 2005; 196

Claude Lorrain *Landscape with Psyche outside the Palace of Cupid, (The Enchanted Castle);* © The National Gallery, London; 124

Constable, John *Sketch for Hadleigh Castle* © Tate, London 2005; 162

Correggio *School of Love (Venus with Mercury and Cupid)* © The National Gallery, London / Bridgeman Art Library; 102

Cranach, Lucas, the Elder *Adam and Eve* Samuel Courtauld Trust, Courtauld Institute of Art Gallery / Bridgeman Art Library; 16

Crivelli, Carlo *Annunciation with St Emidius* © The National Gallery, London / Bridgeman Art Library; 84

Cuyp, Aelbert *View of Dordrecht* Kenwood House, London / Bridgeman Art Library; 48

Dadd, Richard *The Fairy Feller's Master Stroke* © Tate, London 2005; 172

Dalí, Salvador *Metamorphosis of Narcissus* © Salvador Dalí, Gala-Salvador Dalí Foundation, DACS, London / © Tate, London 2005; 208

David, Jacques-Louis *Jacobus Blauw* © The National Gallery, London; 138

Degas, Hilaire-Germain-Edgar *Two Dancers on the Stage* Samuel Courtauld Trust, Courtauld Institute of Art Gallery / Bridgeman Art Library; 20

Delvaux, Paul *Venus Asleep* © Foundation P Delvaux - St Idesbald, Belgium / DACS, London 2005 / © Tate, London 2005; 210

Duccio di Buoninsegna *Annunciation* © The National Gallery, London; 56

Dürer, Albrecht *Saint Jerome* © The National Gallery, London; 88

Dyck, Anthony van *Equestrian Portrait of Charles I* © The National Gallery, London / Bridgeman Art Library; 118

Ernst, Max *Celebes* © ADAGP, Paris and DACS, London 2005 / © Tate, London 2005; 204

Eyck, Jan van *Portrait of a Man* © The National Gallery, London / Bridgeman Art Library; 62. *The Arnolfini Portrait* © The National Gallery, London / Bridgeman Art Library; 64

Fragonard, Jean-Honoré *The Swing* Wallace Collection, London / Bridgeman Art Library; 230

Friedrich, Caspar David *Winter Landscape* © The National Gallery, London / Bridgeman Art Library; 140

Gainsborough, Thomas *Mary, Countess Howe* Kenwood House, London / Bridgeman Art Library; 52

Gauguin, Paul *Nevermore* Samuel Courtauld Trust, Courtauld Institute of Art Gallery / Bridgeman Art Library; 32

Geertgen tot Sint Jans *Nativity at Night* © The National Gallery, London; 80

Giorgione *The Sunset (Il Tramonto)* © The National Gallery, London / Bridgeman Art Library; 94

Gogh, Vincent van *Sunflowers* © The National Gallery, London / Bridgeman Art Library; 152

Gossaert, Jan (Mabuse) *Adoration of the Kings* © The National Gallery, London; 98

Goya, Francisco de *Portrait of the Duke of Wellington* © The National Gallery, London / Bridgeman Art Library; 142

Greco, El *Christ driving the Traders from the Temple* © The National Gallery, London / Bridgeman Art Library; 112

Grosz, George *Suicide* © DACS 2005 / © Tate, London 2005; 200

Hals, Frans *The Laughing Cavalier* Wallace Collection, London / Bridgeman Art Library; 224

Hilliard, Nicholas *Young Man leaning against a Tree among Roses* Victoria & Albert Museum, London / Bridgeman Art Library; 220

Hobbema, Meindert *The Avenue, Middelharnis* © The National Gallery, London / Bridgeman Art Library; 128

Hockney, David *A Bigger Splash* (1967 96 x 96 inches) © David Hockney / © Tate, London 2005; 184

Hogarth, William *Rake's Progress III, The Rose Tavern* Courtesy of the Trustees of Sir John Soane's Museum, London / Bridgeman Art Library; 158

Holbein, Hans, the Younger *The Ambassadors* © The National Gallery, London / Bridgeman Art Library; 104. *Christina of Denmark, Duchess of Milan* © The National Gallery, London / Bridgeman Art Library; 106

Hooch, Pieter de *Interior with a Woman drinking with Two Men* © The National Gallery, London / Bridgeman Art Library; 122

Hunt, William Holman *The Awakening Conscience* © Tate, London 2005; 170

Ingres, Jean-Auguste-Dominique *Madame Moitessier* © The National Gallery, London / Bridgeman Art Library; 146

Inshaw, David *The Badminton Game* © David Inshaw / © Tate, London 2005; 186
Kiefer, Anselm *Parsifal III* © Anselm Kiefer / © Tate, London 2005; 216
Klein, Yves *IKB 79* © ADAGP, Paris and DACS, London / © Tate, London 2005; 212
Klimt, Gustav *Portrait of Hermine Gallia* © The National Gallery, London, on loan to
    Tate Modern / Bridgeman Art Library; 190
Leonardo da Vinci *Virgin of the Rocks* © The National Gallery, London / Bridgeman
    Art Library; 92
Manet, Édouard *Bar at the Folies-Bergère* Samuel Courtauld Trust, Courtauld
    Institute of Art Gallery / Bridgeman Art Library; 24
Mantegna, Andrea *Agony in the Garden* © The National Gallery, London /
    Bridgeman Art Library; 72
Martin, John *The Great Day of His Wrath* © Tate, London 2005; 168
Masaccio *Virgin and Child* © The National Gallery, London / Bridgeman Art Library;
    60
Matisse, Henri *Portrait of André Derain* © Succession H Matisse / DACS 2005 / ©
    Tate, London 2005; 192
Memling, Hans *The Donne Triptych* © The National Gallery, London; 78
Millais, John Everett *Ophelia* © Tate, London 2005; 166
Monet, Claude *Antibes* Samuel Courtauld Trust, Courtauld Institute of Art Gallery
    / Bridgeman Art Library; 28
Picasso, Pablo *The Three Dancers* © Succession Picasso / DACS 2005 / © Tate,
London   2005; 206
Piero della Francesca *Baptism of Christ* © The National Gallery, London /
    Bridgeman Art Library; 68
Piero di Cosimo *A Satyr mourning over a Nymph* © The National Gallery, London /
    Bridgeman Art Library; 90
Pisanello *The Vision of St Eustace* © The National Gallery, London / Bridgeman Art
    Library; 66
Pissarro, Camille *The Quays at Rouen* Samuel Courtauld Trust, Courtauld Institute
    of Art Gallery / Bridgeman Art Library; 26
Poussin, Nicolas *A Dance to the Music of Time* Wallace Collection, London /
    Bridgeman Art Library; 226
Puvis de Chavannes, Pierre-Cécile *The Beheading of St John the Baptist* © The
    National Gallery, London; 148
Raphael *Pope Julius II* © The National Gallery, London / Bridgeman Art Library; 96
Rembrandt *Girl at a Window (Balcony)* Dulwich Picture Gallery, London / Bridgeman
    Art Library; 38, *Self Portrait with Two Circles* Kenwood House, London /
    Bridgeman Art Library; 50
Renoir Pierre-Auguste *(La Loge) The Theatre Box* Samuel Courtauld Trust,
    Courtauld Institute of Art Gallery / Bridgeman Art Library; 22
Reynolds, Joshua *Nelly O'Brien* Wallace Collection, London / Bridgeman Art
    Library; 232
Rothko Mark *Red on Maroon (Seagram Murals)* © 1998 Kate Rothko Prizel &
    Christopher Rothko / DACS 2005 / © Tate, London 2005; 214
Rousseau, Henri *Tiger in a Tropical Storm* © The National Gallery, London /
    Bridgeman Art Library; 154
Rubens, Peter Paul *Autumn Landscape with Het Steen* © The National Gallery,
    London / Bridgeman Art Library; 116
Sargent, John Singer *Carnation, Lily, Lily, Rose* © Tate, London 2005; 178
Seurat, Georges *Bathers at Asnières* © The National Gallery, London / Bridgeman
    Art Library; 150
Spencer, Stanley *The Resurrection, Cookham* © Tate, London 2005; 180
Stubbs, George *Whistlejacket* © The National Gallery, London / Bridgeman Art
    Library; 132

Tintoretto, Jacopo *St George and the Dragon* © The National Gallery, London / Bridgeman Art Library; 110

Titian *Bacchus and Ariadne* © The National Gallery, London; 100

Toulouse-Lautrec, Henri de *In the Private Room at the Rat Mort* Samuel Courtauld Trust, Courtauld Institute of Art Gallery / Bridgeman Art Library; 34

Turner, J.M.W. , *The Fighting Temeraire tugged to her Last Berth to be Broken up* © The National Gallery, London / Bridgeman Art Library; 144, *Norham Castle, Sunrise* © Tate, London 2005; 164

Uccello, Paolo *St George and the Dragon* © The National Gallery, London / Bridgeman Art Library; 70

Unknown *The Wilton Diptych* © The National Gallery, London / Bridgeman Art Library; 58

Velázquez, Diego *Toilet of Venus (The 'Rokeby Venus')* © The National Gallery, London / Bridgeman Art Library; 120

Vermeer Johannes *A Young Woman Standing at a Virginal* © The National Gallery, London / Bridgeman Art Library; 126

Vigée le Brun, Elizabeth Louise *Self Portrait in a Straw Hat* © The National Gallery, London; 136

Watteau, Jean- Antoine *The Music Party* Wallace Collection, London / Bridgeman Art Library; 228

Whistler, James Abbott McNeill *Nocturne in Blue and Gold: Old Battersea Bridge* © Tate, London 2005; 174

Wright of Derby, Joseph *An Experiment on a Bird in the Air Pump* © The National Gallery, London / Bridgeman Art Library; 134

Index

Académie de France 147
Académie Julian 193, 199
Académie Royale 130, 137, 139, 229, 230, 231
Académie Suisse 27, 29, 31
Accademia Pellegrina 111
Adam and Eve 16–17
Adam, Robert 46
Adoration of the Kings 98–9
Aesthetic Movement 175
The Agony in the Garden
     Bellini 74–5
     Mantegna 72–3
Aix-en-Provence 31, 207
Alençon, Duc d' 221
Allais, Alphonse 212
Allegory with Venus and Cupid 108–9
Allegri, Antonio *see* Correggio
Alma-Tadema, Lawrence 155
Altdorfer, Albrecht 93, 97
The Ambassadors (Jean de Dinteville and Georges de Selve) 104–5
Amsterdam 39, 51, 123, 129, 203, 225
Angelico, Fra 61, 63, 65
Angerstein, John Julius 54
The Annunciation 56–7
The Annunciation with St Emidius 84–5
Antibes 28–9
Antonella da Messina 74, 75
     St Jerome in his Study 76–7
Antwerp
     Bruegel 18, 19
     Hals 225
     Gossaert 99
     Rubens 117
     van Dyck 118, 119
Apollinaire, Guillaume 154, 155, 194, 197, 204, 207
Arezzo 69
Argenteuil 25, 29

Arkwright, Richard 134
Arles 33, 152–3
Arnold, Graham and Ann 187
Arnolfini, Giovanni and Giovanna 63, 64–5
The Arnolfini Portrait 64–5
Arosa, Gustave 33
Artists' Company 191
Artists Indépendants, Groupe des 151, 155, 195
Ascoli Piceno 84, 85
Aurenche, Marie-Berthe 205
Aurier, Albert 153
Austria, War of Succession 40, 41
Autumn Landscape with a view of Het Steen in the Early Morning 116–17
The Avenue, Middelharnis 128–9
The Awakening Conscience 170–1

Baader-Meinhof group 217
Bacchus and Ariadne 100–1
Bacon, Francis 182–3
The Badminton Game 186–7
Baldovinetti, Alesso 71
Baldung Grien, Hans 95
Balla, Giacomo 44–5
Ballet Russe 195, 206, 207
Banks, Sir Joseph 132
Bankside Power Station 188
The Baptism of Christ 68–9
Bar at the Folies-Bergère 24–5
Barbari, Jacopo de' 99
Barberini, Cardinal Francesco 227
Barcelona 207, 209
Barry, Madame du 231
Bartolommeo, Fra 97, 100, 101
Basel 89, 105
Bath 52, 53
Bathers at Asnières 150–1
Battenburg, Fridel 203

Bayeu, Francisco and Ramón 143
Bayeu, Josefa 143
Bazille 23, 27
Beaumont, Sir George 163
Beckmann, Max
    Carnival 202–3
The Beheading of St John the Baptist 148–9
Bellini, Gentile 75
Bellini, Giovanni 79, 88, 95, 100
    The Agony in the Garden 74–5
Bellini, Jacopo 73, 75
Berchem, Nicolaes 123
Berlin 183, 185, 201, 203
Bernard, Émile 29, 30, 33, 152
Bernhein-Jeune gallery 199, 205
Bethlem (Bedlam) Hospital 172, 173
Beuys, Joseph 217
Bicknell, Maria 162, 163
A Bigger Splash 184–5
Bingham, George Caleb 165
Blake, Peter 187
Blauw, Jacobus 138–9
Bloch-Bauer, Adele 190
Boccioni, Umberto 195
Böcklin, Arnold 151, 177
Bolnes, Catherina 127
Bonaparte, Joseph 142, 143
Bonnard, Pierre 45, 181, 197, 203
    Coffee 198–9
Bonnat, Léon 35, 195
Booth, Mrs Sophia 165
Borgo Sansepolcro 68, 69
Bosch, Hieronymus 86–7
Boschman, Cornelia 49
Boston 149, 179
Botticelli, Sandro 79, 81, 85, 177
    Venus and Mars 82–3
Boucher, François 41, 53, 131, 133, 230, 231
Boudin, Eugène 29
Bourgeois, Sir Francis 36
Boursin, Maria (Marthe) 198, 199
Boussod, Valadon & Cie Gallery 35
Bouts, Dieric 73
Bragaglia, Anton Giulio 44
Bramante 96, 97
Brancusi, Constantin 197
Brandon, Alice 221
Brandt, Sebastian 89
Brant, Isabella 117
Braque, Georges 154, 207
    Clarinet and Bottle of Rum on a Mantelpiece 194–5
Breton, André 204, 206, 209, 211

Brittany 28, 33
Broederlam, Melchior 59
Bronzino 108–9
Brotherhood of Our Lady 87
Brotherhood of Ruralists 187
Brown, Ford Madox 171
Bruegel, Pieter, the Elder 111
    Landscape with Flight into Egypt 18-19
Bruges 63, 79
Brugghen, Hendrick ter 225
Brunelleschi, Filippo 61
Brussels
    Bruegel 18, 19
    Klimt 191
    Les XX 23, 35
    Paul Delvaux 210, 211
    van Gogh 153
Buckingham, Duke of 117
Buñuel, Luis 209
Burch, Jannetje van der 123
Burgundy, Dukes of see Philip
Burne-Jones, Sir Edward 27, 151
    King Cophetua and the Beggar Maid 176–7
Burr, Margaret 53
Byron, Lord 137

Cagnes 23
Caillebotte, Gustave 23
Campin, Robert 61, 63
Canaletto (Giovanni Antonio Canal) 131, 159
    Old Walton Bridge 40–1
Le Cannet 199
Cantacuzène, Princess Marie 149
Caravaggio 113, 221
    The Supper at Emmaus 114–15
Carline, Hilda 180, 181
Carlos IV, king of Spain 143
Carnation, Lily, Lily, Rose 178–9
Carnegie International Exhibition 199
Carnival 202–3
Carolus-Duran, Charles 178, 179
Carpaccio, Vittore 89, 99
Carrà, Carlo 197
Carracci, Annibale 113, 115
Carrington, Leonora 205
Casagemas, Carlos 207
Cassatt, Mary 177
Cavallini, Pietro 57
Celebes 204–5
Cenami, Giovanna 64
Cephalus and Procris 90

Cézanne, Paul 21, 23, 27, 29, 33, 194
    The Lac d'Annecy 30–1
Chagall, Marc 197
Chapelle, Madeleine 147
Chardin, Jean Siméon 159, 230, 231
    The Young Schoolmistress 130–1
Charigot, Aline 23
Charles I, king of England 117, 118,
    119
Charles V, Emperor 18, 89, 101, 106,
    119
Charles VI, Emperor 40
Chassériau, Théodore 145
Chatou, Île de 23
Chirico, Giorgio de 201, 204–5, 211
    The Uncertainty of the Poet 196–7
Christ driving the Traders from the
    Temple 112–13
Christ Mocked (the Crowning with
    Thorns) 86–7
Christina of Denmark, Duchess of
    Milan 106–7
Cimabue 57
Clarinet and Bottle of Rum on a
    Mantelpiece 194–5
Claude Lorrain see Lorrain, Claude
Clemenceau, Georges 31
Cocteau, Jean 206, 207
Coecke, Mayken (Maria) 18, 19
Coecke van Aelst, Pieter 18, 19
Coffee 198–9
Cole, Thomas 163
Collins, William 169
Collioure 192, 193
Coltman, Thomas and Mary 135
Constable, John
    Sketch for Hadleigh Castle 162–3
Cookham 180–1
Copenhagen 33, 141
Coram, Thomas 159
Corbet, Gustave 167, 175
Corinth, Lovis 45
Cormon, Fernand 35
Corneille de Lyon 107
Corot, Jean-Baptiste-Camille 21, 145,
    163
Correggio 17, 105
    The School of Love (Venus with
    Mercury and Cupid) 102–3
Courbet, Gustave 147, 171
Courtauld Institute Gallery 14–35,
    15
    Adam and Eve 16–17
    Antibes 28–9
    Bar at the Folies-Bergère 24–5

In the Private Room at the Rat
    Mort 34–5
    La Loge (The Theatre Box) 22–3
    The Lac d'Annecy 30–1
    Landscape with the Flight into
    Egypt 18–19
    Nevermore 32–3
    The Quays at Rouen 26–7
    Two Dancers on the Stage 20–1
Courtauld, Samuel 14
Couture, Thomas 25, 149
Cranach, Lucas, the Elder 105
    Adam and Eve 16–17
Crete 112, 113
Crivelli, Carlo 81, 87, 89, 177
    The Annunciation with St Emidius
    84–5
Cromwell, Thomas 105
Cubists 30, 194–5, 206, 207
Cupid 102–3, 108–9, 124–5, 126
Cuyp, Aelbert
    View of Dordrecht 48–9

Dada movement 201, 205
Dadd, Richard
    The Fairy Feller's Master-Stroke
    172–3
Dahl, Johann Christian 141
Dalí, Salvador 211
    Metamorphosis of Narcissus
    208–9
Danby, Hannah 165
A Dance to the Music of Time 226–7
David, Gerard 83
David, Jacques-Louis 137, 141, 147,
    231
    Portrait of Jacobus Blauw 138–9
de Hooch, Pieter
    Interior with a Woman drinking
    with Two Men 122–3
Degas, Hilaire-Germain-Edgar 23, 35,
    149, 175
    Two Dancers on the Stage 20–1
Delacroix, Eugène 147, 149, 163, 165
Delaunay, Robert 155
Delft 123, 127
Delvaux, Paul 155, 209
    Sleeping Venus 210–11
Derain, André 192–3, 197
Derby, Joseph Wright of
    An Experiment on a Bird in the Air
    Pump 134–5
Devereux, Robert, 2nd Earl of Essex
    220
Diaghilev, Serge 193, 205, 206, 207

Diebenkorn, Richard 217
Dieppe 27
Digby, Sir Kenelm 119
Dilettanti, Society of 233
Dinteville, Jean de 104–5
Dircz, Geertje 39
Donatello 97
Doncieux, Camille 29
Donne, Sir John 78
The Donne Triptych 78–9
Dono, Paolo di see Uccello, Paolo
Dordrecht 48–9
Dou, Gerrit 39
Dresden 141, 201
Duccio di Buoninsegna
    The Annunciation 56-7
Duchamp, Marcel 44, 45
Dudley, Robert, Earl of Leicester 221
Dufy, Raoul 195
Dughet, Gaspard 226, 227
Dughet, Jacques 227
Dulwich Picture Gallery 36–41, **37**
    Girl at a Window 38–9
    Old Walton Bridge 40–1
Durand-Ruel exhibitions 23, 27, 29,
    33, 199
Dürer, Albrecht
    contemporary works 17, 91, 93,
    95, 103
    Giovanni Bellini 75
    Gossaert influence 99
    St Jerome 88–9
Dyce, William 145
Dyer, George 183

Eakins, Thomas 35
École des Beaux-Arts 21, 23, 31,
    147, 151, 193
Edward IV, king of England 78
Edward the Confessor 58
Egg, Augustus 173
Egremont, Lord 165
Eliot, T.S. 182, 186
Elizabeth I, queen of England 220–1
Eluard, Paul and Gala 205, 209
The Enchanted Castle 124–5
Ensor, James 29
Equestrian Portrait of Charles I 118–19
Ernst, Max 155, 181, 197, 215
    Celebes 204–5
L'Estaque 31, 194, 195
Este, Alfonso d', Duke of Ferrara
    100, 101
Este family 69, 95
Estorick Collection 42–5, **43**

The Hand of the Violinist 44–5
Estorick, Eric and Salome 42
Eumenides 182
An Experiment on a Bird in the Air
    Pump 134–5
Expressionist artists 215

The Fairy Feller's Master-Stroke 172–3
Fantin-Latour, Henri 174
Fareham, Viscount Lee of 14
Fauves 30, 193, 194, 195
Federigo II Gonzaga, Marquis of
    Mantua 102
Ferdinand, king of Bohemia and
    Hungary 101
Fernando VII, king of Spain 143
Ferrante, Prince of Capua 85
Ferrara
    Piero della Francesca 69
    Pisanello 67
    Titian 100, 101
fêtes galantes 228
The Fighting Temeraire tugged to her
    Last Berth to be broken up 144–5
Fiquet, Hortense 31
Fisher, Dr John 162, 163
Florence
    Botticelli 82–3
    Bronzino 108, 109
    Leonardo da Vinci 93
    Masaccio 61
    Piero di Cosimo 91
    Piero della Francesca 69
    Raphael 97
    Uccello 71
Foley, Lord 173
Folies-Bergère 24
Fouquet, Jean 69
Fourment, Hélène 116, 117
Fragonard, Jean-Honoré 53, 135
    The Swing 230–1
Francesca, Piero della 67, 73, 74, 77,
    148, 149
    The Baptism of Christ 68–9
Francis I, king of France 93, 108
Frederic, Lord Leighton 31
Frederick the Wise, Duke 16, 17
French Polynesia 33
French Revolution 136, 137, 138,
    231
Freud, Sigmund 204, 208, 209
Frey, Agnes 89
Friedrich, Caspar David 143
    Winter Landscape 140–1
Frith, William Powell 27, 173

frottage technique 205
Fugger, Jörg 75
Fuseli, Johann Heinrich 137, 173
Futurists 44–5, 201

Gachet, Dr 31, 153
Gad, Mette-Sophie 33
Gainsborough, Thomas 41, 48, 133
    Mary, Countess Howe 52–3
Gallia, Hermine 190
Gaugin, Paul 27, 31, 152–3, 192, 199
    Nevermore 32–3
Geertgen tot Sint Jans 91
    The Nativity at Night 80–1
Gellée, Claude see Lorrain, Claude
Gentille da Fabriano 61, 66, 67
George III, king of England 233
Gérard, Marie-Anne 231
Géricault, Théodore 143
Gersaint, Edmé-François 229
Ghent, Joos van 75
Ghiberti, Lorenzo 70, 71
Ghirlandaio, Domenico 79, 83
Gillot, Claude 229
Gilot, Françoise 207
Giordano, Luca 129
Giorgione 101, 120
    The Sunset 94–5
Giotto 57
Girl at a Window 38–9
Giverny 29
Gleyre, Charles 23, 29, 175
Glyndebourne Opera 185
Godwin, Beatrice 175
Goes, Hugo van der 77, 79, 81, 99
Goldsmith, Oliver 233
Gonzaga, Ludovico 73
Gonzaga, Vincenzo I, Duke of
    Mantua 117
Gossaert, Jan (Mabuse) 101
    Adoration of the Kings 98–9
Gouel, Eva 207
Goupil & Co. 153, 180, 181
Gowing, Lawrence 93
Goya, Francisco de 139
    Portrait of the Duke of Wellington
    142–3
Gozzoli, Benozzo 73
Grand Tour 40, 41, 51
Granvelle, Antoine Perranot 18
Gravelot 53
The Great Day of His Wrath 168–9
Great Exhibition 218
El Greco 111, 115, 221
    Christ driving the Traders from the

Temple 112–13
La Grenouillère 23, 29
Greuze, Jean-Baptiste 233
Grimshaw, Atkinson 179
Gris, Guan 199
Grosvenor Gallery 177
Grosz, George 203
    Suicide 200–1
Guardi, Francesco 135, 233
Guggenheim, Peggy 205
Guillaumin 27
Guttuso, Renato 215

Haarlem 225
Habsburgs 40, 106
Hadleigh Castle, Sketch for 162–3
Hals, Frans 25, 125
    The Laughing Cavalier 224–5
Hammershøi, Vilhelm 35
The Hand of the Violinist 44–5
Hartopp, Mary 52–3
Hawarth, Jann 187
Hayman, Francis 53
Henry VIII, king of England 105, 106
Heron, Patrick 185
Hertford, 4th Marquess of 222, 224
Herzog, Jacques 188
Hilliard, Nicholas 220–1
Hobbema, Meindert
    The Avenue, Middelharnis 128–9
Hockney, David 187
    A Bigger Splash 184–5
Hogarth, William 131
    The Rake's Progress III, The Rose
    Tavern 158–9
Holbein, Hans (the Younger) 101,
    103, 109
    The Ambassadors (Jean de
    Dinteville and Georges de Selve)
    104–5
    Christina of Denmark, Duchess of
    Milan 106–7
Hollis, Thomas 40
Hooch, Pieter de
    Interior with a Woman drinking
    with Two Men 122–3
Hoornik, Clasina (Sien) 153
Hoschedé, Alice 29
Hoschedé, Ernest 29
Howe, Mary Countess 52–3
Hudson, Thomas 135, 233
Hughes, Arthur 167, 173
Hunt, William Holman 167, 169
    The Awakening Conscience 170–1

IKB 79 212–13
Impressionists
    Cézanne 31
    Degas 20, 21
    Gaugin 33
    Monet 29
    Pissarro 26, 27
    Renoir 22, 23
In the Private Room at the Rat Mort
    34–5
Ingres, Jean-Auguste-Dominique 21,
    141, 151
    Madame Moitessier 146–7
Inshaw, David
    The Badminton Game 186–7
Interior with a Woman drinking with
    Two Men 122–3
International Gothic style 66
Iveagh, 1st Earl of 46

Jackson, Richard 222
Jacobin Club 138, 139
James I, king of England 119, 221
James, Henry 179
Jas de Bouffan 31
Jeroen (Jeronimus) van Aken 87
Joblaud, Caroline 193
John I, king of Portugal 63
John VIII Palaeologus 67, 69
John the Baptist 58, 68, 78, 92, 148–9
John of Bavaria 63
John, Gwen 207
Johns, Jasper 215
Johnson, Dr 233
Johnson, Philip 214
Jonghelinck, Nicolaas 19
Jongkind, Johan Barthold 29
Jourdain, Lucy 35

Kahlo, Frida 211
Kahnweiler, Daniel-Henry 194, 195
Kandinsky, Vasily 195
Kaulbach, Mathilde von 203
Kenwood House 46–53, **47**
    Mary, Countess Howe 52–3
    Self Portrait with Two Circles
    (Rembrandt) 50–1
    View of Dordrecht 48–9
Keppel, Commodore Augustus 233
Khnopff, Fernand 155
Kiefer, Anselm 187
    Parsifal III 216–17
King Cophetua and the Beggar Maid
    176–7
Kirchner, Ernst Ludwig 197

Klein, Fred 213
Klein, Yves,
    IKB 79 212–13
Klimt, Ernst 191
Klimt, Gustav 33, 193, 201
    Portrait of Hermine Gallia 190–1
Kneller, Godfrey 129, 229
Knobloch, Madeleine 151
Købke, Christen 145
Koklova, Olga 206, 207
Kunstlercompagnie 191

The Lac d'Annecy 30–1
Lamothe, Louis 21
Landscape with the Flight into Egypt
    18–19
Landscape with Psyche outside the
    Palace of Cupid (The Enchanted
    Castle) 124–5
Langmuir, Erika 94
Lapre, Marcelle 195
Lastman, Pieter 39
Late Gothic style 70, 82, 98
The Laughing Cavalier 224–5
Lautréamont, Comte de 204
Lawrence, Thomas 139
Le Brun, Jean-Baptiste 137
Lear, Edward 170, 171
Leenhoff, Suzanne 25
Léger, Fernard 201
Lehmann, Henri 151
Leiden 39
Leonardo da Vinci
    contemporary works 77, 85, 87,
    99
    influence 97, 103, 114
    The Virgin of the Rocks 92–3
Lerma, Duque de 117
Leroy, Louis 29
Leyland, F.R. 174
Leyster, Judith 225
Liebermann, Max 25
Lippi, Fra Filippo 83
Liverpool, Tate Gallery 160
Lochner, Stefan 65, 67
La Loge (The Theatre Box) 22–3
London
    Bacon 183
    Burne-Jones 177
    Canaletto 40, 41
    Constable 163
    Dalí 209
    Gainsborough 53
    Hilliard 221
    Hockney 185

Hogarth 159
Holbein the Younger 105, 106
Hunt 170, 171
Klein 213
Martin 169
Millais 167
Monet 29
Reynolds 233
Rubens 117
Sargent 178, 179
Stubbs 133
Turner 165
van Dyck 118, 119
van Gogh 153
Whistler 174, 175
Lorca, Federico 209
Lorrain, Claude
    contemporary works 39, 51,
    119, 121, 127
    influence 145, 163
    Landscape with Psyche outside the
    Palace of Cupid (The Enchanted
    Castle) 124–5
    Nicolas Poussin 227
Los Angeles 184, 185
Lotto, Lorenzo 109
Louis XIII, king of France 227
Louis XV, king of France 131
Louis XVI, king of France 139
Louvre, Paris 92–3, 119, 139, 155,
    195, 227, 231
Löwenstein, Grete and Arthur 44, 45
Luther, Martin 16, 17, 105

Mabuse see Gossaert, Jan
Macdonald, Georgiana 177
Madame Moitessier 146–7
Madrid 113, 143, 209
Maestà 56–7
Magritte, René 181, 183, 197, 209,
    211
Malatesta, Sigismondo 69
Malevich, Kasemir 199, 212
Malta 115
Mander, Karel van 81
Manet, Édouard 21, 27, 149, 173
    Bar at the Folies-Bergère 24–5
Manguin, Henri 193
Mansfield, Lord 46
Mantegna, Andrea
    The Agony in the Garden 72–3
    contemporary works 71, 89
    influence 74, 75, 88, 102–3, 177
Mantua
    Correggio 102, 103

Mantegna 73, 102
    Pisanello 67
    Rubens 117
    Tintoretto 111
    Titian 101
Marey, Étienne-Jules 44
Margaret of Parma 18
Maria Theresa 40, 121
Marie Antoinette 136
Marinetti, Filippo 44
Marquet, Albert 193
Martin, John 168–9
Mártinez, Sebastián 143
Mary, Countess Howe 52–3
Mary, Queen of Hungary 101, 106
Masaccio,
    Virgin and Child 60–1
Masolino 61
Massys, Quentin 97
Matisse, Henri 191, 194, 195, 209
    Portrait of André Derain 192–3
Matsch, Franz 191
Maximillian, Holy Roman Emperor
    89
Mayer, Gaspar 139
Medici, Cosimo de' 51, 108, 109
Medici, Cardinal Giulio de' 97
Medici, Lorenzo de' 73
Meervenne, Aleyt Goyarts van den
    87
Melbye, Fritz and Anton 27
Memling, Hans 83, 85
    The Donne Triptych 78–9
Menil, John and Dominique de 215
Merisi, Michelangelo see Caravaggio
Messina, Sicily 77
Metamorphosis of Narcissus 208–9
metaphysical paintings 196, 197, 205
Meuron, Pierre de 188
Meyndertsz, Lubbert 129
Michelangelo
    Burne-Jones influence 177
    El Greco's view of 112
    Laurentian Library 214
    Rubens influence 117
    Sistine Chapel 96, 97
    Titian meeting 101
Middelharnis 128–9
Milan
    Caravaggio 114, 115
    Christina, Duchess of 106–7
    Leonardo da Vinci 93, 114
Millais, Effie 167
Millais, John Everett 147, 149, 165,
    171

Ophelia 166–7
Miller, Annie 171
Millet, Jean-François 23, 173
Miró, Joan 215
Modernism 197
Monaco, Lorenzo 59
Mondrian, Piet 183, 205, 211
Monet, Claude 23, 25, 27, 31, 175
    Antibes 28–9
Montauban 147
Monte, Cardinal del 115
Montefeltro, Federico 69
Montmartre 34–5, 195
More, Sir Thomas 105
Moreau, Gustave 21, 193
Morris, William 177
Moulin Rouge 35
Munch, Edvard 193
Murillo, Bartolomé Esteban 49, 51, 123, 127
The Music Party 228–9
Musso, Boniface 169
Muybridge, Eadweard 44

Nabi group 199
Naïve Art 154
Narcissus 208–9
National Gallery 54–155, **55**
    Adoration of the Kings 98–9
    The Agony in the Garden
        Bellini 74–5
        Mantegna 72–3
    Allegory with Venus and Cupid 108–9
    The Ambassadors (Jean de Dinteville and Georges de Selve) 104–5
    The Annunciation 56–7
    The Annunciation with St Emidius 84–5
    The Arnolfini Portrait 64–5
    Autumn Landscape with a view of Het Steen in the Early Morning 116–17
    The Avenue, Middelharnis 128–9
    Bacchus and Ariadne 100–1
    The Baptism of Christ 68–9
    Bathers at Asnières 150–1
    The Beheading of St John the Baptist 148–9
    Christ driving the Traders from the Temple 112–13
    Christ Mocked (the Crowning with Thorns) 86–7
    Christina of Denmark, Duchess of

    Milan 106–7
    The Donne Triptych 78–9
    Equestrian Portrait of Charles I 118–19
    An Experiment on a Bird in the Air Pump 134–5
    The Fighting Temeraire tugged to her Last Berth to be broken up 144–5
    Interior with a Woman drinking with Two Men 122–3
    Landscape with Psyche outside the Palace of Cupid (The Enchanted Castle) 124–5
    Madame Moitessier 146–7
    The Nativity at Night 80–1
    Pope Julius II 96–7
    Portrait of the Duke of Wellington 142–3
    Portrait of Jacobus Blauw 138–9
    Portrait of a Man (Self Portrait?) 62–3
    The Rokeby Venus (The Toilet of Venus) 120–1
    St George and the Dragon
        Tintoretto 110–11
        Uccello 70–1
    St Jerome 88–9
    St Jerome in his Study 76–7
    A Satyr Mourning over a Nymph 90–1
    The School of Love (Venus with Mercury and Cupid) 102–3
    Self Portrait in a Straw Hat (Vigée Le Brun) 136–7
    Sunflowers 152–3
    The Sunset 94–5
    The Supper at Emmaus 114–15
    Tiger in a Tropical Storm 154–5
    Venus and Mars 82–3
    Virgin and Child 60–1
    The Virgin of the Rocks 92–3
    The Vision of St Eustace 66–7
    Whistlejacket 132–3
    The Wilton Diptych 58–9
    Winter Landscape 140–1
    The Young Schoolmistress 130–1
    A Young Woman standing at a Virginal 126–7
The Nativity at Night 80–1
Nelly O'Brien 232–3
Neo-Impressionists 26, 27, 45, 193
Neue Sachlichkeit movement 203
Neumann, I.B. 203
Nevermore 32–3

New York
    Beckmann 203
    Dalí 209
    de Chirico 197
    Ernst 205
    Grosz 201
    Hockney 185
    Renoir 23
    Rothko 214–15
Nocturne in Blue and Gold: Old Battersea Bridge 174–5
Noland, Kenneth 213
Norham Castle, Sunrise 164–5
Normandy 27, 28, 151, 195, 199
Nouveau Réalisme movement 213
Nuremberg 89

O'Brien, Nelly 232–3
Old Walton Bridge 40–1
Olivier, Fernande 207
Ophelia 166–7
Orléans, Duc d' 147
Ostade, Adriaen van 121
Ovendon, Annie 187
Ovid 90, 117

Pacheco, Francisco 121
Padua 73, 89
Pahura 32–3
Pakszwer Far, Isabella 197
papier collé technique 195
Parayre, Amélie 193
Paris
    Bonnard 199
    Braque 194, 195
    Chardin 131
    Dalí 209
    David 138, 139
    de Chirico 197
    Ernst 204, 205
    Folies-Bergère 24
    Impressionists 21, 23, 27, 29, 33
    Ingres 147
    Klein 212, 213
    Matisse 193
    Montmartre 34–5, 195
    Picasso 207
    Poussin 227
    Puvis de Chavannes 149
    Rousseau 154, 155
    Rubens 117
    Sargent 178, 179
    Seurat 151
    van Gogh 153
    Vigée Le Brun 137
    Watteau 229
    Whistler 174, 175
Parma 18, 103
Parmigianino 105
Parsifal III 216–17
Pasmore, Victor 213
Patinir, Joachim 18–19
Pécoul, Marguerite-Charlotte 139
Perugino, Pietro 78, 81, 83, 87, 97
Peterzano, Simone 115
Petworth 165
Philip II, king of Spain 18, 101, 112, 113
Philip III, king of Spain 117
Philip IV, king of Spain 117, 121
Philip of Burgundy 99
Philip the Fair, Duke of Burgundy 87
Philip the Good, Duke of Burgundy 63, 64
Phillips, Sir Thomas 172
photo-collage technique 185
Picasso, Pablo
    contemporary works 45, 183, 191, 199, 205, 209
    influence 193, 194, 195, 197
    Rousseau 154, 155
    The Three Dancers 206–7
Pichot, Germaine 207
Pichot, Ramón 206
Piero di Cosimo 90–1
Piero della Francesca *see* Francesca, Piero della
Pisa 60, 83
Pisanello 66–7
Pissarro, Camille 29, 31, 33, 153
    The Quays at Rouen 26–7
Plympton St Maurice 233
pointillism 27, 151
Poland, king of 36
Pollaiuolo, Piero del 75, 77
Pollock, Jackson 211
Pont-Aven 33
Pontoise 33
Pontormo, Jacopo 101, 109
Pope Clement XI 226
Pope Innocent VIII 73
Pope Innocent X 121
Pope Julius II 96–7, 99
Pope Leo X 91, 97
Pope Paul III 101
Pope Sixtus IV 83
Pope Urban VIII 125
Porto Ercole 115
Portrait of André Derain 192–3
Portrait of the Duke of Wellington

142–3
Portrait of Hermine Gallia 190–1
Portrait of Jacobus Blauw 138–9
*Portrait of a Man (Van Eyck Self
    Portrait?)* 62–3
Portugal 63, 199
Poussin, Nicolas 94, 117, 119, 121
    A Dance to the Music of Time
        226–7
Pre-Raphaelites 166, 167, 170, 171
Predis, Ambrogio and Evangelista 93
Psyche 124
Puvis de Chavannes, Pierre-Cécile
    25, 150, 175
    *The Beheading of St John the
        Baptist* 148–9

Quarton, Enguerrand 69
The Quays at Rouen 26–7

The Rake's Progress III, The Rose Tavern
    158–9
Rakewell, Tom 158–9
Ramel, Delphine 147
Raphael 69, 78, 93, 99, 100, 117
    Pope Julius II 96–7
Rat Mort 34–5
Raymond, Marie 213
Red on Maroon (The Seagram Murals)
    214–15
Reformation 16
Reinhardt, Ad 215
Rembrandt (Harmensz van Rijn) 49,
    117, 123, 127, 134
    Girl at a Window 38–9
    Self Portrait with Two Circles 50–1
Renaissance art 61, 66, 70, 82–3, 96,
    100, 109
Reni, Guido 115, 225
Renoir, Jean 23
Renoir, Pierre 23
Renoir, Pierre-Auguste 27, 29, 179,
    191
    La Loge (The Theatre Box) 22–3
The Resurrection, Cookham 180–1
Reyniers, Liesbeth 225
Reynolds, Joshua 53, 133, 135, 137
    Nelly O'Brien 232–3
Richard II, king of England 58–9
Richter, Gerhard 187, 216, 217
Robert, Hubert 231
Rockingham, 2nd Marquess of 133
Rodin 31
The Rokeby Venus (The Toilet of Venus)
    120–1

Rome
    Balla 45
    Botticelli 83
    Caravaggio 115
    Claude Lorrain 125
    de Chirico 197
    Fragonard 231
    Gossaert 99
    El Greco 112, 113
    Ingres 147
    Mantegna 73
    Masaccio 61
    Piero della Francesca 69
    Pisanello 67
    Poussin 226, 227
    Raphael 96, 97
    Rubens 117
    Titian 101
    Velázquez 120, 121
Roque, Jacqueline 207
Rosa, Salvator 39
Rospigliosi, Cardinal Giulio 226
Rosselli, Cosimo 91
Rossetti, Dante Gabriel 165, 167,
    171, 177
Rothko, Mark 214–15
Rouen
    Gaugin 33
    Monet 29
    Pissarro 26, 27
Rousseau, Henri
    Tiger in a Tropical Storm 154–5
Rousseau, Théodore 167
Royal Academy
    Constable 162, 163
    Dadd 173
    Gainsborough 53
    Hockney 185
    Hunt 171
    Martin 169
    Millais 167
    Reynolds 233
    Sargent 179
    Sir John Soane 156
    Spencer 181
    Stubbs 133
    Turner 145, 165
    Whistler 175
    Wright of Derby 135
Royal College of Art 185
Rubens, Peter Paul 119, 121, 137,
    225, 227
    *Autumn Landscape with a view of
    Het Steen in the Early Morning*
    116–17

Ruisdael, Jacob van 129
Ruiz, Pablo see Picasso, Pablo
Ruralists, Brotherhood of 187
Ruskin, John 165, 167, 171, 175, 177
Ruthven, Mary 119
Ruysdael, Salomon van 121
Rysselberghe, Theo van 27

's Hertogenbosch 87
St Barbara 78
St Bridget of Sweden 80
St Catherine 78
St Edmund 59
St Emidius 84–5
St Eustace 66–7
St George 95
St George and the Dragon
    Tintoretto 110–11
    Uccello 70–1
St Ives, Tate Gallery 160
St Jerome 88–9
St Jerome in his Study 76–7
St John 92
    Knights of the Order of 115
St John the Baptist 58, 68, 78, 92,
    148–9
St John the Evangelist 78
St Julien, Baron de 230
Santa Maria del Carmine 60, 61
Santa Maria Maggiore, Rome 61
St Martin's Lane Academy 159
Saint-Non, Abbé de 231
Sandham, Lieut. Henry 181
Santi, Giovanni 69, 97
Salon d'Automne 23, 31, 155, 193,
    194, 197, 199
Salon des Indépendants 151, 155,
    195
Salon des Refusés 23, 25, 31, 175
Saragossa 143
Sargent, John Singer 178–9
Satie, Eric 206
A Satyr Mourning over a Nymph 90–1
Savonarola, Girolamo 83
Schalcken, Godfried 129, 134
Schlesinger, Peter 185
The School of Love (Venus with
    Mercury and Cupid) 102–3
Scott, Sir Giles Gilbert 188
The Seagram Murals 214–15
Seilern, Count Antoine 14
self portraits
    Jan van Eyck? 62–3
    Rembrandt 50–1
    Vigée Le Brun 136–7

Selve, Georges de 104–5
Sérusier, Paul 33, 199
Seurat, Georges-Pierre 25, 27, 177,
    179, 193
    Bathers at Asnières 150–1
Seymour, Jane 105, 106
Sforza, Ludovico 93
Shchukin, Sergey 193
Sicily 77, 115, 119
Siddal, Elizabeth 167
Siena 56, 57
Signac, Paul 27, 155, 193, 205, 207
Signorelli, Luca 83, 91
Sir John Soane's Museum 156–9,
    157
    The Rake's Progress III, The Rose
    Tavern 158–9
Sisley 23, 27, 29
Sistine Chapel 83, 96, 97
Sketch for Hadleigh Castle 162–3
Slade School of Art, London 180,
    181
Sleeping Venus 210–11
Smith, Joseph 41
Soane, Sir John
    Dulwich Picture Gallery 36
    Sir John Soane's Museum 156–9,
    157
Société Anonyme Co-opérative
    d'Artistes-Peintres, Sculpteurs,
    Graveurs etc see Impressionists
Spain
    Dalí 209
    Goya 142–3
    Picasso 207
    Rubens 117, 121
    Velázquez 120, 121
Spencer, Stanley 203
    The Resurrection, Cookham 180–1
Squarcione, Francesco 73
Steen, Jan 51, 125
Steer, Philip Wilson 153
Stella, Frank 213
Stoffels, Hendrickje 39
Strauss, Louise 205
Stravinsky 45, 193
Stubbs, George 231
    Whistlejacket 132–3
Sudbury 53
Suicide 200–1
Sunflowers 152–3
The Sunset 94–5
The Supper at Emmaus 114–15
Surrealists
    Dalí 209

Delvaux 211
Ernst 204–5
Mark Rothko influence 215
Rousseau influence 155
Swanenburgh, Jacob Isaacz van 39
The Swing 230–1

Tahiti 32–3
Tanner, Henry Ossawa 33
Tanning, Dorothea 205
Tassi, Agostino 125
Tate Britain 160–87, **161**
    The Awakening Conscience 170–1
    The Badminton Game 186–7
    A Bigger Splash 184–5
    Carnation, Lily, Lily, Rose 178–9
    The Fairy Feller's Master-Stroke
    172–3
    The Great Day of His Wrath
    168–9
    King Cophetua and the Beggar
    Maid 176–7
    Nocturne in Blue and Gold: Old
    Battersea Bridge 174–5
    Norham Castle, Sunrise 164–5
    Ophelia 166–7
    The Resurrection, Cookham 180–1
    Sketch for Hadleigh Castle 162–3
    Three Studies for Figures at the
    Base of a Crucifixion 182–3
Tate, Henry 160
Tate Modern 160, 188–217, **189**
    Carnival 202–3
    Celebes 204–5
    Clarinet and Bottle of Rum on a
    Mantelpiece 194–5
    Coffee 198–9
    IKB 79 212–13
    Metamorphosis of Narcissus
    208–9
    Parsifal III 216–17
    Portrait of André Derain 192–3
    Portrait of Hermine Gallia 190–1
    Red on Maroon (The Seagram
    Murals) 214–15
    Sleeping Venus 210–11
    Suicide 200–1
    The Three Dancers 206–7
    The Uncertainty of the Poet 196–7
The Ten group 215
Thackeray, William Makepeace 145
Theotokopoulos, Domenikos see
    Greco, El
Thoré, Théophile 126
Thornhill, James 159

The Three Dancers 206–7
Three Studies for Figures at the Base of
    a Crucifixion 182–3
Tiepolo, Giambattista 41, 131, 159,
    231
Tiger in a Tropical Storm 154–5
Tintoretto, Jacopo 19, 221
    St George and the Dragon 110–11
Tissot, James 23
Titian
    Bacchus and Ariadne 100–1
    contemporary works 17, 19,
    103, 107, 109
    El Greco 112, 113
    Giorgione influence 93
    Tintoretto 110, 111
    van Dyck influence 118
    Velázquez influence 120
The Toilet of Venus 120–1
Toledo, El Greco 112, 113
Toulouse-Lautrec, Henri de 31, 155,
    199
    In the Private Room at the Rat
    Mort 34–5
Tour, Georges de la 227
Tube, Minna 203
Turner, Joseph Mallord William 141,
    143, 160
    The Fighting Temeraire tugged to
    her Last Berth to be broken up
    144–5
    Norham Castle, Sunrise 164–5
Two Dancers on the Stage 20–1

Uccello, Paolo 69
    St George and the Dragon 70–1
The Uncertainty of the Poet 196–7
Urbino 69, 71, 97
Uriel, archangel 92
Uylenburgh, Hendrick van 39
Uylenburgh, Saskia van 39

V&A see The Victoria and Albert
    Museum
Vallotton, Félix 33
van der Rohe, Mies 214
van Dyck, Anthony 117
    Equestrian Portrait of Charles I
    118–19
van Eyck, Jan 76
    Portrait of a Man (Self Portrait?)
    62–3
van Gogh, Theo 35
van Gogh, Vincent 29, 31, 33, 35, 151
    Sunflowers 152–3

Varengeville 195
Vasari, Giorgio 70, 83, 90, 96, 101
Vauxcelles, Louis 193, 194, 195
Velázquez, Diego 39, 49, 117
    The Rokeby Venus (The Toilet of Venus) 120–1
Vellay, Julie 27
Veneziano, Domenico 69
Venice
    Bellini 74, 75
    Canaletto 40, 41
    Crivelli 85
    Dürer 88, 89
    Ernst 205
    Giorgione 94, 95
    El Greco 112, 113
    Kiefer 217
    Pisanello 67
    Tintoretto 110, 111
    Titian 100, 101, 118
    Uccello 71
Venus and Cupid 108–9, 120–1
Venus and Mars 82–3
Venus with Mercury and Cupid 102–3
Vermeer, Johannes (Jan) 51, 123, 125
    A Young Woman standing at a Virginal 126–7
Verona 67, 73
Veronese, Paolo 19, 111
Verrocchio, Andrea 93
Vespucci family 82
The Victoria and Albert Museum (V&A) 218–21, **219**
    Young Man leaning against a Tree among Roses 220–1
Vien, Joseph-Marie 139
Vienna, Gustav Klimt 191
Vienna Secession 31, 191
View of Dordrecht 48–9
Vigée Le Brun, Elizabeth Louise
    Self Portrait in a Straw Hat 136–7
Vinck, Eeltje Pieters 129
Virgin Mary 56–7, 58–9, 78, 80, 85, 98
Virgin and Child 60–1
The Virgin of the Rocks 92–3
The Vision of St Eustace 66–7
Vlaminck, Maurice de 193
Vollard, Ambroise 31, 193, 199
Volpini, Café 33
Vuillard, Édouard 35, 199

Wagner, Richard 23
Wallace Collection 222–33, **223**

A Dance to the Music of Time 226–7
The Laughing Cavalier 224–5
The Music Party 228–9
Nelly O'Brien 232–3
The Swing 230–1
Walter, Marie-Thérèse 207
Warhol, Andy 185, 211
Waterhouse, John William 31
Watteau, Jean-Antoine
    The Music Party 228–9
Watts, Miss Fanny 179
Waugh, Edith 171
Waugh, Fanny 171
Wedgwood, Josiah 133, 134
Weight, Carel 183
Wellington, Duke of 142–3
West, Benjamin 139
Weyden, Rogier van der 65, 67, 71, 75
Whistlejacket 132–3
Whistler, James Abbott McNeill 21, 23, 177
    Nocturne in Blue and Gold: Old Battersea Bridge 174–5
The Wilton Diptych 58–9
Winter Landscape 140–1
Winterhalter, Franz Xavier 169
Wittenberg 16, 89
Wolgemut, Michael 89
World War I 179, 181, 199, 200, 202, 203, 205
World War II 182, 201, 203, 207, 217
Wright, Joseph, of Derby
    An Experiment on a Bird in the Air Pump 134–5

Young Man leaning against a Tree among Roses 220–1
The Young Schoolmistress 130–1
A Young Woman standing at a Virginal 126–7

Zola, Émile 25, 31
Zurbarán, Francisco de 123, 227